DATE DUE

MAY 23 03			
AUG 1 5 03			
OCT 9 03			
APR 1 8 05			
DE 07 06			

RN'S ENTERPRISE COMPUTING INSTITUTE

Technology Strat

HARRIS KE

- ▼ Data Ware
  Mark Hu
- ▼ Software
  Marc H
- ▼ IT Auto
  Howie
- ▼ IT Or
  Harr
- ▼ High
  Mi
- ▼ Te
  C

ISBN 013027957-9

90000

9 780130 279576

HARRIS KERN'S ENTERPRISE COMPUTING INSTITUTE

Technology Strategies

Cooper Smith

Prentice Hall PTR, Upper Saddle River, NJ 07458
www.phptr.com

Editorial/Production Supervision: *Mary Sudul*
Acquisitions Editor: *Gregory G. Doench*
Editorial Assistant: *Brandt Kenna*
Marketing Manager: *Debby vanDijk*
Manufacturing Manager: *Alexis R. Heydt*
Cover Design Direction: *Jerry Votta*
Cover Design: *Talar Agasyan*
Composition: *FASTpages*
Series Design: *Gail Cocker-Bogusz*

© 2002 Prentice Hall PTR
Prentice-Hall, Inc.
Upper Saddle River, NJ 07458

Printed in the United States of America

10 9 8 7 6 5 4 3 2 1

ISBN 0-13-027957-9

Pearson Education LTD.
Pearson Education Australia PTY, Limited
Pearson Education Singapore, Pte. Ltd
Pearson Education North Asia Ltd
Pearson Education Canada, Ltd.
Pearson Educación de Mexico, S.A. de C.V.
Pearson Education — Japan
Pearson Education Malaysia, Pte. Ltd
Pearson Education, Upper Saddle River, New Jersey

Contents

Chapter 3

Managing Technological Change   41

Chapter 4

The Limits of Technology   59

Chapter 5

The Future of Technology   79

Chapter 6

The Internet   **101**

Chapter 7

Developing Technological Strategies   **121**

Chapter 8

Developing Business Strategies   143

Chapter 9

The Integration of Technology in Our Business and Personal Lives   161

Preface

▶ Technology as the Strategic Advantage

When I began writing this book I struggled with the direction I wanted it to take. Is this book to be about business, technology, or even the business of technology? I found it was hard to choose a particular direction because so much of business is now tied to technology, and so much of the interest in technology is provided by business. It finally dawned on me that if this was something I was struggling with, then others must be too.

Technology, like it not, is more a part of our daily lives than ever before, whether we are "technical" or not. Technology is inescapable, but how many of us really understand it, or more importantly, understand how to use it to our own best advantage?

Let's start with the basics. Just what is technology? The word itself takes on a transcendental meaning in our culture, as do terms like *politics* or *religion*. We use the term *technology* to express intangible concepts, much like the words *talent*, *skill*, and *insight*. Technology today is gadgets, mostly electronics, and we also recognize mechanics as a form of technology. But few of us look at technology as something much more than doodads and gimmicks. According to the following definition, technology is less defined by the items it produces than by the body of knowledge it comprises.

Main Entry:	*tech•nol•o•gy*
Function:	*noun*
Inflected Form(s):	*plural* -gies
Etymology:	Greek *technologia* systematic treatment of an art, from *technE* art, skill + -o- + -*logia* -*logy*
Date:	1859

1 a : the practical application of knowledge especially in a particular area : *ENGINEERING* 2 <medical *technology*> b : a capability given by the practical application of knowledge <a car's fuel-saving *technology*>

2 : a manner of accomplishing a task especially using technical processes, methods, or knowledge <new *technologies* for **information storage**>

3 : the specialized aspects of a particular field of endeavor <**educa-tional** *technology*>
- tech•nol•o•gist /-*jist*/ *noun*

—*http://www.m-w.com/dictionary.htm*

People frequently lament, "My life is controlled by technology," as they struggle to unlock their car door with a keyless entry device while simultaneously attempting to respond to the pager vibrating on their hip. Technology is the body of knowledge that is required to first implement useful tools and then to put them to practical use. Technology transcends gadgets by giving meaning to the processes that make these tools a reality and give them their value.

Which leads me to the purpose of this book: *to give you a strategic advantage in your personal and professional life by providing you with insight to and instruction on the use and effects of technology, knowledge, and innovation.* More specifically, its purpose is to identify and develop the concept of *digital* technology and the intelligence that it introduces to your complex communication and computing devices, in addition to your mundane household appliances, such as your dishwasher, toaster, and microwave.

My goal is to help you become a technologist (or at least to sound like one)—someone who understands technology. Now, there are many people who will read this, myself included, who would immediately claim no understanding of technology whatever! Few of us can sit and tell someone else just how a cellular phone works. However, it is not the role of the technologist to understand how a piece of technology actually works. That is left for the designer, the architect, and the engineer. It is the technologist's job to understand the purpose and use of specific technologies and how they can either be used separately or in combination to satisfy a particular need or set of needs. In other words, the technologist, given a specific task to accomplish, must decide not on how a cellular phone works, but if the cellular phone can help accomplish his or her goal, either entirely or in part.

▶ But I'm Not an Engineer!

Often, people assume the term *technologist* is synonymous with scientist or engineer, and indeed there are times when these terms can be used interchangeably. But technologist can also be just as easily interchanged with businessman, artist, playwright, or homemaker. A technologist, essentially, is anybody who uses a tool for a specific purpose. Tools and technology are almost synonymous. However, tools are concrete objects, such as hammers, shovels, and computers, while technology is not only the tools themselves, but also the knowledge of how to use them. Let me illustrate this point with a well-known example.

Leonardo da Vinci was a technologist as much as he was an artist. There is little doubt that da Vinci was greatly gifted in a number of areas, painting being foremost among them. But it wasn't the canvas and paintbrush that made da Vinci the extraordinary artist he was; it was his God-given ability to see a subject or a view in his mind's eye and to recreate it, in detail, with the tools of his trade. In other words, anybody can put paint to a canvas, but it is vision, insight, and talent that determine whether or not that person is an artist.

The same can be said for da Vinci's insight into mechanical devices. Da Vinci was responsible for hundreds of mechanical designs, if not actual implementations, from airplanes to tanks. He dabbled in architecture, anatomy, sculpture, engineering, geology, hydraulics, and the military arts, all with success, and in his spare time he doodled parachutes and flying machines that resembled inventions of the 19th and 20th centuries. He made detailed drawings of human anatomy, which are still highly regarded today.

These achievements are even more remarkable because the extension of his own imagination redefined sources from nature (birds and tortoises) into man-made inventions—or early technologies. Since models of these technologies existed only in nature, it was left to da Vinci's imagination to just "dream up" his own mechanical versions. All the more astounding is the fact that although most of these imaginative creations have been realized in the present, such as the tank, the helicopter, and the transportable crane, hardly any were actually realized in da Vinci's own lifetime or for several generations afterward.

But, you argue, da Vinci was a genius! Laugh if you like, but imagination and the ability to extend ideas to practical use are available to anybody with a healthy amount of common sense. Every time someone "flashes" the telephone to give the person he or she is talking to the impression that someone else is calling, he or she is using technology for a specific purpose—to lose the boring conversationalist who just won't stop! You don't have to know how call waiting works technically; you just have to know what it does.

▶ What's Ahead?

Within the last 20 to 25 years, digital technology has provided the cutting edge. What the telephone and lightbulb have done in this century, the digital chip will do in the next. Digital technology, processors on silicon wafer chips, can combine and/or support numerous diverse technologies as one! The result is a kind of *pan-technology*. As the digital chip introduces "intelligence" into a variety of electronics beyond desktop or mainframe computers, that intelligence in turn communicates with other intelligent devices that communicate with us.

Twenty years ago, a telephone and a television (except for the "tele") were two entirely different entities. Now both telephones and televisions are digital—telephones carry television signals and telephone calls can be made through televisions. Although this technology may not be commonplace today, there is a good deal of time, effort, and money being spent to make sure that one day it will be. It is widely expected that AOL, given the vast content and production resources of Time Warner, will provide this content to its customers via the World Wide Web. Soon, almost every sight and sound, except those provided by nature, will be digital. Because of the pervasiveness of digital technology, even the most robust technophobe will have no choice but to conform. This new pan-technology will usher in the 21st century the way the automobile helped usher in the 20th, but on a much faster and more overwhelming scale.

However, our basic living and working rules will not change, even as the landscape does. Everyone will still have to decide for him- or herself where, what, and how these technologies are going to affect everyday life. You do not have to be an engineer, a scientist, or even an artist to be a "pan-technologist." You simply need to be aware of what technology is doing, what technology can do, and what technology can do against you as well as for you. Rather than describing ourselves as either technical weenies or technophobes, we'll label ourselves as technologists because of the significance digital technology has in our personal and professional lives.

Of course, there will always be differences in terms of professional category and status. An engineer is an engineer and a sculptor is a sculptor. But soon even the sculptor will be "digitized," using the Internet to display wares, buy materials, and review other people's works. At the same time, the engineer, when transporting schematics and system designs across the Internet, will take time to muse over the latest work of our renowned sculptor. Does this mean our artist sidelines as a techie, while the engineer daydreams of being an artist?

The purpose of this book is not only to philosophize on the impact that changes in technology will have on the future of mankind, but to also use these changes to shed light on the ever-turbulent seas the information technology professional will face. Computers and the networks that linked them formally defined IT. But computers were singular entities that did specific tasks and were operated by specific people who were educated and trained to run the computer. Pan-technology is leveraging computers in television, refrigerators, and automobiles. People do not need degrees and years of training to use them.

The current trappings of the modern office environment will remain: desktops and laptops, printers and scanners, and network boxes. But even these familiar icons of "hi-tech" are undergoing rapid transformations. These transformations will have the same impact on the business environment as did the introduction of the desktop computer, and of the typewriter 50 years before. Ten years ago, business computing meant terminals connected to a million dollars' worth of equipment sheltered in its own environment. Twenty years ago, the computer was even more isolated, with only a selected few getting to see it!

As we are at the point where computer technology is all but inescapable, we have to understand how to manage this pervasive technology. Specifically, the modern information technology manager has to be part technician, part businessman—the business of technology and the technology of business are rapidly becoming one. Information technology managers, programmers, and systems administrators must re-evaluate how we look at technology's role in business. Traditionally, technology, and computers in particular, have been viewed as "add-ons," like office supplies and copiers. However, from manufacturing to insurance to publishing, technology's integration with the process of doing business has resulted in managers and financial people viewing it accordingly. Business can go on without the copier, but try running it without the corporate mainframe!

▶ How This Book Is Organized

The best way to understand anything, in my opinion, is from the ground up. This book is generally divided into two parts:

- Part 1 – A look at technology's past and the best way to understand it in the present.
- Part 2 – Using this newfound understanding of technology's roots to develop practical methodology for dealing with technology for both individuals and organizations.

Chapter 1, *The History of Technology,* reviews the history of technology from my own perspective. It is much easier to understand technology as a whole when we understand the effect technology has had on our society since the first "society" was understood as such. By putting technology's role in the past into perspective, it is easier to put technology's role into perspective today, as well as to foresee where it is headed. Knowledge and experience can alleviate a lot of uncertainty and frustration when opting for one technology over another, or when learning how disparate technologies work together.

Chapter 2, *The Business of Technology,* explores the current status of technology in today's world of business in terms of its role in modern business, and as a business unto itself.

Chapter 3, *Managing Technological Change,* explores how to deal with technology and its shifting time, using both fictional and actual examples taken from the today's business world. These are real problems that IT managers, in particular, must struggle with every day.

Chapter 4, *The Limits of Technology,* explores what technology can and cannot do. In the context of a real-world technology company, creating a business, growing a business, and losing a business, we look at how technology can be a fast-track avenue to wealth and success, and how the same fast track can lead just as quickly to failure. Using the former Digital Equipment Corporation as an example, we look at both the general picture of the mesh between technology and business as well as at the individuals principally involved in shaping the direction.

Chapter 5, *The Future of Technology,* examines what we can expect if the current trends in technology continue in both our professional and personal lives and how to best prepare to understand and exploit those changes.

From here we move to Part 2, where we try to understand technology's impact in the "real world" from both a professional and personal perspective. How are the events that are happening around us going to affect the decisions we make and how we make them? By looking at particular cases of how technology is actually used, we can get a better understanding of how decisions, both good and bad, are made.

We will begin at the most obvious and inescapable form of technology that has come our way since the atomic bomb. We take a close look at the Internet and why it has had such an overwhelming effect in shaping not only our present-day economy, but also, perhaps, the economy of the entire 21st century.

Chapter 6, *The Internet,* explores the new and burgeoning universal access to computers. Computers were once reserved only for very large corporations, and then moved into medium-sized businesses and into the private homes and businesses of a privileged few. Now, the computer in one form or another is rapidly entering everyone's lives—old and young, rich and poor—all over the world. These computers (and the resulting emerging technologies) together form the Internet. This chapter will discuss why the Internet has had such a tremendous impact on our technology, economy, and way of life.

Chapters 7, 8, and 9 define strategic methodologies for both organizations and individuals. We explore what we can do to make the most beneficial decisions when dealing with this "new" economy—for ourselves as individuals as well as for the organizations we work for and support.

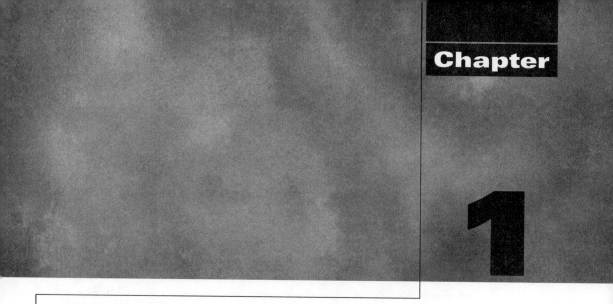

The History of Technology

Why should we look to the past in order to prepare for the future? Because there is nowhere else to look.

—James Burke, *Connections*

You might find that some of the oldest technologies known to man are also some of the most familiar today. For example, a compass represents as much technology as a Global Positioning System (GPS) location finder. In fact, when you get right down to it, a GPS is really just a fancy, updated compass. Surprisingly, most of the technologies on the list below, although ancient, are still in common use today.

- the plow
- the compass
- the lateen sail
- the stirrup
- the water wheel
- the coin
- the loom
- the clock

- the chimney
- the piston

Each of these relatively simple devices has had a profound impact on day-to-day existence as well as on the progression of mankind. You might hesitate to include a chimney as one of the greatest achievements in the history of man, but when you consider what the invention of the chimney *led to,* its overall importance is significant.

> Yet the alteration of life-style brought about by the chimney included year-round administration and increased intellectual activity, which in turn contributed to the general increase in the economic welfare of the community to a point where the increase in the construction of houses brought about a shortage of wood. The consequent need for alternative sources of energy spurred the development of a furnace which would operate efficiently on coal, and this led to the production of molten iron in large quantities, permitting the casting of cylinders (and pistons) which were huge early steam engines. Their use of air pressure led first to the investigation of gases and then petroleum as fuel for the modern automobile engine, without which, in turn, powered flight would have been impossible.
>
> James Burke, *Connections*

As evidenced by the impact of the simple chimney, true technology goes beyond any number of inventions, ideas, gadgets, and gizmos. Technology expresses the relationships between all of these things as mankind creates, understands, and uses everyday items to make life somewhat easier.

Technology is frequently a matter of terminology. From a historical perspective, some might say that technology has defined the human race, while others might champion our ability to reason. Consider, however, that many animal species, from chimpanzees to octopi, can reason. For example, if a dog or an ape or a zebra happened to wander by a bush that had just been struck by lightning on a rather cold night, they could easily "reason" that it is warmer there than anywhere else and a good place to rest for the evening. However, a horse or a dog or a raccoon cannot (as far as we know) pick up a nearby stick, light it from the burning bush, and carry it home to heat its resting place. In my opinion, this application of understanding is what has set the human race apart from any other.

Chapter **1** I The History of Technology

Since the first human learned to bring fire home, or broke an oyster with a rock, or strung more than one bead together to create something "more than just the sum of its parts," technology has been with us. In many ways, it has defined us. Ancient civilizations are often described by technologies that were created and put to use at the time. Anthropologists know there is a significant quality of life difference between the average Stone Age resident and the average Iron Age resident. The time span from the Stone Age to the Iron Age, ranging from 5000 B.C. to about 800 A.D., or the approximate beginning of the Dark Ages, is relatively brief compared to the millions of years of mankind's evolution. But the last seven thousand years have played almost as great a role in our "evolution" as natural selection played in the previous million or so. You see, only after technology was invented did "civilizations" begin to form.

Of course, man's progress, at least from a historical point of view, has tended to be geared toward a military perspective, since early civilizations are generally seen as "empires." Groups with strong political and military leaders frequently gave themselves an identity and took up arms against those who did not share that identity. They attacked and brutally massacred as many people as possible who did not share this identity—in the process, keeping any economic gains, absorbing religious cultures into their own, increasing their own population exponentially, and having plenty of cheap labor for building incredible works of splendor out of raw stone and other natural materials.

This, understandably, has influenced how humans have evolved. But, although frequently brutally barbaric, ancient military empires balanced this bloodlust with incredible, if not indulgent, creations of beauty in both architecture and science, creating monuments like the Hanging Gardens of Babylon, the Laws of Hammurabi, and the Pyramids.

But was it only the level of savagery that allowed one civilization to dominate the next, sometimes for a few hundred years, sometimes for thousands? For example, the First Assyrian Empire, the Middle Assyrian Empire, and the New Assyrian Empire extended from 2000 B.C. to 612 B.C., a period of 1,328 years! Even today, without any country on the world map called Assyria, a large population of people in the world still consider themselves as culturally Assyrian.

If we observed the world today from an anthropologist's viewpoint, the "New World Empire"—generally the United States and her European and Asian allies—would be about 55 years old. This Empire was the result of the decline and fall of the European Colonial Empire that began in 1492 and ended about 450 years later. The European Empire was preceded by the Moslem Empire, from about 600 A.D. to 1500 A.D., which was preceded by the Roman Empire, which lasted about a 1,000 years, and so on. It is fairly noticeable that large, powerful empires' lifetimes are getting shorter and shorter. Today, empires rise and fall in a matter of decades, years, months, or even weeks. Although loss of a financial, religious, or military colossus overnight may give some people a hard time, in general, the rest of humanity is not much the worse for it. For example, the Nazi Third Reich lasted only 12 years, although it was powerful, heavily dependent on technology, and brilliant. The Nazis were a 20th century form of empire, self-proclaimed at inception, and rarely missed upon decline. On the other hand, when the Roman Empire fell, it was seen by the "civilized" western Europeans as the end of civilization itself, a concept we now can envision only as a nuclear holocaust or asteroids smashing into the earth. Fifteen hundred years ago, the nuclear holocaust was losing the war with the Vandals.

My thesis is that technology was the driving force behind these empires. Of course, we can't dismiss religion and greed, but let's speculate for a moment to help you understand my thesis. Early man, for example, an australpithecine, not only discovered fire, but took it home with him. Once our australpithecine returned home with his burning stick, he quickly learned that he could pass the fire on further to another stick or group of sticks. In fact, if he was diligent and located in an area abundant in easily accessible combustible material, he could stay warm *every* night! The australpithecine began to understand that, "Hey, if I could create my own fire, I never need to be cold again!" This, shall we say, was the metaphorical leap from Homo erectus to the technology-aware Homo sapiens.

Let's explore this idea a bit more. Let's go back, say, 10,000 years. The earth was in the middle of an ice age; the few mammals that we would call "human" today lived in cool equatorial regions or in an arctic-type environment year round. Fire was not a commodity; it happened at random by an extraordinary set of circumstances that could only be fashioned by nature. Fire seemed like the Promethean gift from the gods; therefore, "possessing" the power of fire was viewed as having the power of a god.

One day, after thousands or even millions of years, a very lucky person rubbed two sticks together, enabling unbelievable change for man. For the sake of this tale, this "inventor" of fire was named Homer. And let's say a small group of early men and women, say 20 or so, including Homer, lived on an open plain. Homer had been rubbing sticks together for years, and one day he spun a large stick on top of a bigger stick between the palms of his hands. Suddenly, some of the dry grass surrounding both sticks began to smolder, and to Homer's complete astonishment, to burn! This had been rumored to happen from time to time, but was generally attributed to gods—not to Homer! Homer, at first frightened, soon called attention to his ability to make fire. And more importantly, he created fire again! Suddenly, everyone in the group slept by one of Homer's fires every night. Fires were lit because the group learned that both predators and spirits shunned fire. And eventually, the idea of large groups extended throughout the world, creating communal living centered around heat and the benefits it provided.

Homer's fire sticks became a big hit! He was made the leader of the group, which was now on the verge of being a cult. The "Homerians," grateful for the incredible power Homer gave them, worshiped him and sacrificed to him. The Homerians soon learned to do other things with their fire. They picked or caught more food because it was easier to find and consume. They learned to protect themselves from fire by building shelters. Their population grew because children were not carried off by wolves when the parents were scavenging for food.

Soon, there was a noticeable difference in the quality of life between the Homerians and those who did not know how to harness this awesome power. At first, people were eager to become Homerian and be accepted into the well-fed and warm fold. But soon, those that did not find acceptance became envious, realizing that without this awesome power, they did not have the same protections afforded the Homerians. Afraid of this power, the non-Homerians feared their own extinction until their leader, Eboja, decided to take it by force.

A small band of "outsiders," led by Eboja, attacked the Homerians and captured the "fire priest." In return for his life, the fire priest agreed to create fire for the outsiders. Soon the Ebojans had all the Homerians had. But the Ebojans, afraid of someone taking fire from them, ensured that the Ebojan way of life would not be destroyed similarly to the Homerians. Any non-Ebojan they crossed paths with was either conscripted into the Ebojan way of life or killed. This was brutal, but very effective. Soon the Ebojans dominated as far as they could see. The Ebojan empire was born.

Eventually, however, someone did come across the Ebojan empire and returned home with stories of enormous power and wealth, and the cycle began again. The new outsiders, with their clever leader Ting, found a way to make Ebojan power their own. By this time, Ebojans were sophisticated in their creation and procurement of fire. Sticks had now given way to stones. This secret eventually fell into the hands of Ting. It took time, but his people learned how to make fire almost as well as the Ebojans. Ting, an ambitious man, had his "scientists" investigate, and eventually they discovered that a concentrated fire could be created using certain black rocks that could burn as well as wood and last longer. In fact, these rocks could burn so hot, other hard shiny rocks melted if put on top of them. Ting's scientists knew that the melted rocks, if handled carefully, could be shaped into points and, when cooled, become remarkably hard, making very effective weapons. In no time at all, the Ebojans were consolidated into the Ting empire or else were wiped off the face of the earth.

Historians have divided the story of human development into a number of ages. The following description comes from a popular video game.

> This Age of Empires covers roughly four periods—the end of the old Stone Age (or Paleolithic period), the Tool Age (or Neolithic period), the Bronze Age, and the Iron Age. These periods are named after the predominant tool and weapon materials. Stone Age tools were large stone chippers and spear points. Tool Age tools were small stone blades, called microliths, struck from stone core. The small blades were fixed into hafts to make scythes, knives, and other specialized tools. The Bronze Age was dominated by tools and weapons made of bronze metal, an alloy usually of copper and tin, two "soft" metals that combined became something much harder than either. The Iron Age was dominated by tools and weapons of iron.

> Technology was the underlying dynamic for the rise of civilization throughout this period. Those cultures that learned a key new technology first often had an advantage over their neighbors. Technology was often the key factor in survival, expansion, and longevity. Egypt and Mesopotamia grew strong early, once they mastered irrigation. The Minoans established a monopoly on sea trade and grew rich. The Greeks expanded on the basis of trade, mining, and a culture that encouraged

and rewarded original thought. The Hittites mastered metalworking and fielded well-equipped armies. The Assyrians, surrounded by enemies, forged a powerful and innovative army out of necessity.

Tools and other technologies were cumulative in nature. Cultures had to master the preceding technology to proceed and advance. Newly rising cultures were built on the technologies of their predecessors. The advance from one age to another was often a slow process that required a gradual but extensive conversion of an entire economy. New raw materials and new fabrication techniques were required. New skills and workshops came into being. The eventual cost in time and resources was enormous, but the new efficiencies recovered those costs quickly.

The Sumerians are credited with inventing both the wheel and a system of writing around 3500 B.C. The invention of writing, especially, was a gradual process. Both technologies provided immediate and easily understood benefits that persist today. The wheel made carts possible, greatly improving the efficiency of moving goods. The wheel was also a prerequisite for the chariot and other engines of war. The pottery wheel came into use at the same time as the transport wheel. Writing was so important to the storage and communication of knowledge that it became a technology research accelerator. After its appearance, the rate of technology advances increased.

—The Age of Empires

▶ The Age of Ancient Technology

As society became accustomed to technology, technology became accustomed to "society." In time, it was almost impossible to separate the two, as man's crafts provided both practical and aesthetic uses for the natural resources which surrounded him. Although these tools were basic, practical, and immediate, they became more sophisticated as man's imagination began to influence his creations. Abstract sciences were first merged with religion and philosophy but gradually came into their own.

There is no doubt as to the influence of economics on the development of the arithmetic in the older period....Canals, dams, and other irrigation projects required calculations. The use of bricks raised numerous numerical and geometrical problems. Volumes of granaries and buildings and the area of fields had to be determined. The close relationship between Babylonian mathematics and practical problems is typified by the following: A canal whose cross-section was a trapezoid and whose dimensions were known was to be dug. The amount of digging one man could do in a day was known, as was the sum of the number of men employed and the days they worked The problem was to calculate the number of men and the number of days of work.

Morris Kline, *Mathematical Thought from Ancient to Modern Times*

Although there were thousands of years between the Stone Age and the Iron Age, we can see that technology has played no small role in what we know as life on earth. With the exception of perhaps religion, technology as a concept has been with us since man could imagine making the power of the gods his own. Today this concept is part of our collective consciousness. Stanley Kubrick's opening scene from *2001: A Space Odyssey* and Charlie Chaplin's *Modern Times* tap into that innate understanding of ourselves as a species. It is more effective than simply appealing to our sexual urges, violent tendencies, or even greed. We intuitively understand that knowing something works is useless unless you know how to make it work for you.

Interestingly, if we understand the role of technology in our evolution, our understanding of the role of commerce is just as intuitive. After all, things might not have been so disastrous for the Homerians, the Ebojans, or eventually the Tings if they had found a way to "share" or "sell" the benefits of fire. In ancient times, economies were secondary to religious predestination, and then to social class, tied to either religious or military caste. Modern economies, including the capitalist economies of the late European Empire are considerably more fluid in terms of social, political, and even religious influence.

For example's sake, say the Homerians were living in a more perfect world, where jealousy and greed did not exist. Since the outsiders viewed the power of the Homerians as godlike and were more in awe than in fear, they gladly offered whatever resources they had available to either possess or at least take part in the benefits of the fire technology. As long as groups decided that the technology was indeed "shareable," new groups could be incorporated or work in parallel to the mutual benefit of all parties. Not only would the Homerians become fabulously wealthy, but that wealth could be shared by new Homerians. This system worked for the Roman Empire for a thousand years. When the emperor Augustus rose to power, 70 percent of the standing Roman Legions came from the Roman Peninsula. Two hundred years later, it was 6 percent. However, 70 percent of the army was still considered Roman. Although their parents or grandparents may have come from distant provinces, soldiers were granted Roman citizenship for their tour of duty. Of course, a tour of duty could be anywhere between 20 to 25 years, but this, at least, assured that their sons were born Roman citizens with the applicable rights and privileges. This distribution of perceived value was the key to the military success that kept Rome powerful for a millennia.

And Rome, though noted for its military prowess, was really an economic power second to none. Part of that economic power was due indirectly to technology. For example, concrete, the millstone, and the water screw brought unbelievable physical and social wealth to the Romans. I use the term "indirectly" because we don't know how much of their technology was solely Roman. How much came from the conquered provinces? How much had been simply adopted as part of life, handed down from generation to generation by Greek, Phoenician, Egyptian, Nubian, and Sumerian cultures? The Romans absorbed technology from all of these cultures. Technology has been, and always will be, ubiquitous. In our time, how many people know who actually "invented" television? (It was not NBC.) For that matter, how many people actually know how television works? We don't have to. We only need know that TV works and provides something we like or need (such as sports, news and music).

▶ Technology as Necessity

Technology, for this discussion, is engineering or, even more definitively, applied science. It has been generally accepted that it was the ancient Greek culture that "invented" mathematics. The Greeks certainly wrote their knowledge down and continually made copies of this knowledge. Today you or I can still go to a bookstore and find a copy of *Euclid's Elements,* remarkable for a work created almost 2,000 years ago! But although the Greeks were certainly good at understanding and organizing mathematics, they certainly didn't invent it, any more than anyone "invented" fire.

If Homer (in our previous example) had been more mathematically oriented and not just cold, he would have come upon the notion that he was rubbing *two* sticks together. But he did know that nothing happened when you used just one stick; therefore, you must need two. A stick can be picked up, rubbed, touched, tasted, and smelled, so obviously it exists. But "two" has no physical form except in relation to something that does, and more importantly to other things just as conceptual. There would be no two without the concept of one. One and two are abstract concepts that, when understood, can be applied to real-world applications. This is all mathematics really is: the result of understanding and manipulating abstractions to create concrete and practical results.

> [T]he very concept of mathematics was the conscious recognition and emphasis of the fact that mathematical entities, numbers, and geometrical figures are abstractions.
> Morris Kline, *Mathematical Thought from Ancient to Modern Times*

Some could say that the Babylonians "invented" mathematics, because archeological findings have found cuneiform scripts and etchings indicating the existence of a Sumerian "numbering" system based on the number 60. How the ancients themselves felt about these abstractions we can only conjecture. We do know that those who practiced them were usually revered and given lofty social status. Even the ancients knew this kind of knowledge was very important.

Once people learned to count, they basically had numbering systems. Once they had numbering systems, they had to have a way of conveying the concepts numbering systems represented. The concept of two was platonic long before Plato called it as such. Today we do not know everything about how people transacted business and dealt with technology 5,000 years ago. My conjecture is simply that the ancients did... somehow. I further propose that mankind, without communication satellites, biogenetics, and jet engines, was not drastically different than mankind today. With less distractions and more time to ponder the natural world, it is not surprising that an ancient culture spent time looking at the sky, seeing it as a great sphere, measuring distances between one point to the next on that sphere, conceptualizing a degree long before Euclidean geometry was developed, and basing their entire numbering system on the base 60. After all, the Babylonians lived in a spherical universe; it would only be fitting that their description of it should reflect this.

If these abstractions were simple and obvious enough to the Babylonians, it would be logical to assume they were just as logical to the Egyptians, the Sumerians, the Phoenicians, the Seleucids, the Alexandrians, and of course the Greeks. It is the simplicity of these abstractions that give them their power. Like fire, the power of the gods stems not from fire's mere existence but our being able to use that power for our own needs and purpose. In ancient times, the need for food, clothing, shelter, and protection were just as real as they are now. However, with drastically smaller populations and much more formidable natural obstacles, technologies were usually a domestic affair.

Once populations reached some level of basic security, people could then use their imaginations. Creating the Seven Wonders of the Ancient World based upon pharaohs and kings and the like and building monuments to themselves and their cultures. The Hanging Gardens of Babylon, for instance, was built in order to cheer up King Nebuchadnezzar's wife, Queen Amyitis, who was homesick for her mountainous and heavily forested homeland. Whole economies, thousands of laborers, engineers, designers, and architects, and of course expense, could be brought to work at a whim. But regardless of whether technology was pursued for the sake of expression or necessity, technology became indispensable.

> The ascent to the highest story is by stairs, and at their side are water engines, by means of which persons, appointed expressly for the purpose, are continually employed in raising water from the Euphrates into the garden.

Strabo touches on what, to the ancients, was probably the most amazing part of the garden. Babylon rarely received rain, and for the garden to survive, it would have had to been irrigated by using water from the nearby Euphrates River. That meant lifting the water far into the air so it could flow down through the terraces, watering the plants at each level. This was probably done by means of a chain pump.

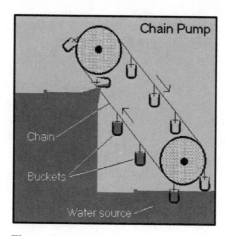

Figure 1–1 Chain Pump

A chain pump is two large wheels, one above the other, connected by a chain. On the chain are hung buckets. Below the bottom wheel is a pool with the water source. As the wheel is turned, the buckets dip into the pool and pick up water. The chain then lifts them to the upper wheel, where the buckets are tipped and dumped into an upper pool. The chain then carries the empty ones back down to be refilled.

The pool at the top of the gardens could then be released by gates into channels, which acted as artificial streams to water the gardens. The pump wheel below was attached to a shaft and a handle. By turning the handle, slaves provided the power to run the contraption.

Construction of the garden wasn't only complicated by getting the water up to the top, but also by having to avoid having the liquid ruin the foundation once it was released. Since stone was difficult to get on the Mesopotamian plain, most of the architecture in Babel utilized brick. The bricks were composed of clay mixed with chopped straw and baked in the sun. The bricks were then joined with bitumen, a slimy substance, which acted as a mortar. These bricks quickly dissolved when soaked with water. For most buildings in Babel this wasn't a problem because rain was so rare. However, the gardens were continually exposed to irrigation and the foundation had to be protected.

Diodorus Siculus, a Greek historian, stated that the platforms on which the garden stood consisted of huge slabs of stone (otherwise unheard of in Babel), covered with layers of reed, asphalt, and tiles. Over this was put "a covering with sheets of lead, that the wet which drenched through the earth might not rot the foundation. Upon all these was laid earth of a convenient depth, sufficient for the growth of the greatest trees. When the soil was laid even and smooth, it was planted with all sorts of trees, which both for greatness and beauty might delight the spectators."

http://unmuseum.mus.pa.us/hangg.htm

These royal whims could only have been met if the basics of society were already comfortably assured. Once local populations had enough food, could produce enough goods in terms of clothing and living items, and could (and did) create spectacular examples of their own importance, these things had to be protected. Naturally, warfare began to drive technological advancement. Whether for the purpose of protection from aggressive neighbors or to become an aggressive neighbor, warfare propelled mankind further into science and technology.

For example, the principle of the mechanical lever, introduced originally as advancement in building and construction, gives way to the catapult. Archimedes of Alexandria, using his understanding of optics, actually created huge magnifying glasses to focus the rays of the sun on invading ships and set them afire! In fact, Alexandria, the Hellenic capital of ancient Egypt, was the birthplace of a number of ancient scientists whose discoveries and achievements are considered wonders even today. Archimedes, Hero, Ptolemy, and Galen were all present at the catharsis of man's evolution, bringing together the best of what man's imagination could achieve in Asia, Africa, and eventually, Europe.

Their ideas were formally recorded and preserved in writing, and the technological sciences were born. These ancients were not just clever men, but scholars as well. For example, Archimedes is considered by some to be the first scientific engineer (this, by definition, making him the first technologist) Archimedes "...had grasped the secret of the lever, the pulley, and the principle of mechanical advantage," according to Petr Beckmann, in his book *A History of PI* (St. Martin's Press, New York, 1971). These technologies, employed against Roman invaders of Syracuse in 214 B.C., held off a vastly superior military force for three years. The ubiquitous nature of science and technology is often lost to militarism. Ironically, it was actually the Romans who were considered the barbarians in the Hellenic/Asian world. They were in the process of building their empire primarily through force of arms and very little through "science." In fact, it was Rome that actually brought about a sort of "Dark Ages" of their own.

> ...it chanced that he was alone, examining a diagram closely; and having fixed both his mind and eyes on the object of his inquiry, he perceived neither the inroad of the Romans not the taking of the city. Suddenly a soldier came up to him and bade him follow to Marcellus, but he would not go until he had finished the problem and worked out the proof.
>
> Do not touch my circles!" said the thinker to the thug. Thereupon the thug became enraged, drew his sword and slew the thinker.
>
> As long as the Alexandrian Greeks civilization was ruled by the dynasty of Ptolemy it flourished. The first disaster was the advent of the Romans, whose entire role in the history of mathematics was as an agent of destruction.
>
> Morris Kline, *Mathematical Thought from Ancient to Modern Times*

However, even if the Romans were interested in technology only as a direct military help, they were intelligent enough to at least acknowledge the importance of accomplished individuals who did understand and create new technologies. By absorbing Alexandria into the Empire, the power of knowledge and technology became just as much booty as the country's gold and wheat. The ancient scientist and scholars, much like the merchants and farmers, continued on with their daily lives the best way possible. It made little difference if the masters were Ptolemiac or Roman.

The Business of Technology

With limited information-carrying capacity ("bandwidth") per pigeon, it was critical to have additional capacity available at short notice ("network availability" and "expanded capacity"), and the use of several pigeons ("multiple channels") to carry the same message protected the service against unforeseen delays and the possible loss of birds ("redundancy" or "fault tolerance"). Reuter also established two other principles with the new service: He instituted controls to ensure accuracy and secrecy, and he enforced impartial distribution by making sure all customers got market-moving news at the same time.

Anirudh Dhebar and Thomas August Grace,
"Reuters Holdings PLC, 1850–1987: A (Selective) History"

▶ Let's Get Down to Business

Unlike science, which can be indulged in simply for the sake of science, technology should be analyzed as a symbiosis between science, the study of ideas and engineering, and the application of ideas. Technology, by definition, must have some useful, practical purpose or it simply is not technology.

More important than invention in the evolution of technology is the concept of timing. As related in Chapter 1, almost all of the technologies that we are surrounded by today are not independent inventions. Rather, they are amalgamations of inventions, ideas, and concepts, brought together either for a specific purpose or accidentally discovered in the pursuit of something entirely different. Hero, of Alexandria, Egypt, designed a working steam-driven engine in the second century B.C. At that time, Alexandria was a Roman province. Rome relied on slaves as an inexpensive, labor-saving device, giving Rome little incentive to put this technology to good use. It took 16 centuries, after England had finally abolished its own practice of slavery, for the steam engine to come pummeling into everyday life, dragging the industrial revolution behind it!

No technology is the creation of one or two geniuses. Technology is a series of steps that leads into something that someone (not necessarily of any particular IQ) puts to good use. It is simply a matter of context. What if Edison had invented the lightbulb, but there was no way of providing electricity to the public, or the public was unwilling to use it? It was only because of years of development on limelight that Edison thought the pursuit worthwhile at all. Edison was not just an inventor, but a businessman (and a very shrewd one at that). He never took on a project unless he already knew there was a market for it. Edison rarely hesitated to take the necessary steps from successful invention to successful business. Sometimes, his businesses were too successful!

> Edison's film studio, the Black Maria, was the first building designed for the purpose of making commercial motion pictures. The Motion Picture Patents Company was formed by Edison and other movie inventors. They controlled much of the motion picture industry until the United States Supreme Court upheld a ruling that the company was an illegal monopoly. Soon after, Edison was out of the motion picture business.
> "The Original Thomas Edison's 'Frankenstein':
> Biography of Thomas Edison"

Now, you and I are just businesspeople, not inventors. It is our job to take these many marvels of other people's genius and put them to work for us. Simply put, how do we use technology to make a profit?

As expressed earlier, as economies have become more complex, technology has become more necessary. In modern times, as industry became more mechanized, so did the western economy. Horses and carts were replaced with steam-driven locomotives, which were replaced with internal combustion and jet engines. It was only a matter of time before the passing of information also became mechanized. As the world learned to produce economies by producing manufactured items, it learned that it profits from information as well. As markets became more complex, selling not only commodities, but interests in companies and organizations, information about those companies and organizations and the way they do business became just as valuable as, if not more valuable than, the companies and organizations themselves. For example, Reuters hasn't changed its basic business model in 150 years, but would it still be in business if it relied solely on pigeons?

Today we have a reached a technological point focused on networked information and digital computing. Computers and the information they provide play some role in our lives, directly or indirectly, whether we're rich or poor, young or old. For this reason, this book concentrates primarily on digital technology and its relationship with other familiar technologies, such as telecommunications and broadcast. Most books of this type refer to computers and the technology that comprises them as information technology, management systems, and the like. I tend to use these terms interchangeably. However, our focus is on the more ubiquitous digital technology.

Digital technology is primarily the technology of transmitting information electronically in binary form. Represented electronically, binary form is simply a state of being on or off. Your desk lamp, for instance, when turned on, represents "yes" or "come in." When turned off, it represents "no" or "nobody's home." This is a binary message easily and cheaply transferred between two parties capable of understanding the "code."

If you had a series of, say, eight lamps, and the sequences of lamps being on or off had different meanings, you could code 256 different messages—from "I'm not home" to more complex messages, such as "I'm not home but I should be back within an hour, since I only stepped out to do a few things at the grocer's. So leave a message if you prefer not to wait." Both messages would have to be "coded" with a recognizable pattern of lamps being turned on or off. The code would have to be understandable to both the creator and the receiver of the message, and the code could not be changed without the consent of both parties. Obviously, there is a lot of information these lamp "information systems" could provide. For example, increasing the number of lamps to 16, 32, and eventually 64 could generate millions of unique messages. Increase the speed of the message passing to reflect the speed of the electron (close to the speed of light), and you can understand what the excitement is around digital technology.

I want to focus on digital technology as opposed to computers in general because it is the process of being able to digitize and process huge amounts of information that is changing the world. For example, consider the following excerpt from an article that appeared in the *New York Times*:

> ...go uptown to Rockefeller Center, to NBC headquarters. There, on the ninth floor, are perhaps millions of dollars' worth of Internet routers from Cisco Systems. And next to them, sitting no more than 18 inches high, is a cobbled-together system using gear from Lucent and others that cost no more than $100,000 and is transmitting more than 750 million bits a second of television...
>
> Seth Schiesel, "A Little-Known Company May Mirror the Future"

Computers are only tools used in that process. Understanding how computers, networks, telephones, televisions, kitchen appliances, and the automobile can be digitized will make our technology overload less mysterious.

The next thing we need to focus on is the fact that digital technology, like any other technology, is simply a tool or set of tools. The first modern example of binary digitizing actually took place in the textile industry. In 18th century France, an automated loom was created by Jacques de Vaucanson to select particular threads to create patterns "programmed" on a metal cylinder much resembling the device inside a music box. But instead of protrusions that struck against harmonized tines, the loom had indentations to allow ratchets to thread according to holes punched in paper. A hole in the paper was "on," no hole was "off." And although this new technology proved vastly superior to the handlooms that had been used for centuries, the concept never really took off until over 100 years later, when the concept of "punched holes" was finally adopted to calculate the 1890 census and the modern calculating machine came into existence. Herman Hollerith, the son of German immigrants, devised this mechanical device. In 1896 Hollerith founded the Tabulating Machine Company, forerunner of Computer Tabulating Recording Company (CTR). He served as a consulting engineer with CTR until retiring in 1921. Interestingly, in 1924 CTR changed its name to IBM—the International Business Machines Corporation.

Ironically, Hollerith had probably never heard of Jacques de Vaucanson, and even more likely, had little or no interest in the textile industry. But with technology, timing is *everything*! In other words, the real miracle of technology is its ability to adapt from one use to another, when and where it is needed and can be applied. A hundred years earlier, guilds and trade unions saw "logical looms" as a threat to their existence. But in 1890, Hollerith's system—including punch, tabulator, and sorter—allowed the official 1890 population count to be tallied in six months. When all the census data was completed and defined, the cost was $5 million below the forecasts and saved more than two years' time. Although Herman Hollerith may not be a household name, his use of technology in one industry has changed the face of almost every industry in one way or another over the last 100 years.

This chapter, I hope, will provide a managerial, or nontechnical, perspective on the effective use of digital technology in business. We will take an objective look at what business means to technology and, more importantly, what technology means to business. Any self-respecting business school able to pride itself on its modern curricula will have more than a few classes today on managing technology or decision-making in the Information Age. This book is not intended to be as in-depth a treatment as such a class, but we will use case studies to illustrate the types of problems and decisions all of us are going to be faced with in the next few years.

If we were in management school, I would title this course Pan-Technologies 101 (PT-101): Managing Digital Technologies in the 21st century. I'd put an abstract into the online catalog that would read something similar to the following: *Strategic advantage is as fundamental as asset and liability to understanding business concepts. In short, strategic advantage is anything that allows anyone to do business more successfully, more easily, or more competitively. If you have ever heard the phrase Location! Location! Location!, then you have a clearcut example of the strategic advantage created when you open a lemonade stand next to a salted peanut factory or present a "tabulating machine" to a census department that still uses pencil and paper.*

Strategic advantage can be defined as a service, product, or solution that enables a company to position itself in the marketplace to better compete. Initially, let's assume that a strategic advantage implies that our business can do one or both of the following:

1. Do what we do now—better.
2. Create entirely new products, businesses, or both.

These two concepts may seem similar, but are in fact very different. If company A produces widgets and only widgets, it simply wants to find a better, cheaper way to make widgets and improve its profits. The second option is concerned with branching out into other ventures. "We are already successful widget manufacturers but now we want to make doodads!" Will the technologies used for widgets be successful for manufacturing doodads?

We will begin with two premises in the business of understanding and deploying digital technology. The first is that introducing, utilizing, or even creating new technologies must allow a business to do it better with this technology; the second is that the business will generate additional revenue with this new technology.

Before we go any further, however, we should take a look at the subtle difference between doing business in a digital world versus doing business in the more traditional world. Traditionally, technology has always been associated with some kind of invention or innovation that somehow made something difficult easier, and therefore better. For example, before the stirrup, armored knights could not go charging into other armed men because, with one hand on a shield and the other on a lance, they had no hands free with which to hold on to the horse. With the advent of the stirrup, warriors were able to stay in the saddle while leading a charge. Today's everyday technologies may not provide such a striking strategic advantage, but countless technologies have altered how we live.

For example, after Hollerith's tabulating machines became common in the use of census taking, the tabulating company recognized that to stay in business it would need to create additional uses for its technology, beyond census taking once every ten years. Hollerith's little company discovered scores of new and interesting uses for the tabulating machine: calculating trajectories for artillery firing tables, solving early electrical and mechanical equations, and the like. However, the CTR was not an overnight success. The little company viewed itself as a manufacturing concern and not necessarily as a technological one. Technology was not a term people used in business circles at the time. Units were sold simply based on what they did. If an item could do 10 different things but people bought it to do only one thing, that is how it was sold. Today people may spend $3,000 dollars for a computer just to have email, but that wastes the considerable potential of the other things a modern PC can do.

This is the way most companies that produced hardcore manufactured items from Henry Ford to Andrew Carnegie viewed themselves at the turn of the century. Technology and machinery were viewed as pretty much the same thing. The real innovation at the time was the system of assembly line manufacture that had been pioneered and perfected, ironically enough, in the textile factories of the northeastern United States. In America, not France, those mechanical looms had finally been brought to good use in the textile mills of New England in the mid-19th century. What had been a bane in the Old World was a boon in the New World, where free-spirited New England manufacturers had increasingly accepted women and children into the labor force. This cheap and expendable labor force stood behind mechanized looms for 10 to 12 hours a day, with the machines doing the producing. Humans were there to feed in the input, gather the output, and make sure nothing went wrong in between. Hence was born the American system of manufacture, as it became known to the rest of the world, or the assembly line system, as it became known in the United States. This system would shape the 20th century.

▶ New Technology, Old Ideas

...the final causes of all social changes and political revolutions are to be sought not in men's brains, not in men's insights into eternal truth and justice, but in changes in the methods of production and exchange.

— Max Engels, *Socialism: Utopian and Scientific*

This passage is an example of man's innate understanding of the importance of technology to everyday life. Max Engels was an economist, not a technologist, yet his definition of an economy is clearly based on technology: "methods of production" combined with commerce. This is not the historical revelation that made Engels famous, for Adam Smith had written the same thing 70 years earlier. It was

Engels' insight into the relationship of these two things. Engels realized that technology was not the result, but the determining factor, of how people lived their lives.

Prior to the assembly line, all goods, agrarian or manufactured, depended on a distinct and specialized labor pool. This was good for labor, but not for the consumer, because these pools could produce only so many goods. Relatively speaking, anything produced prior to the assembly line was quite expensive. This meant that the poor had to make their own clothing, shoes, and furniture, or simply go without. But with the advent of the assembly line, manufactured goods could be made cheaply and in vast quantities. At the beginning of the 19th century, the vast majority of American households made their own clothing. By the end of the century, making one's own clothes, at least for everyday wear, was relatively rare. Today it is almost unheard of. The New England textile makers made fortunes supplying the United States and eventually the world with high quality but inexpensive shirts, pants, and dresses.

After the success of the textile industry, almost every form of manufacture turned to the assembly line. Soon almost all consumer goods, from bathtubs to automobiles, were rolling off of assembly lines. In conjunction with the explosion of textile manufacturing, artificial dyes were being developed to supplement natural dyes that were expensive and limited in quantity. This led to the intense study and research into pure chemistry. Eventually, petroleum products, first used to replace whale oil, were subjected to chemical processes, and the nascent organic chemical industry was born. Electricity was harnessed and exploited to meet the new demands of a well-dressed populace with more money in its pockets than ever before. The Industrial Revolution began in the 18th century, and by the end of the 19th century, it was in full swing.

This unprecedented consumer demand fueled a number of disparate industries to innovate. These innovations came together to form follow-on innovations that led to whole new industries, and so on. These innovations in manufacturing, chemistry, electricity, and magnetism led to a vast array of inventions in a phenomenally short period of time. From 1859 to 1900, the air brake, telephone, lightbulb, electric generator, Bessemer process, acetylene, typewriter, zipper, celluloid film, movie projector, and scores of other innovations were born. After the turn of the century, economists no longer had to differentiate one industry's innovations from another, but could combine products and services in economic terms to describe the country's entire economic output. With the advent of the New York Stock Exchange in 1817 came the financial market's ability to "value" a company (whether it was a manufacturer, a chemical company, or entertainment) by its products as well as by its ability to innovate. The market for technology was born along with the modern notions of progress that we still accept today: market share, industrial growth, and R&D. Our most recent notion of progress is Internet speed.

By the 1920s, at least in the United States, these concepts of modern business took firm economic root, and the course of the 20th century was set. Countries and governments rose and fell according to the industrial standards they were able to set and meet. The United States became a world power not because of its military might, but because of the American system of manufacturing. It was the American assembly line that turned the tide in World War I, more than it was the doughboy. But it wasn't just America that was following this course: Although the world in general was still very provincial, and peaceful intercultural relationships scarce, the modern global economy was eventually born, and the European colonial economy slowly headed towards a self-destructive end.

The 1930s, however, veered a bit off course. Most traditional businesses still had a 19th century perspective of what business was about. Even though their own economies had become interdependent, a railroad man concerned himself only with railroads, farmers only with their farms, bankers only with their customers and finances, and manufacturers only with what they manufactured. And with the collapse of the stock market system in 1929, most businesses did what any 19th century company would have done: cut their losses and started from scratch.

But because the world economy had become completely intertwined by 1930, drastic measures one business used to save itself only hurt other businesses that supported it. Without this support, businesses fell further into the hole. Soon, the hole became a chasm, resulting in the Great Depression. Politically, of course, both historians and economists have noted the ramifications in great detail.[1] But the Great Depression,

---

1. For more information on the Great Depression, see *http://www.amatecon.com/ greatdepression.html.*

in spite of all its hardships, finally crystallized, at least in the minds of many economists and political theorists in the United States, just how interdependent business all over the world had become. As a side note, Keynesian economics was the result of acting upon this analysis, and modern macroeconomic theory was born.

The crux of modern macroeconomics (and microeconomics, for that matter) is the concept of the consumer, the producer, and the pricing model. If a firm is in business, it is in business to generate a profit. Let's consider a simple example using old-fashioned dollars to measure a profit. If company A spends $2 to make a widget and sells it for $3, it makes a $1 *profit*. The consumer, on the other hand, is out to maximize *value*. If the consumer has $3 to spend, he or she wants to make sure to get the most that $3 can provide. One day, our consumer happens to be looking for a widget. If $2 can buy a widget of the same quality as the $3 widget, he or she will buy the $2 widget and have $1 left; this $1 is referred to as *added value*. Now the important point is, where did the $2 widget come from? If it costs $2 to make a widget, how can a company sell it for $2 and make a profit? Simple. Company B figures out how to make the widget for $1.90. True, this company makes only a $0.10 profit, but it presumably sells more widgets. If it sells 10 more widgets than company A sells, company B profits similarly to company A.

Without going into pure economic theory, let's simply say technology is responsible for the $1.90 widget. There are many ways to trim $0.10 off of producing a widget, including hiring less expensive labor, installing cheaper machinery, and finding lower rent. But the focus of our theory of economics is added value through technology. Company A's widget press can produce 100 widgets an hour. If it tries to create any more, its main piston becomes too hot and breaks down. Company A used the Acme widget press that has been the standard in the industry for decades. Company B, however, uses the Digital Wizard widget press. Digital Wizard's widget press uses a microprocessor to regulate just how many stamps the pressing piston makes in an hour. If the piston exceeds 100, the microprocessor automatically slows the piston motion down to more acceptable levels. With this safety system in place, the Digital Wizard widget press can now run much longer during the course of a business day, producing considerably more widgets at about the same price as the Acme widget press. If the overall incremental cost reduction is $0.20 per widget, then not only can company B reduce the cost of widgets by $0.10 cents, it can even make an additional profit of $0.10 on top of the extra units sold. This, from company B's perspective, is a *strategic advantage* created by technology!

This is an oversimplification (and a fanciful one at that), but it does explain the idea of generating added value by implementing technology. In this case, I used a digital example, but a different processing method or any number of things could have created the added value. By the turn of the 19th century, technology was seen more as an amalgamation of mechanical doodads and machinery to do work, the strategic advantage being gained by simply increasing production rather than by doing work more efficiently. However, by World War II, the idea that technology in and of itself could generate real economic value was settling into the American business mindset. By the end of World War II, this concept was ready to take off.

The technical innovations created by industries around the world in the latter half of the 19th century were exploited to their fullest in the two world wars at the beginning of the 20th century. By the end of the World War II, it was obvious that the 19th century way of life was gone. Instead of empires, kingdoms, reichs, and colonies, the business world would become thousands of corporations, each looking for its own strategic advantage in an acknowledged world economy. Note that both of the world wars had been "technological" wars. World War I introduced long-distance aeronautics, chemical warfare, and the footprints for wireless technology and radio. World War II resulted in an even more diverse explosion of new technologies into everyday life, including the use of radar, the jet engine, the atomic bomb, helicopters, television, and of course, the electronic computer.

▶ Business Enters the Digital Age

The start of World War II produced a large need for computer capacity, especially for the military. New weapons were made for which trajectory tables and other essential data were needed. In 1942, John P. Eckert, John W. Mauchly, and their associates at the Moore school of Electrical Engineering of the University of Pennsylvania decided to build a high-speed electronic computer to do the job. This machine became known as ENIAC (Electrical Numerical Integrator and Calculator).

The size of ENIAC's numerical "word" was 10 decimal digits, and it could multiply two of these numbers at a rate of 300 per second by finding the value of each product from a multiplication table stored in its memory. ENIAC was therefore about 1,000 times faster then the previous generation of relay computers.

ENIAC used 18,000 vacuum tubes, about 1,800 square feet of floor space, and consumed about180,000 watts of electrical power. It had punched card I/O, 1 multiplier, 1 divider/square rooter, and 20 adders using decimal ring counters, which served as adders and also as quick-access (.0002 seconds) read-write register storage. The executable instructions making up a program were embodied in the separate "units" of ENIAC, which were plugged together to form a "route" for the flow of information.

These connections had to be redone after each computation, together with presetting function tables and switches. This "wire your own" technique was inconvenient (for obvious reasons), and with only some latitude could ENIAC be considered programmable. It was, however, efficient in handling the particular programs for which it had been designed.

Jeremy Meyers, "A Short History of the Computer"

The tabulating machines of the1890s had proved useful not only in census taking but also in military use for calculating artillery trajectories. Since the amount of artillery in use during World War I alone was staggering, the need for quicker, more reliable calculating had become essential to the aggressively militaristic economies of the early 20th century. The problem of calculating numerical tables remained largely mechanical, however, until just before World War II. Germany began experimenting with completely electronic calculating machines as early as 1932, but because they relied on the then new vacuum-tube technologies, these electronic calculators were excessively large and expensive. But the electronic technology race was on!

By the end of World War II, the age of technology was ready to take hold. The power of ENIAC and other computers like it were put to immediate use by the military as the first line of defense in the Cold War. However, by the mid-20th century, the electronic digital computer was able to divert some of its power from military to commercial use. By the mid-1950s, the SABRE application was introduced by IBM and American Airlines for the express purpose of real-time flight reservations, meaning that if a seat was booked in New York for a Los Angeles to New York flight at 12 noon Eastern time, a travel agent in Los Angeles would know about it at 9:00 a.m. Pacific time, and vice-versa. This assured that the same seat could not be booked twice. This created a considerable strategic advantage for American Airlines, as double-booking flights was a serious problem for the burgeoning transcontinental airlines business of the 1950s. The implementation of SABRE was a smashing success, so much so that it is still in use today.

From that point on, the value of real-time processing became the instant strategic advantage to any firm whose business crossed more than one time zone, and computers became a necessity for business. Thirty-four years after the Computer Tabulating Recording Company had changed its name to IBM, "Big Blue" generated revenues of well over a billion dollars. The Information Age was here to stay.

But although technology, and digital technology in particular, was now generally accepted as a sound, sometimes even necessary, business stratagem, the cost of entry was still pretty steep. During the 1950s and 1960s, the cost of an IBM computer was astronomical. International and transcontinental companies could justify such an expenditure because of the advantages of doing business in real-time, but local businesses and businesses where processing in real-time really didn't matter so much were unable to quickly make this computing investment. These smaller, local companies, firms, businesses, colleges, universities, and government agencies all turned to the digital computer in a variety of ways. All had to somehow justify the expense. With the mood of the nation decidedly progressive, any excuse would do. If you could not buy a computer from IBM, you could lease it for a few thousand dollars a month. This was palatable to corporations able to directly replace labor in areas such as accounting and finance. For a few thousand dollars a month of computer time, companies could replace 20 accountants—their salaries, pensions, benefits, and sundry "people" issues—with a system willing to work 24 hours a day, able to calculate thousands of times faster, and for the most part, never make a mistake. This was the stuff of both science and popular fiction. But in reality, the cost savings were slow to accrue. The 20 accountants were only replaced by 20 programmers, operators, managers, and technicians to support this new colossus. But what board of directors could resist making such a beast a part of their modern corporate arsenal?

So, by the 1970s and 1980s, computer systems, especially the mainframe, were well established in the international business community.

However, the fiction and romance had given way to experience and bottom-line common sense from a generation that had used these systems both successfully and unsuccessfully. Anyone who knew even the most basic computer programming languages was in very high demand, although the managers hiring or even interviewing these people sometimes had very little knowledge about computers or programming. But by this time, the mainframe had become like the family car—relied on with little idea of how it works.

> As the application of computers becomes pervasive and ubiquitous, it becomes harder and harder to discern the complex and subtle ways that computers change organizations. The premise of this course is that computers can be used to give businesses short and long-term strategic advantages in the marketplace. Firms now allocate about one-quarter to one-half of new capital outlays on computers; clearly many CEOs are sold on the idea that computers do make a difference.
>
> William K. McHenry, MGMT 550:
> Information Technology & Business Strategy, Course Overview

Now that we have established that business and technology are almost synonymous in the latter half of the 20th century, we can take up one of two general points of view: Either we ourselves are the purveyors of technology; (that is, our product or service is technology) or our organization's main business is not technology but rather the use of digital technology to gain a strategic advantage in our particular market. There is of course a third option: that our economic system is comprised of single enterprises that produce technology by relying on other companies' technologies. But this new breed of business is relatively young in the world of digital technology.

▶ The Tried and True

Traditionally, the economy of technology was basically the economy of producers and consumers. Thirty years ago, when the current market was taking shape, there were two major players on the technology playing field, setting the pace of technology for wide business use across the globe: IBM and Digital Equipment Corporation (DEC). IBM has stood the test of time; Digital Equipment did not. We will go into more detail on this in later chapters, but for now all we need to know is that both started primarily as manufacturing companies and IBM managed to make the transition to today's economy. These early pioneers in computing technology were able to make digital technology accessible to the international business community, universally redefining *strategic advantage*.

But what is important to note is not just what these two corporations did, but how each accomplished similar business objectives in two completely different ways. IBM, since its tabulating days, had always been in the business of "computing," long before digital technology was introduced. DEC was created in direct response to the way IBM was developing and deploying IBM's idea of digital technology. By the mid-1950s, IBM was a billion-dollar company; but in terms of how it did business, it wasn't radically different from what it was in 1924. The Watson approach was still a manufacturing approach: Make the machine, sell or lease it, make more machines. The directors, managers, and engineers at IBM considered themselves forward-thinkers, but their business structure was a reflection of the American business ethos of the 1920s, if not earlier. DEC, however, was a "visionary" company; it was selling technology, not just the box it came in. From its inception in 1957, DEC took great pride in being an "engineering company for engineers." But by the 1970s and 1980s, it was not only engineers who were buying into and relying on DEC's technology; it was banks, manufacturers, insurance companies, and publishers. Suddenly, businessmen with MBAs, whose businesses had nothing to do with engineering per se, were making strategic decisions about which computer manufacturer to invest millions of dollars in, affecting the future of their companies for decades to come. Many used the same strategies to buy technology as they used to price, market, and support their own products. This began to draw the border between the Manufacturing Age and the Information Age.

By the 1980s, just having computer technology did not separate a business from its competitors in terms of the open marketplace. The real question was, Did having a computer actually make doing business easier? The answer, many managers found, was yes and no. As computer technology took hold in business during the late 1960s and 1970s, productivity gains became markedly noticeable. The issue for managers then became to determine where productivity could additionally improve. An IBM System 360, for example, could collect, analyze, and report on data a hundred times quicker than, say, a DEC PDP-11. But it would take two days to reprogram a report or database query on an IBM mainframe, and only two hours on a PDP-11. The needs of the business then dictated the best solution to go with: If the business didn't require writing or modifying programs frequently, then an IBM/S360 was the way to go. If there was a good deal of programming required, then the user-friendly PDP-11 was the programmer's choice. This worked as long as it was the middle managers who actually used the equipment firsthand in relation to the business who, for the most part, made these decisions.

But with the 1980s came the personal computer. Soon, everybody from the secretary to the CEO dealt with information technology. No longer was just having the technology enough for any organization. Since computers were used and reviewed by just about everyone in the company, each computer, large and small, had to have a direct "strategic" purpose. In other words, the following question could no longer be shunned: We all know we need computers to do business, but why?!

There are a variety of answers to this question, and none of them are as simple as they should be. In response, not only were hundreds, even thousands, of PCs required to be bought, but they were also networked, supported, maintained, and more importantly, kept up to date. The cost of IT in most corporations skyrocketed! Because of this cost increase, the decisions for accepting these costs were taken out of the hands of middle managers and department heads and sent straight to the boardroom.

> During the 1980s, American firms poured more than $1 trillion into information technology. The results, as one cynic in *Fortune* magazine wrote, was that "... Information Technology is already one of the most effective ways ever devised to squander corporate assets..." The payoff from these applications, which sometimes launched new businesses and radically changed the way the firm operated, was a matter more of faith than of concrete proof, although many CEOs felt that they would lose any ability to compete without them.
>
> William K. McHenry, MGMT 550:
> Information Technology & Business Strategy, Course Overview

One of the most common justifications for the increased spending on computing equipment follows the reasoning that since computers gather and store information so much more quickly, they provide that much more information upon which to base our decisions. This sounds reasonable, but the reality is that with the increase in information, the process of making a decision becomes longer and more complex. We frequently find ourselves paralyzed by the abundance of information, and so choose not to make a decision, or at best, to make the simplest choice. Unfortunately, the tides of business very rarely lend themselves to such simplicity. Consider the following:

> Manager A and Manager B are competing to convince their board of directors which technology their organization should buy. The size of the investment is considerable; therefore, so should be the returns. Manager A argues for a technology that is less cutting edge, but reliable, strongly branded, and made by a blue-chipcompany that has very deep pockets. His argument is that by investing in this technology, his company is in fact partnering with the blue chip company, allowing them to generate the market momentum that will allow the technology to become a de facto standard. If so, the organization will have invested in a strong, well-backed product they will be using for years to come.
>
> Manager B, however, wants the company to invest in a newer, more cutting edge technology, created by a group of brilliant but inexperienced "techies." Her argument is that the technology itself is far superior to that recommended by Manager A, and with the company's support, they can actually enter the market in a dominant position, take an immediate market share, and reap beneficial short-term profits immediately. By placing themselves in such a favorable position in the short term, they all but ensure a considerable return on their investment over the long term.

Which one of these managers is right? They both are, depending of course on what the organization is trying to do. For instance, if the organization as a whole wishes to invest in this market conservatively—that is, they know that if they don't invest in some fashion, they'll be left behind—then Manager A may have the most convincing argument. It is simply better to "piggy-back" on a company that does have a firm understanding of what technology can do and that has already taken most of the risks in bringing that technology to market. For years (and perhaps even today) the most enduring motto among IT executives around the world was, "No one ever got fired going with IBM!" This was seen as acceptable even if the actual technology proved inferior, in performance or logistics, to more cutting-edge technology.

If the company is seeking to enter an unfamiliar market or to create a completely new market, clearly seeing the opportunity for a large economic advantage, they should approach it aggressively to enter the market ahead of any competition. In this case, Manager B's solution sounds the best. In fact, this approach has been the impetus behind the phenomenal growth of the so-called e-businesses and other Internet companies. The current whirlwind over the Internet is a perfect example of businesses looking for new markets to define and exploit. Many companies have found that by simply putting a "dot com" after their name, their stock prices rise considerably. (We will go into detail as to why in later chapters.) Even if a company is not interested in the risks associated with the e-business market, they are all but forced to enter into this realm of business or, at the very least, to devise some type of strategic business plan that takes the dotcom market into consideration.

Most companies find themselves somewhere in between. They want to develop new businesses or find a way to strengthen their current business, or both, which returns us to the strategic advantage discussion. But the idea of gaining a strategic advantage introduces additional questions. For example, even if we do make the right business decisions, how do we know we've accomplished them? In other words, now that we've made our decision and accepted either Manager A's plan or Manager B's, we have to implement the plan. There can be an almost infinite number of reasons why a business plan based on technology succeeds or fails. But more often than not, when one fails it is usually because the organization that created the plan has trouble carrying it off, not because unforeseen market forces or unexpected competition cause it to fail.

Are computers really just a sinkhole for corporate assets? Hardly. The managerial issues that confront upper level managers, however, are not restricted to strategy alone. These computer applications are, naturally, based on computer hardware, software and networks. Without a basic overview of the scope and types of products that are available, managers will not be able to understand or think creatively about how to apply computing technology to their problems. Similarly, the annual reports of numerous corporations are filled with the red ink from information systems projects that have gone over budget, been delayed, or have failed completely. Managers must be aware of the issues surrounding the management of the development of information systems. In an age in which personal information can readily be bought and sold, managers have a special need to be aware of all of the ethical implications of these systems. Finally, managing in the global arena brings additional complexities to the task.

William K. McHenry, MGMT 550:
Information Technology & Business Strategy, Course Overview

Of course, when we discuss business strategies, we are talking at a very high level. Sooner or later, we have to come down to implementing these strategies, either within or outside of the organization. If the strategy is simply one of investment, businesses write the check and wait for the results. If strategy entails implementation, then we have a whole different ballgame. For our purposes, we will assume that the strategy requires some kind of software application implementation at some point in the process. This software has to be written on some form of hardware, either inside or outside of the organization, for the benefit of the organization. As soon as we start factoring in these issues, we start finding all the "slips between the cup and the lip."

Technology should suit one's purposes. Ironically, at least in the United States, the same pliability that allows different technologies to solve different problems is usually what causes so many headaches. This is one of the reasons why 10 different people will install the same software in 10 different ways—with the same instructions. However, I would argue that problems arising from technology usually do not occur *because* of technology. They occur because of people. As illustrated by non-high-tech examples (the chimney, the stirrup, etc.) the fundamental problem is not getting the technology to adapt to people, but getting people to adapt to unknown or new technology. After all, even if William the Conqueror had decided that the stirrup was the way to go, he wouldn't have made it very far if his knights hadn't taken the time to become proficient at using the stirrup.

The most important thing about any strategy, technological or otherwise, is implementation. Although the decisions concerning where and how we use technology have moved up to boardrooms and executive suites, it is still the middle managers, the department heads, and the lowly programmers who must make it all work.

▶ Moving into More Practical Matters

Shift your attention from the generals, and take a look at the soldiers in the wars of technological and strategic advantage, the programmers. For years in American business (and even today), programmers were identified by the language they programmed in and by the systems they programmed on. In hiring programmers, "non-programming" human resource managers and financial officers and other middle managers find themselves interviewing, for example, a COBOL programmer. It can't be left to COBOL programmers to be solely responsible for the hiring process—if so, departments would be taken over by those who know COBOL, alienating and perhaps eventually replacing those who do not. Remember, one of the reasons it took the "automated" loom so long to gain acceptance was the belligerent resistance of skilled weavers who saw the "logical" loom as a threat to their livelihoods instead of as a boon.

The fact that the process must begin with non-technical people asking the questions has given rise to the notion of a standard interviewing process consisting of first a resume showing, for purposes of our example, clear COBOL experience, preferably on the COBOL platform used by the interviewing organization. Note that since it is naturally assumed that programming is a tedious and mind-numbing pursuit, the candidate is expected to be dedicated programming to the exclusion of all other interests; hence the myth of the computer nerd.

Next, the quality of the candidate's ability should be directly proportional to the amount of time he or she has been programming. For instance, someone who has been programming COBOL for 10 years is preferable to someone who has been coding for two. It's assumed that long-term programmers must know all of the "tricks," can do things nobody else has thought of, and hence fulfill the role of the other standing myth, the technical guru.

It is nice if the resume includes other languages, technologies, and skills to show that the individual is a well-rounded person who may be able to help out with, for example, an obscure question on PASCAL. If the candidate can meet these stringent criteria, then comes the "technical" interview, which, depending on the skill of the interviewer, can either be a revealing experience or an abstract discussion on what COBOL means as an expression of modern computer theory.

We can assume that the organization is looking for a COBOL programmer to supplement current COBOL programmers or that the organization needs to add this skill set to the business, and that this expertise is required because the current business strategy requires it. But by the time our programmer is reviewed and selected, he or she probably has only a vague concept of just what that business strategy is, and probably no understanding of the importance of his or her role. Like any soldier, if ordered to take a hill, he or she takes the hill. He or she is not concerned with whether or not the order comes from the

Chief of Staff; the soldier is only concerned that the order came from his or her immediate commanding officer. But what if the soldiers were allowed to offer their own ideas of implementing strategy in the field? Would this notion be radical or revolutionary? We will return to this notion again in later chapters; for now, let's move to the staff officers.

▶ The Real World

If selecting your technologists isn't the easiest thing in the world, what about selecting your technology? Finding people to share your point of view on anything is difficult at best, but when it comes to truly esoteric subjects like religion, sexual morality, and technology, arguments are sure to flare. So let's take a look at real-world examples of how our two technology companies approached their business, and more importantly, how nontechnology companies exploited technology strategies for their own strategic advantages.

Let's return to an earlier stage in the market, at least in digital computing technology, when it was dominated by two major players. As we discussed earlier, 20 years ago most decisions about which technology to adapt in most organizations fell into two camps: IBM or DEC. Each of these companies relied on different strategies to make their products attractive to the market. IBM sold their machines based on reliability and a vast support structure that could and would do everything for the customer, provided of course they were willing to pay. DEC marketed its products based on ease of use, accessibility, and interactivity. DEC's strategic advantage was based on the architecture of their systems. Although an IBM S/390 did the same thing as a PDP-11, they did it differently. DEC's approach was to make its architecture more user-friendly.

A savvy business market would soon learn the differences between these two approaches and would decide which architecture provided the most strategic advantage for their business. And though DEC no longer exists, there are still plenty of DEC computers in use, albeit under the name Compaq. These systems were bought and paid for because they were DEC equipment using DEC's architecture, which still provides a very discernible, if somewhat obsolete, strategic advantage. Most of the New York banking industry still depends heavily on DEC/Compaq computers, although they've consciously been trying not to for the last 10 years. Is this mismanagement or good management? DEC's VAX computer was a very formidable piece of technology at one time—it was DEC's business decisions, not its technology, that led to the company's demise. This is a clear example of how technology, in reference to a business need, can be obsolete without *becoming* obsolete!

Thirty-five years ago, DEC introduced the minicomputer, offering the same processing power as those mythical beasts of the 1950s, mainframes, at a fraction of the cost. Twenty years ago, DEC introduced networked computing via VAX technology. Now every corporation could build distributed networks worldwide if necessary. This was a strategic advantage that no truly competitive international company (or domestic, for that matter) could ignore. Worldwide, universal electronic transfer was made possible by VAX/VMS technology. Of course, IBM and other computer makers had systems that could create the same wide area networks, but they were usually complicated, less intuitive, and more difficult to program. Different IBM products used different architectures, and most couldn't talk to each other the way a related set of VAX systems could. DECNET was simple and elegant, and could slip into the programming language of your choice. Once the Federal Reserve decided to run all its banking consolidations via DEC-NET technology, every American bank had to develop its own VAX/VMS banking systems, if, for no other reason, to communicate with the Federal Reserve. Soon, these same banks found they could communicate not just with the Federal Reserve but with each other quite easily. Before long, foreign exchange, letters of credit, and of course wire transfer were taking place between domestic and international banks all over the world.

If there was ever a case of digital technology creating a clear strategic advantage, this was it. In developing these vast internal and external networks of banks, banking systems took advantage of the second best reason for investing in technology—either doing old business in a new way or creating new business. Banks began branching off into semiprivate networks (where certain banks could handle a block of clients more efficiently) or concentrating in certain markets ,where they either did not have the capital or ability to handle the risks alone. In doing so, they could charge back the costs of such services as foreign exchange, letters of credit, and international money markets to the clients in these markets for a customer's exclusive rights to these services. Because of large-scale distributed computing, all but invented by DEC, international banks, and especially Japanese banks, had a field day during the 1980s, fueling everything from real estate booms to the rampant leveraged buyouts on Wall Street. It wasn't just junk bonds that fueled those deals, but the availability and convenience of large amounts of electronic cash.

These systems and networks are true examples of technology evolving synergies. DEC did not develop technology solely for the use of international banking. For the most part, banks didn't care if they could create these new businesses with DEC or IBM equipment. Somebody, somewhere, in some organization, whether a charismatic DEC account representative or a technically savvy banking executive, had to bring the two together for the benefit of their respective organizations. The question is, how do you or I put ourselves into a situation where we can do the same for ourselves and our own organizations?

This is pretty heady stuff considering all we want to do is take advantage of a good opportunity when we see one. If we are to deal with the realm of technology, either as sellers or buyers, we must start with some fundamentals:

1. Understanding basic technologies: hardware, software, and telecommunications
2. Understanding the process of building information systems

So what exactly does this kind of understanding entail?

- We need to understand the basic building blocks of any digital system in order to understand what it can or cannot do. One of the most important jobs for technologists should be to envision a different future for themselves and their organization and to understand how technological choices influence business strategy, and vice versa.

- We must be knowledgeable about the specific means by which businesses achieve strategic advantages by using computers, including best-case practices, and we must have an increased familiarity with numerous leading-edge technologies in order to define short term choices.

- We must have a fairly deep understanding of the rise and dimensions of electronic commerce and be familiar with the choices involved in managing the information technology function within the corporation.

- And these days in particular, we must be more familiar with the World Wide Web.

▶ The Microscopic Point of View

Now that we've decided that technology is vital to our business strategy regardless of our organization, how do we understand technology as a resource and as a tool? As much as any manager can understand how programming languages like COBOL work, he or she will never understand COBOL without actually using it. But if the manager becomes a COBOL programmer, then where's the line between a technology manager and a COBOL programmer? One of the more common prevailing myths is that it is impossible to do both. It is not impossible to do both; however, I am open to the notion that it may be impossible, or at least unlikely, to do both well! The simple notion that there is a solid line between those who manage and those who do not has choked more than a few technology-based strategies and projects. Programming and management are not mutually exclusive, but people can be. It is simply easier to "specialize." In reality, the most nontechnical manager has to be hands on at some point, and the most entrenched programmer has to look at the big picture periodically, if either is to survive and prosper.

For instance, a senior manager has heard quite a bit about Java during the previous months, and simultaneously, he is put in charge of a new strategic initiative. It is up to him to decide what technology to use to implement this strategy. Should he use Java? He, of course, has no idea until he begins researching Java. He begins to find out what this language can and cannot do. He reads about it, has others tell him about it, and experiments with applications that are written in Java. Although a three-star general may not always be expected to be in the front line with a platoon of infantrymen, he damn well better know how to use a rifle—if for no other reason than to know how the grunt private is expected to take that infamous hill. In fact, it is generally assumed that to command soldiers you must be a soldier first. The same is true of the technologist. You can't be good at making technology decisions unless you are familiar, if not downright comfortable, with technology.

So we will assume that if a person is in charge of making strategic decisions involving technology, he or she should have some experience with technology. If not, then chances are any technology strategy is going to be misguided. Let's say that our senior manager actually started as someone selling COBOL applications, or even writing those applications as a COBOL programmer. It may be years since he has written a line of COBOL code, but he still knows what COBOL is supposed to do in the context of a programming language. Logically, if Java has replaced COBOL as the programming language of choice, it must at the very least do what COBOL is capable of doing, but in some superior way. It is the senior manager's responsibility to find out how Java is superior and how to exploit it.

On the other side of the coin, we have the hard-core programmer, who is less concerned with the long-term business strategy and more concerned with the current programs being written. She has spent years becoming a COBOL expert, but knows that the rest of the world, and in particular younger programmers and businesses, haven't the slightest interest in COBOL. In fact, a younger programmer with half the experience can earn more money programming in Java than in COBOL. There are more opportunities for Java programmers than for COBOL programmers. In fact, more and more peers, placement firms, and people within her own organization are beginning to look at her as a kind of anachronism. The programs and technology she has dedicated her career to are rumored to be on the way out. If she does not want to miss out, she must start looking at why Java is becoming such a force and whether or not she wants to be a part of it. She must find out the difference between corporate rumor and actual strategy to gain some idea of how it will affect her in both the short and long run. In short, albeit from a different perspective, her dilemma is exactly the same as our senior manager's: Where is this technology going, and what does it mean to me?

Just look at the plethora of programming choices over the last twenty years: first COBOL and BASIC, then FORTRAN, PL/I, PASCAL, C, C++, SMALLTalk, LISP, and many others. PASCAL and FORTRAN were just as hot 15 years ago as Java is now. How do we decide right now which technology is going to pay solid dividends in the future as an investment in terms of money and time? What if our senior manager opts for a Java technology only to find that two years from now, the Squid programming language does everything Java can do and more? So all the old Java software companies are out of business and finding Java programmers to support the new strategic initiative is next to impossible, because now everyone wants to be a Squid programmer. Other businesses have already turned over to Squid applications, so now the old Java technology is incompatible, old hat, and legacy.

What if you're a programmer and decide to redirect your career to Java through re-education or a new job at an up and coming Java company, giving up whatever tenure and security you've developed, only to find that Squid is the hot programming language? What do you do? The only thing either the senior manager or programmer can do is put the latest hot technology in perspective regarding the last hot technology and hope they make an educated and correct decision. The problem is that most, if not all, technologies will eventually become obsolete. Fifty years ago this wasn't such a big problem because that obsolescence could take years, if not decades. But in the 1990s and the early 21st century, obsolescence can happen in a matter of months, or even weeks. This doesn't leave much room for error. Given the prevailing style of technical interviewing, you can see the difficulties that would arise for our COBOL programmer trying get a job writing Java programs unless his or her resume already reflects Java skills. Fortunately, there are ways to gauge whether a technology is fly-by-night or will be around for a while.

Managing Technological Change

A firm's IT architecture defines the technical computing, information manage-
ment, and communications platform of the firm; the structures and controls that
define how the platform can be used; and the categories of applications that can
be created upon the platform. The IT structure provides an overall picture of the
range of technical options available to a firm—and, as such, it also implies the
range of business options.

—Professor Lynda Applegate, *"Managing in an Information Age:*
Organizational Challenges and Opportunities"

▶ Technology and the Workplace

Over the last 50 years, the old fashioned "deal on a handshake" has
been replaced by deals over the cellular, the Internet, and now the wireless Internet. With all the information zipping around in wires and airwaves, the complexity and speed of an average business deal would
leave a mogul one generation removed from today's movers and shak-
ers with a headache. Every corporation, manager, and individual must
now adapt to an ever more complex set of economic realities. However, there is minimal precedent for businesses and technologists to follow from the traditional IT structures that arose in the latter half of the

41

last century. But, fortunately, the business of human nature dealing with human nature is as predictable and reliable as ever. In other words, although the nature of technology and its impact on business worldwide defines the "New Economy," many of the tried-and-true business rules of the "Old Economy" are still valid.

Managing technology is still managing value, however that value is perceived, judged, and understood. The same can be true for managing any kind of commodity or person, but in technology, measuring value can be considerably more elusive than evaluating a luxury car or a hard-working employee. The economic principle behind technological value is simply, "If you make something work, you are valuable." Whether the technology is blacksmithing or Internet management, this common principle *never* changes. In the real world, however, everybody gets things to "work" in their own way. Whether they are teachers, scientists, accountants, or engineers, making things work is how we provide economic value to others. In addition, we must provide for ourselves as individuals by making things work, from complex office social systems to automobile engines. But what happens when a restaurant suddenly asks the resident chef to fix the owner's car? In fact, the chef is told that if he doesn't fix the car, he'll be fired! This seems like a preposterous notion, but situations similar to this occur every day in IT departments all over the world.

What happens when an individual has spent 10 years learning everything there is to know about cooking, but is suddenly asked to cram 10 years of auto mechanic learning into a single day? What happens when an individual has spent years becoming a Windows NT expert, but suddenly is asked to cram years of UNIX learning into a single day? Interestingly, a digital technologist skilled at some type of technology is often asked to not only become familiar with other technologies, but to master them on a dime. Ironically, because of the very ambiguous nature of technology, people making these requests rarely have any idea of the complexity involved.

Do managers and executives make unreasonable technological requests because of a human inability to grasp the complexity of technology? Or is there something more like a platonic "truth," where the quixotic nature of technology exists in and of itself, whether mankind is around to be perplexed by it or not? As technology is based on logic, it appears logical to assume that one can adapt from one form of logic to another with only a shift in paradigm. A nice idea, but people aren't always so logical. This is often apparent when creating "logical" systems. This is why almost everybody has a certain love/hate relationship with technology. We all love it when it works. We all hate it when it doesn't. But the trick in using technology to generate value is learning how to make it work for you. Learning, understanding, and managing new and different technologies are part of any IT manager's job, but new technologies are not learned in the timeframes usually requested by others in the organization. Most managers see a technology job as any other job. Jobs are created by businesses. If the strategists behind the business decides it is time to change technologies, the business strategist makes this decision regardless of whether the company's IT managers have been immersed in the old technology for the last 10 years! This lack of understanding as related to the difficulty of switching or modifying legacy technologies, combined with the diversity of human nature, has developed some very interesting patterns in the way most businesses relate their business needs to the needs of IT managers.

The modern functional dilemma for most businesses, large or small, technological or nontechnological, is, Where does technology end and businesses begin? As we explained in previous chapters, this question is key to any technology's success in the real world. Almost every business today must have some level of IT capacity to do business outside of itself. The tasks for principal owners are to first understand the relationship of technology to their core business and then to manage that relationship. More specifically, how do businesses manage the people who manage the relationship between business and technology?

▶ Business Case Models: Life in the Real World

If a company's business is publishing, manufacturing, or insurance, then chances are its IT services will be either a completely separate business unit or a subunit within a segment, division, or department. Traditionally, there was some definitive organizational line between business managers and IT managers in most organizations, even technology organizations. For some reason, this line—real or imagined—can, and often does, seem considerably more difficult to cross than other organizational boundaries. For instance, it is not too difficult for a human resources manager to understand the job of a purchasing or office manager. But beyond "making the computers" work, it is difficult for most non-techies to know just what technical managers do and how they do it.

This complexity can have many forms and variations, depending on the nature of the business, the technology it uses, and of course the people who use it. But we can still learn a great deal from general examples. Let us examine our first two cases studies.

Case 1: Driven by Business

Harrison-Murphy, a Fortune 500 publishing company with a 130-year history, has a dilemma. Having been one of the first major publishing companies to embrace computer technology in the 1950s, 40 years later they find themselves in a quandary similar to that of their allies, competitors, and rivals. Their technical infrastructure, consisting primarily of mainframe applications and the systems and people that support these applications, are no longer applicable or sufficient. The most modern application to support the fulfillment of their publications to over 30 million readers a month is almost 20 years old.

Although the application still performs its function adequately, it is constantly asked to do more. More and more often, the demands of the publisher and marketing managers are being unfulfilled by the application's limited abilities. More importantly, the technical support staff does not have the ability to easily reprogram the application to fit current needs. This failure is not because of any lack of competency or skill; there is simply not enough money or staff to handle the programming load. In addition, the fulfillment software's pricing is based on the mainframe economies of 20 years ago. Software updates alone can cost hundreds of thousands of dollars.

There are many reasons why the organization should turn to more flexible and less expensive software. The technical personnel are, in fact, quite eager to learn new and more marketable technology. However, since most of the staff have been there almost as long as the application has, upper management feels it does not have the time or money to teach "old dogs new tricks." The software itself may be less expensive to purchase, but it is the cost of implementation and integration that frightens senior management.

Senior management's view is that it would be far more cost effective to outsource new product development to cutting-edge technologists to develop the applications their publishing staff and customers demand. In the meantime, a younger, more savvy technical group can be put together to replace the veteran COBOL programmers. Of course, in adopting this policy, the overall morale of the current IT staff plummets. Middle-aged programmers feel betrayed after giving years of loyal service to a company noted for its loyalty to its employees. In fact, the programmers have been working in their current environment for so long that they have missed out on several technological trends and feel it is too late to catch up.

In addition, when trying to find new personnel with this cutting-edge technical savvy, senior management finds they are running into a labor market where, with only two to three years of experience, a 20-something demands as much, if not more, money than the 20-year veteran already on board. Additionally, these new programmers make it clear that they have no interest in long-term commitments to or from the company. As long as the technologies they work on are current and marketable, they will stay. When they are no longer interested, they will move on. With so many opportunities available, *why become technically obsolete like the programmers they are meant to replace?*

Case 2: Driven by Technology

A division of a large pharmaceutical company delivers pharmaceutical information nationwide to hospitals, chemists, researchers, and pharmacies on new developments in their local areas. This division has developed several electronic products to deliver this information via a proprietary distributed mainframe network. Customers must subscribe to the service and lease the required terminals to access the network that distributes the information. Almost a monopoly for 20 years, the business is profitable, but suddenly finds itself besieged by competitors. First, competitors formed around the PC-based client-server model; now they're competing via the Internet.

Earnings, though relatively strong, are rapidly being eroded. There are fewer and fewer new customers every month. Within two years, operating expenses could exceed operating income for the first time in decades. Senior management's response is to implement a series of initiatives to migrate the company's legacy-based products to PC-based network applications, and then, as the technology matures, to the

Internet. However, they find the progress in launching these initiatives is not what they had hoped. The core group of technical managers and programmers that comprise the technology division seem to actually be resisting these initiatives, even though these initiatives are clearly in the best interest of themselves and the entire company.

Although, in this case, senior management is willing to foot the costs of training, reengineering, and development, it is the technical managers and programmers who resent having new technology forced upon them. The resistance is not forceful or dramatic. It consists primarily of discussions within the technical staff about their perceived inability to migrate their current technology to ones they do not know, do not understand, and, at heart, feel they do not need. They do not have, or cannot find, the people who know these new technologies in time to meet senior management's deadlines. And it would take even longer to retrain a talented, albeit one-dimensional, staff of already skilled programmers.

Clearly, we can see that in both situations we have interesting dilemmas with no easy answers. But how do these situations arise? If we understand the more typical points of view of how technology is managed within an organization, we can gain considerable insight into how to handle these two very real scenarios.

Technology as a Cost Center

Management's point of view is typically that "Computers cost us money!" But before we jump to the present, let's look back 100 years at another industry that was as on-the-rise then as digital technology is now. We'll start with a growing railroad company with row after row of clerks checking, logging, signing, and reading the sea of paperwork an intercontinental railroad system generated daily. As the years passed, typewriters, stenographic machines, and calculators were added incrementally, replacing paper, pencils, clips, ink, blotters, and erasers. Although these were all items vital to the railroad's business, they were simply tools to allow the railroad to carry out its business of moving people from one place to another. Or, is it possible that they were as much a part of the business as the trains themselves? An owner, an office manager, and an accountant will most likely give you three different answers to this question. (I would actually like to implement a poll, asking managers this very question.)

An accountant thinks a pen or a typewriter may be essential for someone to implement a specific task, but these tools certainly do not transfer Mr. Jones from point A to point B. These items cannot be inventoried because they are not seen as contributing directly to the bottom line in terms of sales or deliverables. In fact, they seemingly do not add revenue in any way. Therefore, in simple accounting terms, if these items do not add revenue, then they must be expenses. Expenses are paid for out-of-pocket and therefore decrease total net profit. From an accountant's point of view, company's should not want to spend money on these items unless absolutely necessary. And, once purchased, the items must be kept long enough to at least recoup any extra expense through tax incentives and depreciation. These items are *costs*, and as any good businessperson will tell you, controlling costs is essential to any business's hope of survivability and growth.

But let's look at the scenario from the perspective of a typical railroad employee, the secretary of a trainyard manager. His job is to keep track of the destination timetables and schedules, monthly payroll, rail yard expenses, and most importantly, reports to and from corporate headquarters. This person receives up to 65 items a day, each related to one of these aspects of doing business. Remember that this railroad spans the entire nation, and this particular railroad yard acts as a central hub. At least 40 of the letters have to be responded to in the form of answer letters, telegraphs, or cables. To save expenses, the secretary must do all the work in pen and ink. There is no typewriter, there is no telephone, and there is no direct connection to a telegraph service.

Our secretary starts the day at 7:00 a.m. The first thing he does is open the morning correspondence. Now, let's assume a well-trained secretary can open, read, and assess the content of a letter in three minutes. For 65 letters, that is 195 minutes, or approximately 3 hours and 15 minutes. It is now 10:15 a.m. The next task is to respond to the 40 or so letters that need an immediate reply. By hand, a good secretary can write, edit, and envelope an average response in 10 minutes. For 40 letters, that is only six and two-third hours. It is now 5:55 p.m. Responses due either that day or early the next day must be brought to the telegraph office, sent, and acknowledged. The trip to and from the telegraph office is approximately one half hour, and it takes another half hour for the actual transmissions and replies, totaling an hour. It is now 6:55 p.m. Also, there are messages that need to be delivered within the rail yard, itself. The railway manager wants to talk to several engineers about their drinking while on duty. To round up these people takes another hour, and now it's 7:55 p.m. Since meticulous records of all the day's transactions must be kept, each letter must be organized and filed, adding two and a half more hours to the day. When this task is finally finished at 10:25 p.m., our secretary can call it a night and go home for dinner, kiss his wife goodnight, and sleep until 6 a.m., when he must start a new day. This is a bit of an exaggeration, but a century ago, this was not an uncommon way to do business. If the workload did become too much for one person, another could always be hired to improve efficiency. Labor was cheap compared to the cost of the then newly invented typewriter or the cost of telephone and telegraph service. Why spend $10 on telegraph when you could have your own messageboy for less than $10 a month?

The main advantage to this type of business economics is not the cheap labor costs but something far more difficult to define: *productivity*. It has taken years and a rudimentary education for our example secretary to hone his skills to the point that he can carry out his daily duties in a little over 15 hours, not including time to eat or chat with a colleague or two. But say our secretary becomes ill one day or one week. He would be replaced, but finding someone with such honed skills would not be easy. A century ago, businesses, even transcontinental businesses, recruited locally, and generally from people they knew. There would be only so many secretaries in an area, much less secretaries with the applicable skills. It was generally easier to start from scratch, promote the messengerboy just hired, and wait for him to come up to speed…in a year or two.

Although the simple office items we discussed were very expensive in their day, what if they could enable our secretary to type, envelope, and send his mail responses in half the time? The time spent traveling to the telegraph office and messaging about the yard could be eliminated. Our secretary could wrap up his day by 5:00 p.m., leaving another five hours for him to do other administrative tasks he previously had little time for. (It's been generally accepted that technological advances may eliminate some human tasks, but this does not generally create more leisure time; it only allows people to do more with the same amount of time.)

But productivity does not show up on an income statement, balance sheet, or cash flow statement. So, in the world of accounting, productivity does not exist. Traditionally, office technology (everything from paper clips to mainframes) within nontechnology based businesses has been viewed as pure cost. Money is spent with little or no direct return.

In the case of computer technology, this more often than not includes the people who maintain and support that technology. This cost was often bearable when technology primarily consisted of centralized mainframes from a single vendor. Although there could be an enormous initial expenditure (often in the millions), this expenditure would eventually be offset by simple capital depreciation. Buying a mainframe computer meant the firm would own a million-dollar asset without having to pay appreciable taxes on it, a corporate accounting bonus.

However, during the 1980s and with the introduction of distributed, client-server computing, operating costs skyrocketed while capital expenditures hardly moved, in spite of reliance on smaller, much cheaper PCs and workstations. Although unit for unit, PCs were less expensive, businesses now had to replace their one or two mammoth mainframes with hundreds, sometimes thousands, of individual systems scattered around the country or the world. In addition, private networks had to be set up and maintained to distribute all the data from location to location. And, although businesses were becoming more and more empowered by these technologies, a senior executive dependent on his own PC for spreadsheets, reports, and electronic mail was constantly presented with exponentially increasing costs. These costs seemed to constantly gyrate compared to the days when he received the same information on oversized green and white "hole" paper.

The solution frequently implemented for the increase of technological assistants is to treat them as office expenses. And if office expenses get to high, the senior executive frequently mandates cutting them. No new typewriters this year! And if there are any purchases, purchase manual typewriters instead of electronic!

In other cases, the solution is to send the work to an outside vendor that will do the work for fixed monthly costs. The number of corporations relying on outsourcing began to rise in the late 1980s, and these firms continue to provide truly reliable solutions to such cost escalation problems. However, we are not talking about typewriters anymore. In fact, due to PC technology and software, typewriters are all but a thing of the past. But is a PC only a typewriter with memory, or is it something more? PCs are "intelligent" and can talk to other PCs, the mainframe, and outside vendors. By being able to network and be networked into new and existing information channels, business is obviously easier and more productive, hence the senior manager's reports and spreadsheets. This is what gives the PCs their value and justifies their expense. But if they justify their own expense, then why all the spiraling costs?! Why can't PCs simply replace these mainframes that are paid for but costly to maintain? Why can't the costly networks, which link all these PCs, workstations, and mainframes, be maintained by some other company devoted exclusively to such service? After all, businesses were never asked to run their own telephone systems. For a reasonable monthly rate, this service was always provided for them by an outside telephone service provider. Are computer networks that radically different from telephone networks?

From the senior manager's viewpoint, just what should and shouldn't she be paying for?

Technology as a Profit Center

Management's point of view is, "Computers make us money."

> Operating employees...traditionally had limited understanding of the impact of their local decisions...information to gain a deeper understanding of the firm's overall objectives and the relationship between local decisions and corporate-wide business dynamics.
>
> —Lynda Applegate

Now let's look at another example. A midwestern farming equipment business relies on salespeople to find prospects, make sales, and return orders to corporate headquarters. Traditionally, the salespeople would write up purchase orders for specific items as they were ordered. The salespeople would have to phone in the actual orders by a particular time of day to ensure that the delivery information was processed by the next day. The purchase orders themselves would be mailed or taken directly to the central office for reference and record keeping. The clerical staff at the home office would then be responsible for fulfilling the order by finding the stock in their warehouses, boxing and shipping it, and making sure the product arrived at the designated location on time and in one piece. The entire process generally took three days to a week. Since the company was in a relatively strong business cycle for the farming sector, business was relatively brisk, with about 20 orders per day. At an average cost of $50 per item and 5-day workweeks, the company averaged about $5,000 a week in sales, or a modest $250,000 in sales per year (including two weeks off for holidays).

But the director of sales has heard of a new technology available to allow salespeople to use laptop computers to electronically deliver sales requests. Each laptop could deliver these orders directly to a centralized database stored at the warehouse itself. If an order was received before, say 3 p.m., the order could actually be shipped overnight and delivered the next day. The director goes for the idea, spending $2,000 dollars per laptop for his 20 best salespeople ($40,000) and another $10,000 for the fulfillment system, software, and peripherals.

With the promise of overnight delivery, orders zoom up to 50 a day. Everything else being equal, with a $50,000 investment, sales revenue for one year has gone from $250,000 to $1,250.000, an 800 percent return on investment (ROI). In other words, new technology is directly responsible for adding a million dollars to the bottom line!

Of course, the previous scenario is an oversimplification. There are many more variables and costs that enter the day-to-day operation of any business. The farm equipment example still falls under the same general accounting rules as the railroad example. The new product delivery system can easily be classified as "office equipment," devalued as cost, and treated as such. But what is the big difference in perception? The electronic farm-product delivery system can be directly credited with increased cash flow that not only pays for the initial expense but also considerably adds to net profit.

But how much does the technology investment really add when the "intangibles" are thrown in? In this case, introducing, maintaining, and integrating the new order system was not without its own costs, the *cost of integration*. Like productivity, this concept has little meaning in terms of standard accounting practices, but a very real meaning in terms of economic value, both real and potential.

> In terms of new technology, there is a direct inverse relationship between the productivity gains and the cost of integration of any new technology is ROI = Productivity – Cost of Integration. The mathematical formula is simple; defining in "real terms" productivity and the cost of integration is not so simple, but it is the technical manager's job as well as the business manager's job to be able to understand, describe, and utilize these concepts.
>
> —Cooper Smith

Now, let us return to the pragmatic from the theoretical. How do we test our theories in the real world to make the best management and technology decisions?

The technology managers in both case 1 and case 2 are essentially dealing with the same situation. New technology is being introduced, and each needs to know how much it is going to cost. The difference between the two scenarios is simply a matter of perspective. Is technology an asset or a liability? Older corporations are naturally inclined to assume any investment in software is an expense. It is hoped that the investment will eventually provide returns in terms of either increased strategic advantage or increased productivity. But corporations' biggest concern has been the allusiveness of measuring either. For years, corporations have poured millions, even billions, into state-of-the-art IT systems in order to stay competitive. But very rarely, unless the corporation is itself a technology company, have they seen a clearcut and immediate advantage in terms of market position, sales, or net profit.

Because of this lack of obvious ROI, most business cases for technology investment involve primarily internal resources that can be clearly understood and controlled. A million-dollar inventory management system is not going to increase sales. In fact, its very existence depends on goods that have not been sold. So how does one justify paying a million dollars unless a million dollars can be made or saved? Since it is unlikely that the company will be able to sell, lease, or rent the use of the inventory to either internal or external users, then chances are that the only cost benefit will be seen as savings. This has been both the bane and the boon of the typical IT manager since SABRE was first introduced in the 1950s. SABRE alone did not necessarily allow American Airlines to increase sales, but it did allow American to manage sales more efficiently. By putting an end to overbooking, poor flight scheduling, and irate customers (or lessening the number of irate passengers), American Airlines could focus on filling up planes and fulfill their schedules more simply and easily with a real-time information system. But how are these business advantages recorded in the accountants' books?

▶ The Trade-Offs

No technologist or technology manager is going to disagree with the notion that investing in technology requires more than investing in equipment. People should still be a company's primary investment for any company regardless of its technology. But with that said, since technologies change so quickly, it is difficult to determine which technologies should be emphasized for employee training. Since the 1990s, this topic has been, and continues to be, a hot issue in IT. Do you train your technical staff on the latest technologies, or do you go out and recruit the technical talent? As our case examples imply, there are no easy solutions. But perhaps we can at least get a few clues from what some IT organizations have done in the past.

The Data Processing Center developed during the 1960s, 1970s, and 1980s. The knowledge (through continuous training) and hands-on experience gained during any tenure within the mainframe world was focused on single technologies. Businesses owning IBM mainframes enabled everyone to learn and work using today's data center can contain two, three, even four operating systems, three or four types of networks, and several different application languages from COBOL to Java! IT staffs cannot go to cookie-cutter courses any more and come back with unified methodologies addressing all the company's computing needs.

In the mainframe environment, an entire IT organization was given the opportunity to be trained. The key words are *entire* and *opportunity*. Not everyone could adapt to new technologies, but the curriculums were provided across the board. No one was excluded. Exclusion to anyone or any group always resulted in poor morale. For arguments sake, let's say only 30 to 40 percent of the MIS staff had the initiative to take on new challenges on their own time. Further, let's say this percentage kept morale high for the rest of the department and the MIS operation as whole could be viewed as a smoothly running success.

Today, these kinds of opportunities are almost a thing of the past. There is training for certain technologies provided for a select few who are usually isolated from the rest of the department to work on some hot technology in the hopes of it generating millions of dollars for the corporation, but not necessarily for the individuals being trained.

In today's IT organization, where technologists are jumping from one company to another faster than ever before, is it worth spending the time, effort, and money? In many instances, after someone works his or her way up through the ranks, having been trained by the organization, he or she seeks free agency out in the marketplace, where the rewards are very lucrative for technical personnel. This can never be completely prevented. My answer is that it's better to have this individual on board for a few years than not to have them at all.

Today, morale problems are atrocious and getting worse. Much of it has to do with this lack of attention to people issues. Providing the opportunity across IT organizational boundaries (i.e., UNIX, NT, etc.) is unheard of. Herein lies one of the biggest problems in IT today. Boundaries and walls need to come down. Organizations need NT experts and UNIX experts, but these gurus should also have a career path made available to them, whether in management or technology. The opportunity was rare in IT in the past, resulting in poor morale and substantial turnover. Even in today's dotcom business environments, employees having thousands of stock options will pick up and go if their personal as well as financial needs are not met. When will IT management realize that this is a huge problem? Some people do actually care more about their career that about the number of company stock options they have.

During the 1960s through the 1980s, developing technical resources was common practice in the data processing department. It's now disregarded because everyone is focusing on the latest and greatest technology. Get the application on that server as quickly as possible! Forget about the people issues—we can always go out and get consultants if need be. Sound familiar? We're not condoning this—finding the top skill should be a priority, but at the same time, putting people issues on the back burner is a huge mistake.

▶ The Most Common People Issues

Lack of Senior Technical Resources = The Organization Structure

The most common and frustrating problem in supporting today's hectic and wild pace of technology is the lack of skilled technical resources. This is nothing new, depending on the technology we are looking for. C++ programmers are not as hard to find as Java programmers because right now everyone needs Java programmers. Five or six years ago, when everyone was looking for C++ programmers, they were hard to find. Such is the nature of the beast! Management is always scampering for additional technical resources. I'm betting that at the rate technology is evolving and changing, there will never be enough technical resources to meet the demands of the marketplace.

IT organizations I surveyed complained about not having adequate technical resources. For a quarter of these companies, this complaint was legitimate. They are low on senior technical resources, and finding talented help is increasingly difficult. Most of their efforts are being spent on external recruiting. This needs to continue, but there also needs to be skill development within the organization as well. Developing technical IT staffs is just as important as recruiting external resources. The current organization structures do not promote effective technical career development. This needs to be a priority.

If you take a closer look at the problem, you will see (based on the hundreds of one-day infrastructure assessments performed with Fortune 1000 companies and emerging-growth dotcom startups) that 90 percent of the technical staff's time is spent fighting fires. Most efforts are tactical-problem resolution. There is never enough time or resources to perform the proper strategic planning for infrastructure development (processes, systems management design, automation, etc.).

The problem is not only the shortages of resources, but determining how to properly structure the organization to leverage the current technical staff. Today, most IT organizations are structured to focus on a particular technology, usually with one to two levels of support. The first level of support would be from the help desk, and the second level would be a company's most senior technical resource. These two groups are usually in separate organizations.

There needs to be three levels of support built into the infrastructure. Level one is the traditional operations function (monitoring systems) and/or the help desk (first-level problem resolution). Level two is the mid-level technical staff. Level three is comprised of technical gurus (systems administrators, database administrators, etc.). This structure could be used for all mid-sized to large-sized environments. For the smaller dotcom startups that have their platforms outsourced to hosting companies, such as Exodus or Frontier, this structure should already be in place at the hosting facilities. The table below breaks down the percentage of time required for the requisite activities for first-, second-, and third-level personnel.

Table 3–1   Time Requirements for Levels of Support

LEVEL OF SUPPORT	JOB FUNCTION	PERCENTAGE
First	Monitoring	80
	Problem resolution	20
Second	Problem resolution	75
	Architecture development and technology analysis	25
Third	Architecture development, systems management planning, and technology analysis	80
	Problem resolution	20

▶ Ineffective Systems Management Planning/ Implementation = The Organization Structure

Designing and supporting new technologies is an organization's biggest challenge. Keeping up with changes puts stress on the staff. According to the hundreds of assessments we have performed, one of the areas scoring very low is systems management planning, implementation, and customization. System management tools are rarely fully implemented. Management spends millions of dollars on these sophisticated tools, but unfortunately, the technical staff never has the time to properly implement and then customize these tools. Understand that technology is awesome, but organizations need to give technical staff the time and resources to effectively implement the proper system management solutions. The only way to effectively do this is to structure three levels of support and have an effective problem management process in place.

Focusing on Technology

In over half of the companies I visited, I found that IT organizations were divided to focus on technology, usually on the basis of operating systems as shown in Figure 3–1. This is one of the most frequently used structures in the corporate world today.

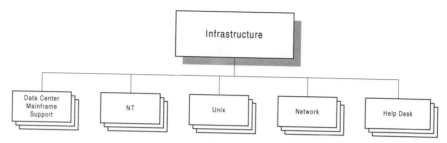

Figure 3–1 A common infrastructure operating system

This approach worked with legacy shops, but after designing and implementing this structure and after management's reassurances to the staff that one day the walls will come down, it rarely happens. The issues with structuring an organization in this manner include:

- Limitations on existing resources
- Morale problems
- Territorial boundaries
- Cross-training constraints
- Duplication of processes and tools
- Poor communication among the different groups
- Lack of enterprise-wide systems management solutions
- Limited skill development

There should be no boundaries within a technical support staff.

All in all, although technology has fundamentally changed the way we do business, business itself has stayed fundamentally same. For an organization to be successful, it needs successful people. But we are still faced with the problem of measuring success. Should success be measured by managers and high-level executives, or by the people who must do the work, produce and maintain the products, and in today's technological society, produce, maintain, and use that technology?

* See Appendix B.

The Limits of Technology

With the creation of new industries and the restructuring of many existing industries, massive investments will be made in information technology and telecommunications. The key question that arises is whether or not this investment will afford firms sustainable competitive advantage. Many of the firms justifying these investments on the basis of gaining competitive advantage are likely to be disappointed.

—Richard L. Nolan, *"Note on Information Technology and Strategy"*

Now that we know what technology can do for business, the logical question to ask next is, What can it *not* do? Throughout the ages, technology has been touted as the cure for the ills of mankind and, much more so, for the ills of business. In reality, this is far from the truth. Technology can help make some aspects of our lives easier, but it cannot replace common sense when dealing with most of life's problems. And of course, the same can be said for business. Technology is not a panacea; but it can be a very useful tool. However, "new" technology, can create its own set of problems—anything "new," whether technology or not, inevitably will. A simple book of matches can be a miracle tool, given the right circumstances, or can cause enormous problems if used carelessly and irresponsibly.

For many of us, the mere mention of technology is enough to stimulate feelings of fear and dread. Most people think that if they are not technically inclined, than anything mechanical or logical is well beyond their intuitive grasp. Perhaps there is a superstitious thread within us that equates technology with "magic," which is possibly why the term *technology* does not encounter language translation problems. Even the most pristine, "untechnological" society still knows what technology is, no matter what words or language they use to describe it.

> The world is becoming a smaller place to live and the transformation of the world into a global village has allowed computer technology to affect even the most desolate, rural villages in third world nations.
> —Jennie Duran, *The Advancement of Computer Technology in Third World Countries: Detriment or Benefit?*

Technology stirs real emotion with a sense of pathos and an innate understanding that it is something greater than we are. If technology is greater than we mere mortals are, then it potentially has the power to consume us. In many ways in western society, technology has been identified with "horror." Frankenstein is the ultimate creature of technology. From Godzilla to Darth Vader, technology can be as much a villain as it can be a hero, or at least the tools associated with our heroes, from Flash Gordon to Captain Kirk, from Dick Tracy to James Bond.

Although technology is a manifestation of our own imagination, our own need to make our lives better, many of us still feel separated from our own creations. Some of us even fear technology. Like anything else, technology is only as good as the people who use it. Technology has no feelings, no sense of purpose, no right or wrong, no good or bad. It is simply there for people to do with as they see fit. Now, this is not a philosophical discussion, but a pragmatic one. Technology, whatever its form, is just another tool. As the saying goes, "It is a poor craftsman that blames shoddy work on his tools."

Technology does have its limits, but those limits are usually due to the human soul more than to the intricacy or simplicity of technology. In other words, technology's only limits are the limits we ourselves reach. Think of it this way. Technology is like an immense jigsaw puzzle, made up of an infinite number of pieces. Each one of these pieces, when added to a particular puzzle, makes up only a small part of a greater, grander picture. But each piece must be added one at a time. Without any one piece, the puzzle is never truly complete. Of course, at any given time, the average person finds himself or herself dealing with a piece here and a piece there, but who really spends time thinking about a grand picture? If our car works, fine. If my cellular phone works, fine. How many people concern themselves with whether or not this makes the world a better place? Yet, more often than not, this is an underlying motivation for our preoccupation with technology to begin with!

Technology is not something we find in nature, like trees and crude oil. It is something that springs from the human imagination. Therefore, it is as much a part of us as music or art or literature. But alas, we may all like to sing, but we are not all destined to be singers! The same is true for a technologist. There is quite a difference between someone who likes to know how things work and the person who just thinks its cool that it does work. The "technical" person is the one with the interest to actually dig into the details. This is the person who takes the time to know the difference between a carburetor and a spark plug or the difference between a bit and a byte. Why people take interest in such things is as arbitrary as the color of their hair or their favorite kinds of food.

Alternatively, it is just as naïve to think that if someone does have a knack for technology, he or she always know the best ways of applying it. Technology has always been closely associated with science, and science, for the most part, has always been associated with the "Truth." Contrary to some western beliefs, technology for its own sake does not make life "better" simply because it exists. According to Ilya Prignogine and Isabelle Stengers,

> It is natural that this quest for an eternal truth behind changing phenomena aroused enthusiasm. But it also came as a shock that nature described this way was in fact debased: by the very success of science, nature was shown to be an automaton, robot.
>
> —Ilya Prignogine and Isabelle Stingers, *Order Out of Chaos*

"Better," as we all know, is a *very* relative term. Even technologists can fall prey to their own love of technology, often overlooking faults and shortcomings in their tools. Like any other professional, the technologist, experienced or amateur, has to constantly work to improve his or her craft. But, no matter how hard any individual or group works at understanding technology, the use of technology can only be successful when circumstances, direction, and imagination fall perfectly in line.

With that in mind, let us return to the integration of technology with the world of business and economics. If we think of a technologist as someone who offers a service or product, either as a group or as an individual, there is a ready and profitable market for a technologist's products and services. Technology sells. Sex sells too. To some this is a good thing, to others something deeply disturbing. But that's the economics of the situation. Max Engels was not the only economist who noted that controlling technology is controlling the means of production. Without the means of production, nothing is produced. Means of production could be anything from a plow to the Intel Pentium III. Human beings are simply in the business of "producing."

But technology will not make people more attractive, smarter, or more at ease with their place in the universe (though to some, it may help). It will not bring an end to war, since war existed long before technology; and it will not cure disease and aging. It can greatly assist in the pursuit of these and just as easily prove detrimental. At the turn of the century the invention of powered flight was seen as a boon for peace, helping to forge better communication and understanding between different nations and cultures. World War I proved that powered flight was also a good way to bomb, strafe, and cause general mayhem between different nations and cultures. People are, and always will be, the key to the success or failure of any technology. Again, technology is only as good or bad as the people that use it.

Now, as we delve into decrypting the secrets of the human genome for profit and clone sheep for productivity, it is ironic that if nature's secrets are ever deciphered, their discovery will immediately fall under the onus of "technology," technology that is both feared and respected. But there will always be limits. Technology can turn lead into gold, but it takes a lot of technology and it is very, very expensive—unfortunately, more expensive than the actual value of gold. It cannot yet make a perfect diamond. It cannot (despite great strides in genetic engineering) make a baby, or an olive, or an ant.

What technology does do is provide tools, which allow us to do the fundamental things in life more easily—eat, clothe and shelter ourselves, and of course work. Each new tool is valued according to how much it saves in time, effort, and labor. But this is a simplification. We use dollars, marks, and yen to value the use of technology. When technology is commercialized, its value reflects the tenets of business, with all of its complexities and subtleties.

Humans have, on average, a relatively constant lifespan of 70 or so years. Technology, on the other hand, can last millennia (like the plow), or just a few decades (like the electronic vacuum tube), or just a few years (like 8-track audio tape players). The important thing to remember about the lifetime of any technology, however, is that if a successful technology enters our everyday lives, no matter how briefly, it will inevitably have a profound, usually significant impact on the technologies that follow, even if that impact is not immediately obvious. Remember the vacuum tube? Well, that vacuum tube gave us transistors, transistors lead to miniaturized electronics, and miniaturized electronics make the laptop computer I'm writing this book with possible.

▶ Life in the Real World

Case Study: Digital Equipment Corporation

> You're always scared you're not going to have the best products and not enough orders, so you have to design as if the whole world is after you. I don't know whether its strategy or terror.
> —Ken Olsen, in *The Ultimate Entrepreneur*

To help us understand the results of the integration of business, let's consider the rags-to-riches-to-rags story of Digital Equipment Corporation, or DEC.

In 1957, Ken Olsen and Harlan Anderson, two MIT graduates, founded DEC by borrowing $70,000 from the American Research and Development (ARD) Corporation in return for a 70 percent interest in their fledgling company. Thirty years later, DEC was a Fortune 100 company, second only to IBM in sales and revenue of computer-based business equipment. In 1987, DEC had revenues of well over $6 billion, and ARD still owned 70 percent. Eleven years after this financial peak, DEC as a corporation no longer existed.

DEC's technology, however, still exists, although repackaged, reformatted, and remarketed. How does DEC no longer exist but its technology still flourish? DEC's "engineering for engineers" is the solid basis for technology that can still be applied by any number of industries around the world. DEC was the first organized business to successfully build and market a minicomputer processor. DEC was the first organization to create a network-based, distributed brand of computers with a single, generic operating system. DEC was the first organization to produce a chip with processing speeds upwards of 650 MHz. But although its technology is still influential, DEC as an organization could not survive the departure of its driven, brilliant, and sometimes overbearing founder.

Is this because of the tenuous nature of any relationship between business and technology? I don't think so—after all, the Edison Electric companies have far outlived their own highly driven and even more famous founder, Thomas Edison. Or is digital technology, more than any other, easily embroiled in turmoil when combined with the volatile ingredients of business and human nature?

A Closer Look at DEC's Failure as an Organization[1]

When Ken Olsen was a young man fresh out of MIT, he had worked for Lincoln Labs in Lexington, Massachusetts. Lincoln Labs at the time was an extension of MIT, funded by the U.S. government and the Department of Defense (DoD) to research electronic and eventually design digital computer systems and radar. Since Lincoln Labs worked with several other agencies also working on the same or similar DoD contracts, Ken Olsen was able to work at IBM's Poughkeepsie site on a collaborative project. Interestingly, Olsen hated IBM's bureaucratic infrastructure. Coming from the informal, loosely structured atmosphere of a pure technology lab to the rigid hierarchical maze of the private company rankled him. Deciding that engineering design in digital computing could much better serve business without IBM's so-called structure, he decided in 1957, at the age of 31, to found DEC.

We tend to picture the originators of new technology or, in the case of Mr. Edison, persons combining a number of hitherto unrelated technologies, as "visionaries." In general, when someone wants to do something outside the norm, they naturally assume they can do it better. Maybe their innovations will come to the notice of society as a whole, or maybe not. But it is obvious that they see or understand the implications of a new technology or an old technology applied in new ways that the rest of us do not immediately recognize.

---

1. *The Ultimate Entrepreneur: The Story of Ken Olsen and Digital Equipment Corporation.* Glenn Rifkin and George Harrar. Contemporary Books, 1988.

Olsen's vision can be summarized as understanding the significance of enabling people in general to easily access an electronic computation machine. In the 1950s, only a select few were able to access the huge, million-dollar processing system that sat behind a "glass wall." Olsen's vision was simple: From a business perspective, there must be a market for people who already use computers to be able to use them whenever they want. This may seem somewhat obvious to us now, but it was wildly radical in the 1950s.

Assume you were fortunate enough to have access to a computer in the 1950s; you would spend hours, sometime days, writing the program logic, punching the code correctly onto stacks of punched cards, and then scheduling time to have the cards formally processed. Waiting hours, days, or weeks to get back your processing results obviously didn't enable quick debugging and rapid turnaround times.

Olsen simply wanted to make the programmer's life easier by allowing him/her to write, test, and debug his/her own programs directly on the machine—no punch cards, no operators.

This idea, when viewed from a business perspective, follows the principle that instead of paying an iceman to deliver ice to your door and being subjected to the iceman's schedule, availability, and supply, you could have your own ice whenever you want by simply purchasing a Frigidaire. It is even more remarkable when the person who comes up with the radical idea of ice on demand can extend that idea to inventing the Frigidaire. Now, Ken Olsen and Harlan Anderson were not the first such technology entrepreneurs, but they were certainly two of the earliest in the digital age. These two men, along with General Georges Doriot, head of the ARD Corporation, made it possible for the worlds of Bill Gates and Steve Jobs to be created 20 years later. Gates and Jobs may have used radically different technologies but their basic business vision was still the same: The more accessible you make computers, the more people will use them.

But our mixture is not yet complete. Now that we have the human factor (Olsen and Anderson) and the technology concept (interactive computing), we now need the business aspect, the quest for profit. The original reason why Olsen and Anderson turned to ARD was not for startup capital but because they were engineers, not businessmen. They could design and build their interactive technology but had no idea of how to actually turn a profit by doing so. If ARD could supply this vital expertise, then naturally they were entitled to their fair share. The thought that 70 percent was deemed a fair percentage for such an incredible idea illustrates how technology was viewed in the 1950s in relationship to "traditional" business. Olsen and Anderson were simply glad to have the money, no matter how many strings were attached.

In fact, the idea of a company dedicated solely to digital technology was so new and radical; Olsen, Anderson, and ARD eschewed the original name of the company, Digital Computer Corporation. That name sounded as if they were trying to compete with the ubiquitous IBM. The founders opted for the more conventional Digital Equipment Corporation. ARD, besides providing the finances, lent some general accounting and business acumen and, above all, a simple credo:

> Gentleman, if you want to be a success in business, you must love your product.
> —General Georges Doriot, in *The Ultimate Entrepreneur*

With this in mind, Olsen and Anderson set about their work with passion and desire, first producing electronic memory circuits and modules and eventually the device that would prove Olsen's vision correct. The Programmable Data Processor One, or PDP-1, was the first of DEC's interactive programmable computers to roll off the assembly line. The PDP-1 provided a cathode ray tube monitor and a keyboard so programmers could enter their processing instructions directly into the machine, without bulky and time-consuming key punch cards and overnight batch processing.

At $120,000 apiece, PDP-1s sold like the technical equivalent of hotcakes—53 units were sold. For a fledgling computer business, a sale of 53 units was gangbusters. By DEC's tenth year in operation, it was an international company with over $23 million in revenue. The PDP-1 and its follow-up machines, the PDP-5 and the PDP-8, became the first widespread minicomputers. By coining the word minicomputer, DEC expressed the opposing relationship DEC had with IBM's imposing and enormous mainframes. The minicomputer, although not exactly portable, still had a fraction of the footprint of a typical IBM at a fraction of the price, but performed almost as well. It couldn't beat an IBM 390 for sheer number crunching, but the few thousandths of a second difference was hardly a big deal to the public at large.

▶ Technical Innovation Meets Business Motivation

The minicomputer was DEC's early contribution to technology, but DEC was also pioneering new ground in business. Although DEC was an engineering company, Olsen, Anderson, and Doriot took their management responsibilities seriously and worked to find the best way of mixing creative engineering with sound business principles. In 1965, the year it launched the minicomputer business, DEC also launched the concept of *matrix* management, in which line managers would share such resources as sales, manufacturing, and marketing, negotiating to buy these services from the central functions. This organization structure, DEC's hallmark, came to be known as the *matrix,* a term that was unused in 1965. "In a matrix organization, employees or managers may combine two or more dimensions in their jobs—a functional specialty, such as sales, and a responsibility to a particular product line or market area" states Rosebeth Moss Kanter in Rifkin and Harrar's *The Ultimate Entrepreneur.*

DEC's goal was to rid the business environment of the endless bureaucracy and inefficiencies of hierarchical management by setting a new example. Olsen's approach was to try to meld the freewheeling spirit of the designer/engineer with the hard-core "get-the-job-done" approach of the entrepreneur.

In the late 1980s and early 1990s, the concept of matrix management was a well-documented method for organizing the modern information organization. In pure business terms, the idea of throwing away hierarchical management allowed the highly focused and well-informed manager to make quicker, more insightful decisions on a day-to-day basis. Without the delays created by information flowing upward and waiting for orders to float back down, information within an organization would flow freely to any node or individual that needed the information for either approval or deployment.

By the 1990s, the number of DEC's matrixed networks, both internal and external, far exceeded what management had foreseen 30 years earlier. Networks, both simple and complex, are matrix management's keys to the success. A great deal of responsibility is placed on the individual in terms of making his or her own ideas and insights come to light. This is the price paid for greater lateral freedom to make decisions. Managers not only had to think like entrepreneurs but act like entrepreneurs. DEC salespeople had to cajole and persuade their own internal units as much as DEC's customers. Engineers had to develop their internal and external supply networks. Business managers had to strike as many deals with other DEC units as they did with customers and suppliers.

> Traditional authority virtually disappears; managers must instead persuade, influence or convince. The subordinate is expected to be the resolver of the conflict, integrating the demands in these two dimensions. Conflict is thus built into the matrix.
>
> —Rifkin and Harrar, *The Ultimate Entrepreneur*

DEC successfully employed this style of management into the 1990s, but not without problems. Although the demand for DEC's technologies was always high, its business direction was always much less focused, even awkward. The matrix proved to be an exceptional tool in producing quality computers, but seemed to complicate every other facet of business. If a product or marketing decision had to be made, it had to be made by a committee, sometimes without the staff knowing who should or shouldn't be on the committee. There was considerable in-fighting and innumerable turf wars, and senior managers generally perceived Olsen as "managing by ridicule," according to Rifkin and Harrar.

These conflicts were not restricted to low and middle management, but were also pervasive among senior managers as well. In fact, Ken Olsen's perception of a real or imagined "palace revolt" eventually forced cofounder Harlan Anderson out of the corporation. If not for the sheer strength of personality and resolve shown by Olsen, DEC may not have been able to make it into the 1970s, much less the 1990s. Olsen was an engineer, and his engineer's sense convinced him that building a better mousetrap was DEC's goal and that any other problems would eventually sort out themselves. As Rifkin and Harrar point out, Olsen's overall perspective on business was simple and to the point: [P]roduct drove the market; marketing did not drive the product.

However, any first year business student knows that although marketing may not make or break business, it certainly doesn't hurt. But because Olsen seemed so unconcerned with marketing, engineering and business factions quickly arose within the matrixed company. Olsen would speak his mind, and although his points of view were very pragmatic, from time to time they seemed to defy normal business logic for technology. As an example, Olsen once stated, "There's no such thing as personal computing"—a seeming contradiction, since he himself had championed personal computing as the reason for DEC's existence.

Chapter **4** I The Limits of Technology

Olsen made that statement in 1972, only 15 years after his vision of the "interactive" computer. His statement was a reaction to the then theoretical notion of the personal computer. DEC's PDPs, although designed for the convenience of the individual programmer, were still centralized, multiprocessor units. This meant individuals still worked on a single, centralized processor, even though their personal view of the data was unique to their own unique stations.

There is no quantum leap of logic from the concept of an individual using a shared machine to an individual using a single, personalized computer. But this was not in DEC's business plan going into its 20th year of operations. Olsen simply was not willing to make such a leap. Why? Perhaps because the PDP series, especially after the introduction of the PDP-11, was still selling like wildfire and the basic premise of the PDP was interactivity, but interactivity between a number of users with a single computer. If individuals had their own computer, why would they need a PDP-11?

By seeing only as far as his original vision, Olsen doomed DEC to obsolescence. No matter how far ahead of its time a vision might be, it still has a finite existence. It would have been just as simple to view interactive computing as personal computing in 1959, but the components simply hadn't been invented. Being an engineer, Olsen viewed the world in terms of what he had to work with and the best way to utilize existing technology. Given the technology of his day, he could make computers smaller, but given the equipment at hand, the smallest computer could only be so small. But after 1957, each successive year brought new technologies and new ideas that did not belong to DEC. Some ideas were integrated successfully into DEC technology, but many were not. If they did fit in or improve upon Olsen's vision of the interactive multiprocessor, they were adopted. If they did not fit this vision, they were simply ignored. Ironically, it was DEC's self-reliance and ability to engineer its own product that allowed it to grow so rapidly, but this exclusivity and inability to adapt to change eventually caused its demise.

The point of this discussion is that technology can only prosper when its point of view is kept squarely on tomorrow. Businesspeople are consumed with what was; technologists are consumed with what will be! The natural tension between these two philosophical poles is what makes balancing the needs between business and technology such a tricky job. The simple truth is that "buy low, sell high" will always be true in business, no matter where, no matter when. But there are no simple rules when it comes to technology's role in good business.

▶ The End of a Dynasty

With the introduction of the IBM PC in the early 1980s, the technology landscape began to change at a feverish rate, a rate DEC found increasingly difficult to keep up with. During the 1970s, with the introduction of the VAX line of computers, DEC had not only become a hardware company but also a large developer of software built on its proprietary VMS (virtual memory system) operating system. DEC found it sold as many VAX systems because of VMS as it did for VAX's processing capabilities. This may have seemed like a good thing, but it soon became a double-edged sword. Increased exposure in the world of software also meant increased competition.

The matrix system of management was effective in an insular environment with a singular direction, but it became cumbersome and ineffective in an organization the size that DEC had become. Matrix management did not lend itself easily to dealing with the changing tides of competition. As other operating systems, such as DOS, UNIX, and eventually Windows became more prominent, DEC became more insular and self-absorbed. Again, being a sound engineer, Olsen probably saw the logical merits of an operating system like UNIX, but because those merits had no direct bearing on his vision for DEC, he refused to see the commercial benefits. As a young man with innovative ideas and a willingness to prove them right, Ken Olsen was a visionary. As a mature leader of a multinational organization, Olsen misunderstood and misread the marketplace.

However, that doesn't mean that everyone at DEC was unclear about the direction in which digital computing was heading. In fact, C. Gordon Bell, the real inspiration behind the PDP and DEC's flagship technology, VAX/VMS, saw these market changes and tried to respond by extending the processing capabilities of DEC's systems across networks. He foresaw different machines talking to each other across buildings, cities, even countries. Bell was the second computing engineer hired at DEC and maintained a productive, if stormy, relationship with both DEC and Olsen through most of DEC's existence. But by 1979, even he knew that distributed computing would inevitably be the technology of the next millennia:

> VAX would become a way of computing life, the basis for tying an entire organization together. The key was networking—that was the fuel that would turn DEC's smoldering present into a blazing future.
>
> —C. Gordon Bell, in *The Ultimate Entrepreneur*

Of course, Bell's view, like Olsen's, was tempered by his exclusive immersion in DEC equipment, the brilliant but proprietary VMS operating system and DEC's Decnet networking technology. But Bell was quite aware of the flaws in DEC's brilliant combination of hardware and software. He understood that DEC, with its market clout and exceptional engineering and manufacturing ability, could lead the way into the world of networking as it had once pioneered minicomputing—as long as the world was willing to use DEC technologies. But other technology companies were now doing what DEC had pioneered in the 1950s. They were making smaller, faster, and more importantly, cheaper processors than DEC. In an attempt to keep up, DEC began producing redundant product lines in niche markets for personal computers, desktop VMS systems, and numerous minicomputers, confusing both their salespeople and customers. Although older organizations remained loyal to DEC, newer, smaller, and more streamlined companies and business units were rapidly turning to alternatives.

When the PC introduced additional competition in 1983, Bell himself had been forced out of the company, clearly eschewing views that were not shared by Olsen. Olsen had never seen the market value of personal computing, Bell anticipated nothing else. He could see that Olsen's pragmatic approach was almost counter-intuitive to the very instincts that had brought them success.

During the 1980s, both DEC and IBM were getting surprise competition from not only PC manufacturers but from "microsystems," or workstations, based on 32-bit RISC (Reduced Instruction Set Computation) technology. RISC workstations were pushing their way into the world of the exclusive DEC "mini." The advantage they offered was comparable performance and uniform networking at a fraction of the price. Why were these new systems so cheap? Workstation manufacturers found that buying a generically manufactured processing chip was much cheaper then designing and manufacturing their own. The same could be said of using easily accessible third-party software. And, UNIX was free and VMS was not. To use VMS, companies needed to buy a VAX, and VAX systems relied on components manufactured exclusively by DEC. Additionally, only DEC software could run on DEC hardware, unless companies developed their own software from scratch.

UNIX was not as easy to use or as beloved among the traditional programmer community as VMS, but it was powerful. It had its own built-in networking protocols, could be programmed directly, and, although partitioned into many "flavors," had been favored by ARPANET to create a universal networking protocol for the Department of Defense and the worldwide academic community. Although Olsen and DEC denied it vehemently, the momentum of UNIX was quite clear to everyone except DEC and, ironically, IBM.

▶ The New Revolution

By the early 1980s, it was becoming evident that the business of technology was continuing its evolution. Since IBM's rise in digital computing from the late 1940s, technology was manufactured and sold like any traditional manufactured commodity—refrigerators, cars, and sewing machines. At IBM, the software was completely secondary to the hardware. Although software was integrally more important to DEC's business than it was to IBM's, DEC still viewed itself at the core as a manufacturing company. Success and failure were still measured according to number of units sold.

When DEC did try to keep up with the times, it found the traditional approach of designing and manufacturing a competitive product from scratch to now be ineffective. Several ventures into the PC and desktop computing market proved all but disastrous, because the DEC Rainbow was designed to be a miniature VAX system. This should have been to their advantage, since VMS, no matter how compact, was still a powerful and well-established operating system. The product line followed nicely into Bell's concept of the homogenous network. But where DEC's and Bell's plan went slightly awry was in thinking that the demand for brand homogeneity was as powerful as the demand for networking solutions.

With the popularity of the IBM PC, desktop computing became a fixture on the American business landscape. Those tasked with managing and supporting that landscape now had to deal with hundreds of desktop applications as well as with traditional DEC minicomputers and IBM mainframes. System management departments began to segregate, and the inefficiencies in costs and labor to support different technologies began to mount.

A way of centrally managing these heterogeneous systems had to be found. Some form of networking was needed outside the limited scope of a single vendor. DEC's original view of networking only incorporated its own technologies. This clearly wasn't enough for a marketplace now bristling with numerous vendors, and there was nothing DEC could to do to change this. Although an IBM AT was more limited, slower, and had fewer applications available than a DEC Rainbow, the simple DOS-based applications they supported, Visicalc and eventually Lotus, became industry staples. These type of "shrink-wrapped" applications could be bought off-the-shelf, allowing much greater flexibility in how, when, and what to buy for technology professionals. In other words, software and hardware were rapidly becoming two separate commodities. Each was designed, developed, and sold separately, although neither could exist without the other.

When UNIX workstations entered the picture, a third component was added: the concept of "open" technology. "Open" simply meant that code for software and specifications for hardware were made available to anybody interested in learning, using, or expanding on them. IBM, needing to introduce an affordable desktop system, purchased the computer parts off-the-shelf and designed the technology, called BIOS (basic input/output system), that allowed the CPU and system memory to talk to each other. Since this was the only technology in the PC that IBM designed from scratch, it was the only technology it could patent, thereby leaving the remainder of the computing system available for cloning.

With the smashing success of the IBM PC, it was inevitable that competitors would quickly enter the market. This time, however, unlike IBM and its mainframe technologies, the design of the PC held no secrets, except for one: the BIOS. Compaq's Ben Rosen knew that a BIOS design was really standard electrical engineering design. Since the specifications of how the BIOS should operate was not patented, he assembled a group of engineers who had never heard of BIOS and told them to engineer a system of data transfer between the memory and CPU components that met specific operational standards. Once this was accomplished, Compaq quickly brought its own PC to market, and computer price wars were born. The real key to Compaq's clone success, however, was not the duplication of hardware but the availability of the same operating system that could run the same applications as IBM's PCs.

Ironically, although it was open hardware that enabled the production of the PC clone, it was a "closed" proprietary operating system that ignited the digital technology revolution: Microsoft's DOS (disk operating system). When IBM searched for an "off-the-shelf" operating system to tie together their hardware components, there were only a few to choose from, and even fewer hardware manufacturers willing to accept IBM's Byzantine rules of ownership. One company, however, seeing a golden opportunity to ignite its own struggling business, was perfectly willing to supply the components: Microsoft. However, after signing away everything but the kitchen sink to get the contract, Mr. Gates and Mr. Allen shrewdly held on to a single ace in the hole. Although IBM could license the DOS software as much as it liked, Microsoft would keep the rights to sell it to whomever else it chose. Naturally, this was not a sticking point with IBM, since at the time there simply was no one else to sell the software to. By the time there was competition, IBM thought it would be sitting firmly on top of the PC market.

Simultaneously, on the UNIX workstation front, the industry pioneers were all using essentially the same hardware and software. A RISC chip was a RISC chip, no matter who manufactured it. UNIX, in all its flavors and forms, was still UNIX. Workstation manufacturers like Silicon Graphics, Sun Microsystems, and Apollo had to compete head-to-head in performance and price. IBM and DEC simply were not used to multiple competitors.

While the rest of the technology world was concerned with getting the most bang for the buck, regardless of the technology, DEC was waging an empty and futile war for homogeneity. Behind its back, the "open" age of technology had introduced itself and had begun setting its own standards. And DEC, despite its huge position in the technology workplace, had nothing to do with these standards.

But despite its lack of foresight, DEC still had the resources to adapt to, but not stem, the tide of change. Ironically, DEC's matrix management missed the opportunity.

> In 1984, Jeff Kalb...envisioned opening up the Microvax's proprietary chip.... He hoped it would become the industry standard in workstations.... [W]orkstation companies like Sun and Apollo would never have existed if DEC had tried this bold move.
>
> Rifkin and Harrar, *The Ultimate Entrepreneur*

Kalb's part of the matrix had been paying close attention to the open standard developments and saw an opportunity. With its dominant position in the minicomputer and desktop marketplace, DEC should have been establishing most of the new ground rules. In the mid-1980s, a Microvax chip in the hands of a RISC competitor would have been worth millions, perhaps billions, of dollars. But the marketing side of DEC's matrix balked at the idea of selling the precious proprietary technology that had locked customers into buying DEC systems. The business side could not see the logic of selling an extremely valuable DEC asset to Sun Microsystems, Hewlett-Packard, or any other competitor. Did anybody see IBM licensing its proprietary technologies? So, while the rest of the world evolved, DEC wrangled and wrangled about the best way to compete in this brave new world of open systems and simultaneously keep its best technologies to itself.

By the late 1980s and early 1990s, the OpenVMS system was introduced. OpenVMS was of course open only to VAX users, but could cooperate to some degree with other operating systems and other networks. And TCP/IP integration could be added for a price. But of course, DEC still maintained a centralist view that other technologies not developed by DEC were peripheral add-ons that DEC would simply have to accommodate. DEC, along with other rapidly growing workstation manufacturers, including IBM, sponsored the Open Software Foundation (OSF). Simultaneously, DEC began closing its Uni-Bus and Q-Bus structures, the DEC equivalent of PC BIOS systems. It withdrew from long-held OEMs to avoid giving access to DEC's internal technology. On one hand, DEC was talking a good game about open system; on the other hand, it was dealing cards that played to a closed VMS.

By the time Decnet V was released in the early 1990s, this "open" operating system was simply a convoluted, poorly thought-out version of the once elegant and wonderfully simple Decnet IV. This newest version of Decnet promised easier connectivity to the expanding network of heterogeneous systems. But Decnet V held neither the simplicity nor the power of the TCP/IP network protocols built into every flavor of UNIX. In fact, even among the hard-core DEC aficionados, there were few advocates of Phase V. Most saw the cumbersome new technology as a dreaded nuisance to install and maintain. Many long-time DEC shops even refused to upgrade until they were forced to by DEC, who would no longer support older versions of Decnet.

By the early 1990s, DEC's world was in turmoil. Long-time supporters of DEC technology were being pressured both internally and by the marketplace to begin looking for alternatives to improve IT efficiencies. Over a 10-year period, UNIX-based hardware, software, and support had not only caught up with DEC but had surpassed it. Many businesses, sometimes quite reluctantly, began to turn over both the internal and external enterprise applications to UNIX as DEC fell further and further into the legacy category. (Legacy, simply translated, refers to old systems that still work and need to be maintained, but no longer support newer, more efficient systems or applications.)

In 1993 Olsen was ousted, having lost his grip on DEC's matrix management system and whatever influence he had with the ARD board of directors (ARD still owned most of the company). Doriot's death a few years earlier, along with the financial losses that had begun to mount, had impacted Olsen's influence. For years, Olsen had relied on the matrix form of management both to keep a finger on the pulse of technology and to drive DEC in the direction that technology demanded it go. But by the early 1990s, the matrix was failing miserably. While some elements in DEC's organization saw the writing on the wall as early as the late 1970s, other elements saw only their own bottom lines and the need to protect their business units. The resultant internal wrangling among DEC's management teams produced only conflicting product lines, ambiguous marketing strategies, demoralizing reassessments, and in the end, cumbersome, almost useless software. Throughout, Olsen either was ignorant of his corporation's ineffectiveness or simply could not (some say, would not) get DEC back on track.

Olsen was replaced by Robert Palmer. Palmer had been a leading executive in DEC's chip-making facilities, one of DEC's last business units still turning a profit. The Alpha chip was introduced to compete head-to-head with both RISC and Intel. This approach of "if you can't join them, beat them," seemed like the only real direction DEC could take to compete on every front with the now overwhelming flood of UNIX-based and Windows-based technologies.

DEC had grown enormously over the last 30 years by developing little companies within the larger corporation. The database division had developed Rdb, Datatrieve, and ACMS. The storage product divisions of storage hard drives and RAID sets were second to none in the industry. Not only was its service and support organization the best trained and knowledgeable in the industry, but it turned a significant and reliable profit. But with the diminishing presence of the VAX in the organization's technology plans, the core base of revenue continued to falter. Wall Street and investor demands began to catch up with DEC, and DEC, in need of cash; sold its profitable business units.

At a company that once prided itself as never having had a layoff under Olsen, layoffs became commonplace and chronic. Even the vaunted Alpha chip seemed to be making little headway against the inferior but open and well-marketed RISC and Intel chips. In 1998, Digital Equipment Corporation, or what was left of it, was sold to, ironically, Compaq Computers. It wasn't as if Compaq had finally managed to buy out IBM, but it was the next best thing. The mouse had finally swallowed the elephant.

The Beginning of the End

The final picture of success is how well the company does after you're gone.

—Ken Olsen, in *The Ultimate Entrepreneur*

Technology is like the human imagination. There are no limits except the ones we create for ourselves. DEC started as a company that simply intended to build a technology that people could use in a different and meaningful way. The idea of interactive-computing was a revolutionary one at the time, and essentially, this is the creative core of all technology: finding a better way to do the things we do. But this is the role of technology in an ideal world, and like any ideal, it is easily lost behind the day-to-day realities of business and human nature. Once we lose site of our own vision, our own ideals, either as a producer or consumer of any kind of technology, then the technology no longer serves us. Rather, we serve the technology. Technology is only a mindset, a group of ideas, methods, and concepts that when combined allow any or all of us the opportunity to do great things or little things better. Olsen succeeded in grasping a relatively simple idea and making it an everyday, working reality. But Olsen failed to hold that same simple idea as DEC's reality began to include payrolls, shareholder responsibility, manufacturing deadlines, and cut-throat competition. He did not follow the natural path along which interactive computing was naturally destined: the basic empowerment of any individual to access the information they need, anytime, anywhere.

The ultimate failure of DEC is not solely because of Olsen. Visions and lost ideas are still commonplace in industry, business, and society as a whole. It is very easy for any CEO, president, or middle manager to forget that ideas do not exist only for profit or shareholder equity. They exist because every now and then a visionary can see the potential of some form of technology. And if that visionary is in a position to invest in or exploit this idea, than he or she is in the position to profit by it. This is the core of the economic revolution we are living in. But ideas can be transient visions and are often limited. If we choose only one or two and set all our hopes by them, they will inevitably be replaced by better ideas. If we are in business, than our business should not simply be to exploit and benefit from a single good idea, but to take the idea and exploit it to its ultimate end.

This chapter has focused on the technologies of the past. It is time to take these lessons to the next level. But remember that not all things beneficial are measured in dollars and cents. Value is the most intangible and personal item that economics and the sciences, not to mention religion, politics, and nature, are constantly trying to define. Simply stated, the real value of any technology is limited only by the imagination of those who use it, and the value of a good imagination is always priceless.

The Future of Technology

It would appear that we have reached the limits of what it is possible to achieve with computer technology, although one should be careful with such statements, as they tend to sound pretty silly in 5 years.

—John Von Neumann (1949)

In my opinion, between understanding technology's past, trying to manage it in the present, and understanding its future, understanding the future is by far the easiest. The future of a technology can be generally mapped by observing and following logical progression using known precedence. When observing new and pervasive technologies, almost all technologies fall into the simple S-curve pattern.

> Substitution increases slowly at first, faster as acceptance grows, and more slowly again as saturation is reached.
>
> —James Brian Quinn, *"Technological Forecasting"*

For example, Figure 5–1 contains a diagram of market saturation of black and white and color television sets in American consumer households. This chart was created in 1967. Now let's project the same chart, using only extrapolation (Figure 5–2), and we can see just how remarkably accurate these predictions were.

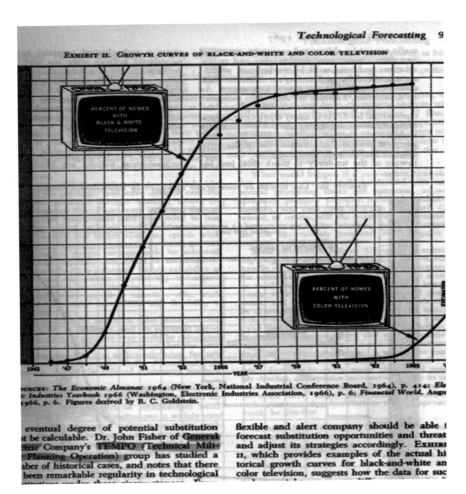

EXHIBIT II. GROWTH CURVES OF BLACK-AND-WHITE AND COLOR TELEVISION

PERCENT OF HOMES
WITH
BLACK & WHITE
TELEVISION

PERCENT OF HOMES
WITH
COLOR TELEVISION

SOURCES: *The Economic Almanac 1964* (New York, National Industrial Conference Board, 1964), p. 414; Ele
ic *Industries Yearbook 1966* (Washington, Electronic Industries Association, 1966), p. 6; *Financial World*, Augu
1966, p. 6. Figures derived by R. C. Goldstein.

eventual degree of potential substitution
t be calculable. Dr. John Fisher of General
tric Company's TEMPO (Technical Mili-
Planning Operation) group has studied a
ber of historical cases, and notes that there
been remarkable regularity in technological

flexible and alert company should be able t
forecast substitution opportunities and threat
and adjust its strategies accordingly. EXHIBI
II, which provides examples of the actual hi
torical growth curves for black-and-white an
color television, suggests how the data for suc

Figure 5–1 Need caption and source for this figure.

But plotting technology is the easy part. Deciding which technologies
to chart is the difficult part. Yet that is what we are all asked to do, in
some way or another, almost every day.

Technology Forecasting

> At the outset, let us dismiss a source of great confusion concerning technological forecasting—that is, the purpose of this activity. To be useful, technological forecasts *do not necessarily need to predict the precise form technology will take in a given application at some specific future date*. Like any other forecasts, their purpose is simply to help evaluate the *probability* and *significance* or various possible future developments so those managers can make better decisions.
>
> —James Brian Quinn, *"Technological Forecasting"*

Of course, charting and predicting technology in the 21st century will be drastically different than it was in the 20th. The 19th and 20th centuries were marked with technological expansions in particular and concise areas. Vacuum tubes and transistors were the products of electronics, propellers and jet engines of aeronautics. These and many others were tangible, insular examples of technological progress over the course of time. But the Digital Age will be judged quite differently.

The pervasive nature of digital technology and the role it plays in conjunction with other technologies makes it more difficult to insulate areas of progress. Almost every branch of science, from biogenetics to geographical tectonics to quantum physics, depends on the power of digital computers to process, record, and display collated data. Manufacturing and engineering have also become increasingly dependent on digital automation. Even the social and political sciences now rely heavily on digital statistical analysis and demographic data. The entertainment industry uses almost as many computer-generated characters as real ones. Knowing this, it becomes evident that even a small incremental improvement in digital technology can lead to a wide variety of advancements on numerous economic fronts. When viewing the classic corporation as a whole, we can see that the modern manager is now faced with a twofold problem. On one hand, corporate leaders must first understand what their internal dependence on digital computing systems means to their core businesses. Second, they must understand how digital computing affects their entire interdependent value-chain network. As if it wasn't hard enough to keep track of the inhouse expenditures on PCs alone, now you have to keep track of everyone you do business with. This is more than a little daunting. Inevitably, even the smallest business or businessperson must be able to respond to, or at least understand, technology. Larger corporations with their greater resources must do more. Large industries and the corporations that comprise them can no longer afford to wait for external innovations. Even the largest businesses must be more proactive in determining what type of technology they need to create, utilize, or disseminate.

> R&D spending...is treated as a current expense in financial statements even though it produces intangible assets with extended lives. By reducing current earnings and book values, the expensing of R&D raises price-earnings ratios and lowers the book value of equity.
>
> —Gene Koretz, *"Investing in High R&D Stocks"*

Insurance companies, banks, and retail chains all invest in technology R&D to a certain extent. Many nontechnology companies do not assume they need to do R&D in technology. They may not formally have a category for this in their general ledger or a full-time staff devoted to it. But every company, small or large, has some investment in computers, networks, and software; therefore, there is commitment to get these technologies to work. Every time a company upgrades Microsoft Word, for example, it is actually reaching into the R&D budget, whether that budget is real or imagined. Usually, this investment is paid in time and effort spent by individuals to perform the basic tasks and ensure workability.

But that's just the beginning. There will be more phone calls to the help desk when a company upgrades, perhaps significantly more. Not only is the corporate help desk the first line of defense in addressing new and unknown issues, but the help desk staff is also expected to find answers. This is a formidable task, considering there are few Ph.D.s in technology available to answer calls and solve problems. My point is that once a company or institution *decides* to adopt technology, in whatever form, it is therefore also agreeing to either make the technology conform to its needs or have its needs conform to the technology. New technology results in one or the other, because no technology, unless created for some express purpose, is going to meet 100 percent of an organization's needs right out of the box! There always has to be some degree of customization.

When technology is developed in-house, either for internal or external use, the R&D costs are straightforward. The ambiguity in R&D expenses within a firm begins when purchasing technology. From Chapter 3 we remember that the cost of integration of any new technology is ROI = Productivity − Cost of Integration.

The cost of integration for inhouse technology is usually easy to assess, since it can be quickly calculated from the original budget and project plan. The costs are usually fixed in labor hours (time and materials) for analysis, design, coding, testing, and integration with fixed cost for hardware, installation, and training. This cost breakdown is pretty similar in the case of "purchased" technology as well. Very rarely, even in technology organizations, are the specific costs of design and coding taken into consideration other than in man-hours. Most firms assume that since they do not have to design or code the application, then these costs do not have to factor into total costs. This may be true, but they are simply replaced with the internal costs of integration. It is widely assumed that as soon as a new technology is put into place, it starts paying dividends right away. However, hard-core experience has taught almost all of us that this is a fallacy.

Change *always* means costs in some form or another. Perhaps this is one of the reasons why most people have a general tendency to try to avoid change. Cost, in an economic sense, is the same as price. Price is an extension of value. Value is the meeting point between the supplier and the consumer. Without these two parties agreeing on value, there is no interaction. If there is no interaction, there is no market. We must take into consideration that although synonymous, price and cost are still different. Price is a definitive, agreed-upon value expressed in terms of money, livestock, or human values.

Cost can be the same as price, but it can also include other values that are not associated with material goods. Time has a definite value but can rarely have a single defined price for everybody. The value of time is usually measured by the value of a service. But how do we value that service? How do we value our own time? Economics terms the price of spending time, effort, and energy on one exercise as opposed to another as *opportunity costs*. For instance, after graduating from high school, you have a choice to go to work for $25,000 per year or go to college and probably pay $25,000 per year. Initially, it appears that college puts you $25,000 in the hole. But without a college education, your "opportunities" for increasing your income over time become dramatically reduced. Going to college, on the other hand, increases opportunities (at least, in theory). You may earn $25,000 a year straight out of high school, and let's say that 20 years later you are earning $50,000. However,

...remember that the average annual wage in this country is $27,845. The average starting salary for college graduates with software related degrees is over $40,000.

—Remarks by Harris N. Miller,
President Information Technology Association of America,
April 21, 1998, before the House Subcommittee on Immigration,
http://www.house.gov/judiciary/6095.htm

Theoretically, the average college graduate should take far less than 20 years to increase his or her salary by $10,000. (Ideally, two individuals with equal talents and skill should eventually achieve the same level of income, but this is an ideal.) Opportunity costs simply measure the trade-off between what you have and what you could have had.

Every time one is forced by scarcity to make a choice, one is occurring.
—Lipsey & Steiner, *Economics*

However, the concept of measuring opportunity costs in a business rarely arise, except at the highest levels of management or under the direction of an actuary. Apparently, since the interpretation of these costs has always been somewhat subjective, either they are given scant notice, thereby becoming absorbed by the final "price tag," or they are simply ignored altogether. This can lead to enormous problems when whole businesses try to re-engineer or outsource.

Projected budgets only take into account the price of actual goods and services on a timely basis. Future costs of doing business a new way, let's call it System B, can always look more attractive than doing business the same old way, System A. What's difficult to measure is the true cost of migration from System A to System B. Sooner or later, the reengineered company must retrain its own drivers in a new way of driving or in new routes. Similarly, companies that outsource can't leave all the technology development or deployment in the hands of strangers. Additionally, technology all by itself can rarely solve large problems. However, technology in the hands of people who are knowledgeable and trained can solve almost any problem. This goes for technology applied within an organization as well as for technology created for consumer use.

In light of the history of technology, we can theorize that options analysis (similar to the kind used for pricing financial futures) is the most reliable way of predicting the possible impact of new technologies. Options analysis is *not* a technique based on an opportunity or situation that may or may not present itself; rather, options analysis allows positioning for *any* number of opportunities that may or may not arise. The law of averages will eventually dictate that even if most of these opportunities do not pan out, one or some of them must. Technology is just as conducive to hedging as a commodity or stock price.

But the real question about technology is more than a matter of economic potentials. Technology is powerful because it actively and genuinely improves our lives, at least in theory, and occasionally in practice. To really take advantage of these improvements, we simply must be able to predict "potentialities." Thomas Edison saw the need for motion pictures but never saw the need for motion picture projectors. This is what makes technology so interesting both as an investment and as a mental exercise—this ability to branch into new and different technologies like a fractal. I believe that technologies, like fractals, can be mathematically predicted. This book is not concerned with the mathematical view of technology. However, this knowledge helps us by identifying the idea that if something is predictable, it must be tangible.

Into the Crystal Ball

It was the advent of the transistor that paved the way for miniaturized electronics. It was miniaturized electronics that lead the way to digital computers (originally the size of refrigerators!). Now we have computers that fit in the palm of our hand. Using technology to develop and enhance existing technologies has allowed us to make chips that carry the same amount of memory as the original ENIAC (the first computer built in the United States) in just a square millimeter or less. (When referring to memory chips, knowledge really is power. A single germanium wafer can hold trillions of transistors.) So what are we going to do with all this power? We can assume that we will continue down our current path of using advances in technology to make other technologies more useful.

Currently, PDAs, or personal digital assistants, are all the rage. PDAs are small, handheld receptacles that allow us to store and gather knowledge anywhere, anytime. They are capable of storing a fair amount of data, run relatively small programs, and interface directly with larger desktop computer systems. The cutting-edge models allow Internet and email access. Now that we can use PDAs to access Internet-based applications and email from anywhere, it is a relatively safe assumption that voice will eventually be added, blurring the line between digital telephones with Internet access and the common analog telephone. When this occurs, we will have a completely interconnected personal communications device. The device will become smaller and smaller, replacing cumbersome button pads and digital writing displays with a voice command system. In conjunction, digital video will be able to transmit, error-free, over wireless connections. We will actually be able to see to whom we're talking.

Once the device is the proper size, say about the size of a large wristwatch, we will strap it on and go about our business. Want to phone a friend? Press a button, raise the watch to your lips, and simply say "Dick Tracy." This may sound whimsical, but start paying close attention to business articles on the advancement of wireless and PDA technologies. In the next year, we will begin to see actual examples of what was once farcical. If it can be conceived, it can become real. The motivation is simple: What would we pay for a device like this? If the elements of these technologies exist, it is just a matter of time before someone has both the imagination and the resources to put them together. Because digital logic chips are produced on an almost microscopic scale, programmable "intelligence" will allow almost anything, such as coffee makers and digital alarm clocks, to be "smart appliance" technologies. The question then becomes, do we need our appliances to be any smarter than they already are? Do you want your refrigerator to order groceries if it detects you are running low on milk? Perhaps, perhaps not. It is up to the real world and the good old-fashioned "invisible hand" to determine.

But in the meantime, the iron that turns itself off and the oven that can cut its own temperature a few degrees after 20 minutes would be immensely useful items to anyone who uses one or both of these appliances on a regular basis. But how do you interface with irons and ovens? Button pads are simple and easy and work well with appliances already (microwave ovens), but a button pad would seem oddly out of place on an iron. And even if buttons could be made more embedded, would the average consumer want button pads on everything? Where do we start setting limits? Basic human instinct, more than any other force, has driven the direction of technology. Somehow a "collective consciousness" has separated the genius from the crackpot.

So, what if we could talk to our appliances? I'm not interested in chatting with my dryer, but I'd like to be able to enter simple direct commands like, "Tea, Earl Grey. Hot." Ah, there we go again, off to the realm of science fiction. But the technology to do this already exists; we are simply waiting on voice recognition software to catch up with the hardware. But if this technology were on the mass market right now, we still want our teapots to look like teapots and not like the office desktop PC. But what if our standard of a home desktop system could handle a sophisticated voice recognition software system and could also communicate with various appliances and conveniences? What if we simply used the following phrase: "Computer? Tea. Earl Grey. Hot." We now go from the plausible to the very probable. Let the desktop become like *Star Wars'* R2D2 and turn our complex English-based commands into simple, digital, infrared signals and binary beeps; how electronic alarms and garage door openers communicate every day. Of course, if it were this simple, I could wire my home right now to make my coffee, start the shower, make the oatmeal, and wake me up at 6:30 every morning. Interestingly, if I did have the time, the money, and of course the inclination, I could actually wire my own house to accomplish these things.

Now let's take the next logical leap. The idea of intelligent devices starts as a personal one, such as a television or a coffeepot. The idea is limited to our personal realm. But what happens when we go beyond our world to the world at large? When we add wired and wireless communication to our technology immersion scenario of the 21st century, not only can we now talk to our teapot, but we can talk to it from 2,000 miles away! Will we have communication at the speed of thought? Will we be able to transport around the globe at the speed of light? If this is what we're able to do here on Earth, than what won't we be able to do in outer space? Will we have intergalactic star ships? These are noble notions, but a bit beyond the scope of this book. The question for this book is, how will these technologies affect our personnel and business lives both as individuals and as organizations? We will no longer be able to assume our level of knowledge at any given point cannot be reaffirmed, reassessed, or re-evaluated by an event happening anywhere in the world, at anytime. With such enormous *reach*, how in the world are we going to be able to determine the *richness* of all the information we can access and can put to work for us?

One major problem will be how to measure the economic value of information and knowledge. A Nobel prize will be granted to the economist who develops an effective theory of the economics of information.

—Joseph F. Coates, John B. Mahaffie, Andy Hines,
"2025: Scenarios of U.S. and Global Society
Reshaped by Science and Technology"

As these questions are answered one at a time, humankind will witness subtle but profound changes in our economic and social thinking. We will begin to merge into a truly interglobal society, not just an economic "global village." Decisions will be made on a global scale. We will watch television from Moscow, buy shoes from Mali, and make a date in Singapore. And it will not require excessive wealth to do so. True, the idea of first, second, and third worlds will not go away simply because of technology, but technology will definitively become the borderline between all three, for the economics of technology, more often than not, is simply based upon accessibility. Once obtained, its value is based on technology's ability to act in a predictable and reliable fashion.

Unfortunately, a good deal of current economic thought centers on control and predictability. This can be good when kept in the context of what can be controlled and predicted, but in business, as well as in life, control and predictability usually make up the smallest portion of the pie. DEC was a prime example of a company trying to control the uncontrollable. For example, networks currently exist because someone installed them. Certain companies, which began putting together our current telecommunication systems at the turn of the last century, have almost as much power to recreate those telecommunication systems in the next century. But the challenge becomes how to do so without losing out on the investment of the prior century. This is why wooden telephones poles with copper wire that were conceived 100 years ago still exist and remain the dominant form of telecommunication, at least in this country. See Appendix C (FCC statement).

Whether pushed by federal intervention or the demands of the marketplace, some form of broadband Internet access will be as common in every household as the standard telephone line is today. It is then that the seemingly enormous potential of the Internet will come to fruition. According to Joseph F. Coates, John B. Mahaffie, and Andy Hines,

With regulatory paths opened up since about 2005 and the standards jungles being cleared, all new building complexities and nearly all new homes have been fully wired for broadband.

As broadband becomes more prevalent, our personal world can link into the real Net, the network which will perhaps finally begin leading man back to the tower of Babel. Although humankind will continue to be separated by thousands of native tongues, the Internet will define some level of standardization across the globe, despite the objections of France. Some of those standards will be hard-fought and perhaps some even foolish, but they will exist for the world as a whole! This alone will be the shining pinnacle of technology's role in making the world a better place. This worldwide standardization should make our lives simpler— our experiences, for better or worse, will become much more universal.

This empowerment will bring about the political and sociological changes that will add considerably to forecasting the role that technology will have as communication standards solidify. The time is coming when information technology will be everywhere and in everything. This doesn't seem to narrow down the gamut of possible directions technology can go, but in truth, it actually does. According to Coates, Mahaffie, and Hines, technology can be narrowed down to three fields that will impact universal standardization and the ubiquitous effects of information technology on most: telecommunications, computation, and imaging.

Now, let's try to catch a glimpse of where this convergence should be going in real terms. We'll start by taking a close look at how technology has been converging.

Information technology in the last half of the 20th century has affected information in four stages:

1. **Collecting, processing, and presenting data.** We are most familiar with this use, for example, the original Hollerith census.

2. **Interpreting data into information.** Only in the last 20 years have we begun to consider the immense amount of data we create and store every day. By simply selling databases to telemarketers and to artificial intelligence systems, raw data, if formatted and used correctly, can become value-added constructs of knowledge itself. In other words, we are rapidly becoming a society that never forgets. Almost any small minutia

of data, once recorded and stored, will always be there for somebody to access.

3. **Generating knowledge.** This, in my opinion, is the current borderline. Right now, the technology we have available to gather and store knowledge does not necessarily create new knowledge. That still requires human intervention, because the actual border between data and knowledge is very difficult to define. After all, a silicon chip can contain data, but the technology that creates the chip is also knowledge. How do we capture that differentiation on a chip?

4. **Generating wisdom.** When we can generate more wisdom from a computer than we can from our own experience on earth, will this be a step forward, or a step backward?

Not only will humankind begin to merge, with notable exceptions of course, but so will technology. Like our cellular phone/PDA example, the lines between technologies will begin to blur. As digital integration becomes widespread beyond teapots and toasters, the "digital revolution" will be complete.

With the convergence of technology and our lives, will we be able to tell where users start and technology ends? Of course, the most rapid changes will first creep into the way we do business and then into our personnel lives. Whether we are at work or at home, or in some instances, both, we will most likely be using the same networks. You may think this is the case now, since telephone networks are generally the same for a business or the home. But there are different services, different prices, and obviously different ways of making a connection provided by an ever-increasing variety of companies. But as the Internet grows, and broadband Internet in particular, the equivalent to the "Baby Bell" will be the ISP. But there will be a dramatic difference. Where the Baby Bell has a localized monopoly on all telephone access in a local area, ISPs cannot "control" access to the Internet. And as the demand for Internet access continues to heat up, so will the competition between ISPs. It is this competition that will spur an ever-increasing swell in productivity among media companies, network providers, and all the companies that will provide the technological infrastructure of the Internet Age, surpassing the productivity of the Steel Age at the end of the last century.

Slowly but surely, every piece of information that can be digitized will be accessible, recordable, and processed on the Internet. Other than the obvious security and privacy issues, this means that the Internet will allow a single individual to renew a driver's license, order groceries, send invitations to the latest party, and watch personalized television, old movies, and home videos. The home entertainment unit, which now exists as a group of units (television, VCR, stereo) merely spaced together in the same area, will be a single, universal, digital, individually programmable unit.

As a result of this personalization, the industrial revolution in the 21st century will be driven by the exact opposite force that drove the industrial revolution of the 19th and 20th centuries. Until now, the focus of most economies has been to produce goods and services inexpensively in mass quantities. The assembly line has been the focal point for increasing output by decreasing costs. But as information is gathered about just our day-to-day working and business lives, the true level of success in the information economy will be the degree of personalization manufacturers and services can embed into their goods and services.

This personal information, though sometimes intrusive, should be benign but still enable a coffeemaker to not only brew coffee in the morning, but to brew it to just the right temperature every time, and, perhaps, have it measure the amount of coffee to brew (a feature I anxiously await). This more acute degree of electronic knowledge will slowly take precedence over the more common attempt to combine as much knowledge into specific categories as possible. Although artificial intelligence has been available for years, it has never developed a strong niche in any product or service. As such, computers can store vast amounts of knowledge, but cannot store instinct, intuition, or insight in order to use that knowledge in ad hoc situations.

But artificial intelligence on a smaller, more personalized scale is useful in a variety of ways and is being implemented on a growing scale. This "soft intelligence" (termed by Coates, Mahaffie, and Hines) is the subtle key to the coming "Era of Personalization."

Soft intelligence (SI) is commonly used via "cookies" and home entertainment boxes. Cookies are simple files created on local systems across networks. They store the information needed to tell information providers whose PC they are talking to and, possibly, what that PC's user wants. It is hoped that, with some restraints, information providers can personalize their content to our tastes. As tools to access information evolve, our personal choices will as well. Our entertainment centers will soon begin to aggregate all of our home activities through a central area; we will access all this information from one common appliance, "the flat screen."

See Appendix D.

How Much Is too Much?*

▶ The Second Industrial Revolution

Now that we have a good idea of what the era of personalization will look like for individuals, what about for businesses and organizations?

Throughout the second half of the 20th century, the automobile accounted for 10 to 11 percent of the GDP, counting original sales, servicing, maintenance, repair, and collateral industries; information technology now accounts for 40 percent of the GDP.

Here, too, the grounds for economic advancement and growth are determined by the drive to meet the demands of individuals. A furniture manufacturer will no longer be able to simply manufacture a thousand bureaus, and then inventory, distribute, and sell them. The furniture manufacturer most likely will provide an online catalog with global distribution. Consumers will browse the catalogue at home or at work, select the items they like and, more importantly, the *customized* features they are particularly interested in. This order will be received at the "just-in-time" manufacturing facility, built to order, and shipped to the customer in a few days. The impetus for this point of view is the simple fact that as the Internet is global, so will be the marketplace of the future. This means almost all economic competition will be global, eroding the advantage that regionally based companies enjoyed in terms of where and how they market. Ten years ago if the Acme Furniture Company resided in North Carolina, its only competition was typically from other furniture companies in the North Carolina area. Today, market differentiation is much harder to create and maintain because every furniture manufacturer is showing at the same bazaar.

* See Appendix E.

The only way to create any market segmentation is to sell very specific products to a very select market. Production is to order, not to stock and sell.

For example, our furniture company must learn to specialize not only in bureaus, but also in contemporary, rustic, and art deco bureaus. It must offer a variety within each group, narrow drawer, wide drawer, wood or lacquer finishes. It must offer a variety of color and styles to capture the attention of a specific user looking for a particular color and style. This also means that the manufacturer must now maintain the capacity to not only collect all this information from the prospective buyer but also to produce the product and ship it in a short turnaround time.

Automation is seen as the key to keeping manufacturing output high while decreasing the actual number of workers involved. It is estimated that by the year 2010, manufacturing will account for 18 percent of the GDP and employment only 4.1 percent. But manufacturing extends well beyond just making products. It also includes the vast value chains involved in acquiring and preparing the resources and materials used to create these products and then, once made, storing and distributing products. Even traditional manufacturing requires a good deal of logistics to produce standard assembly line goods. What will be the implications of producing just as many goods, in different varieties, shapes, and forms, on demand? And this question is not confined only to the realm of manufacturing; all other services and products that must be customized "on the fly."

For this to occur, the creation of almost each and every product must be a very specialized affair. If a single factory can make 10 variations of a particular cabinet, does that factory keep all the resources required to produce those variations onsite, or does it maintain an ongoing link with 10 suppliers that can provide the necessary resources with minimum turnaround time? Obviously, the answer depends on what is the most cost effective. If the networks available to order and receive goods in a matter of days or even hours are less expensive than purchasing a direct inventory 10 times the size, then go with networks. This is an even greater advantage to manufacturers and suppliers when that same inexpensive network is available to everyone anywhere in the world!

With the addition of SI to specific business-to-business (B2B) networks, a single supplier can make a variety of parts always accessible to a variety of clients. As we move up the value chain, these parts, in turn, are included in a variety of parts that may exist in an entirely different value chain. In short, distribution value–chains will no longer follow the linear link-by-link pattern but will begin to resemble a living, organic web of continuous supply and demand first between businesses (B2B) and then between businesses and consumers (B2C).

The same effect occurring daily in B2B affairs will occur for the personnel producer-consumer relationship. SI will begin to not only comprise external and internal value chains but to actually define them! Businesses will compete within the value chain as ardently as they compete in the open market.

> As open markets continue to emerge, a combination of these three process arrangements need to be supported simultaneously in a given ecosystem. Players in a value chain will have differing technological capabilities and readiness for process sharing. For example, a mom-n-pop specialty manufacturer of components may not have a computer but can participate in an e-commerce a value chain by fax, just like in the traditional world of commerce. Others in the same value chain may participate only by email, while yet other participants are connected in real time, 7x24. New Web standards for data and document sharing, such as the eXtensible Markup Language (XML), will ease the interoperation challenges and bring the benefits of traditional EDI systems to all businesses, big or small.
>
> —Peter Fingar, *"E-Commerce: The Third Wave"*

This will be one of the driving forces behind the blurring of the line between the producer and the consumer. This is similar to the infamous IBM e-commerce commercial where the Japanese conglomerate turns to Al's Parts Shop in Texas for vital parts when its local supplier becomes to expensive. Worldwide distribution will rapidly become commonplace.

If enterprises can no longer rely on location to define and exploit their markets, those that can understand and exploit the network that accesses these markets will be the ones most likely to survive. The technologist of the future, regardless of his or her area of specialization, will be the most valuable asset in any organization, if only to keep track of the value chain of information flowing freely across the universal network.

The Rise of the Knowledge Base Economy

According to Coates, Mahaffie, and Hines, as early as 1993, 60 percent of the workforce was in information. By 2006, this will peak out at 66 percent; well over 98.5 percent of all work will involve some use of information technology, whether direct or embedded.

As the concept of work changes, so will the notion of how people should do their work. There will always be a need for direct physical labor, but there will also be an equal need to know when, how, and why that labor needs to be applied. This flow of information will not always be constricted to office buildings of the traditional corporate network structure. In fact, the new economics of a knowledge-based economy will eventually erode most of the financial incentives for extensive internal networks.

Most organizations, with the exception of some government agencies and some particularly large corporations, will become more and more reliant on the public Internet for access to all pertinent information, particularly as both security and filtering technologies advance. This information will be even further enhanced by the continued use of desktop applications. These applications won't be radically different from their current forms. The most notable difference will be their "thinness," since there will be less of a need to store large programs on everybody's personal systems. The main role of these applications will be to customize a user's information and give the user a better ability to handle and manage information. Since the applications themselves will not be bound to a specific system, they will be used just as easily at home as at work.

Since nearly everybody in the workforce will be using some form of information technology, just about everybody will have some set of highly specialized skills that contribute to an organization or group of organizations. This system can viewed as a series of interlinked value chains concentrating on select core businesses, such as entertainment, publishing, and manufacturing. The skill to navigate these value chain webs will be highly prized, demanding both a strong individual knowledge base and even stronger teamwork efforts. As labor is replaced by knowledge, even the mythical boundaries that once defined industry segments will begin to melt away. If an individual or teams of people are skilled at navigating an organic value chain, it might not matter what the core business of the value chain is. The same skill set for acquiring and utilizing doorknobs will be just as valuable in acquiring and utilizing widgets. The next logical step will be to move away from singular product delivery to delivering a group of products designed to solve problems or produce results on a much larger scale. As this new economy evolves, business in the information era will deliver total services packages.

So what does an era of customized economy actually mean for the future? What exactly will it be like when a person can press a button on a flat screen and order a custom-made suit for dinner that evening? What kind of CEO will one have to be to run an online clothier that supplies the suit, made-to-order in terms of size, material, and cut, in a matter of hours? To stay competitive in the industry, the clothier will introduce efficiencies in the manufacturing of these goods that are unheard of in the era of mass production. The Internet will eliminate market inefficiencies in terms of pricing, meeting demand for both the consumer and the supplier. Every item made will no longer simply be a manufactured good, but the sum total of these new efficiencies that create not just a suit but a product of a universal problem solver.

Will this mean an economic utopia? Hardly, although markets will most assuredly be more efficient, they will also become more complex. It is this complexity that will provide the core of the problems we as individuals will face in the 21st century that we did not face in the 20th. In 1900, wouldn't a world without polio, a world where people in the United States could go from coast to coast in a matter of hours instead of weeks, a world where communication anywhere in the world could happen instantaneously, seem like a utopia? Well, it's 100 years later and I'm sure the majority consensus is that we are by no means a utopia! But the real question is, Are we better off now than 100 years ago? The answer is very subjective, but my vote would be yes.

Since Adam Smith, science has cautioned that as the world's population grew, the world's resources would diminish. Every economic theory based on production and consumption met the law of diminishing returns at some point, giving economics the nickname the "dismal science." One reason we may have not all perished today from our own overwhelming greed and avarice may be the advent of technologies. Technology allows us to eke out just a little bit more from less, giving us greater potential to add to our economic basket without drying up the resources that create it. Of course, technology can only do so much. But we are starting to see less of the global competition for natural resources (with the exception of crude oil) that has plagued mankind for centuries.

The 19th century imperialist and nationalistic urges to extract resources wherever they could be found wreaked havoc on non-European economies and cultures until the violent upheavals of the 20th century ended European colonialism. This is what inspired Engels' thought on technology's role in controlling the means of production. Now the world is rapidly evolving toward an economic base where the most valuable resource is no longer oil or gold or natural gas, but knowledge. Knowledge is not a diminishing resource but, we hope, a resource that is continually replenished.

Mind you, this does not mean that new natural resources are becoming any less valuable. But the knowledge base to use them in the most economically efficient manner is growing. These resources will still be the basis for manipulation, redirection, and valuation for the new global economy. But it will be the knowledge of how to manage this ever-changing web of value that will pay the biggest dividends. Because of the ubiquitous nature of global electronic transactions, the free flow of information on the Internet, and, at least in the 1990s, the continuous upward surge of the stock market, a good deal of the standard rigidity in financial and labor markets is beginning to dissolve. In the workplace alone, Internet startup companies are commanding extremely high stock market captializations strictly on the potential markets they are designed to tap.

The savvy employee/entrepreneur now wants a piece of the action and, by and large, is getting it. These new trends of providing stock options, generous profit-sharing plans, cars, and other non-cash bonuses seem to indicate that the dismal science is in reverse. Standards of living continue to rise, but at least so far, inflation does not. A highly skilled technology labor pool continues to shrink, but wages remain relatively low in nontechnology sectors and especially among blue-collar workers. As more money is made, more money is reinvested. Financial markets are becoming 24-hour operations that are complex practically beyond human understanding. The Internet represents the latest "gold rush," and like most gold rushes, it will eventually peter out, but that doesn't mean that fortunes won't be made along the way.

The Internet and the expansion of the global economy are just the result of the 20th century mass-production society coming to a fitting end. With the decline of assembly line manufacturing, it is only logical that assembly line labor must eventually begin to fade. As economies become more liquid and free from the direct control of a few well-placed, powerful individuals, so will the way individuals and groups view how they should work and how they should be compensated. In turn, organizations and businesses have to review how they recruit, hire, and compensate their workers as they try to remain competitive in this new Web-based value-chain environment. This goes beyond mere profit sharing to quality of life issues. Inhouse child care centers or even staying at home to work is not just a trend: soon it will be commonplace.

Eventually, the swell of Internet and technology startups will undergo a form of social Darwinism. The strong will eventually force the weaker players out of business or absorb them through mergers and acquisitions. And as these new companies grow and prosper, they will foster a "lean and mean" culture of independence and individual value. In short, they will begin creating organic Web value chains from within. As larger railroads expanded by gobbling up smaller railroads throughout the 19th century, larger Web value-chains will simply gobble up the smaller ones. Already, precedents are being set for these new labor markets.

> Just as the New Economy is dismantling the old rules of commerce, the new workforce is shredding the contracts between employers and employees. Employees are giving up rigid wage scales in favor of flexible compensation. They are learning to live with high turnover and abolishing seniority-based pay. "We're in a dramatic transformation," says Hewitt Associates LLC compensation consultant Paul Shafer. "We're moving toward person-based pay."
> —Michelle Conlin, Peter Coy, Ann Therese Palmer, and
> Garbrielle Saveri, *"The Wild New Workforce"*

Like any other change, this may bode well for some and ill for others, but on the whole, at least in terms of economics, this is a necessary and obvious evolution. Although the American workplace has been the most productive and creative over the last 50 or so years, the standard corporate structure of the time was almost as stifling. Innate cultural, social, and political boundaries would often seep into day-to-day business affairs. Sexism, racism, nationalism, and a slew of other "isms" permeated American industry, undermining a good amount of its overall productivity. Of course, these social ills are not going to disappear as technology enters the Internet Age, but for the most part, at least in business, typical social ills will become more and more invisible. As organic value-chain webs begin to dominate the way we do business, they will often be faceless, sometimes even nameless, entities that are simply nodes on a network. Like telephone operators that controlled the flow of telephone traffic across the U.S. in the early 20th century, they will be indistinguishable.

Without social and political restraints, economies can begin to exploit their own cultural values in terms of what they can and want to produce. Since customization will be the goal for both manufacturing and service organizations, customers will have greater input as to how they want their products to look, feel, and behave. This will, of course, be a reflection of individual tastes and cultures. A chair manufacturer will be able to produce the same chair just as easily in kinte cloth as Japanese silk, depending on the extent of its material value-chain network. Ironically, this reculturalization will actually exist because of the Internet's ability to cross cultures seamlessly. By and large, the following will mark the general shift of this new faceless economy:

- A shift from mass to custom production
- A change in the world division of labor for producing universal and culture-specific products
- Improved manufacturing productivity through the integration of management and organizational tools and organizational strategies with technologies.

In addition, without social "friction" getting in the way, organizations should find it easier to maximize efficiencies at a much lower cost. Until 15 years ago, manufacturing technologies were more advanced than the strategies for using them. Technology only affects the lives of the people and institutions that use it. Although the Internet is free, or at least relatively inexpensive (a $20 monthly ISP fee is still considerably less than the average monthly phone bill), it is still a new, even emerging, technology. To use any new technology, we have already learned, implies some level of investment. Not everybody will want to or even be able to make these investments in the near future. But the future will come nonetheless, and the individuals and institutions that make their investment in that future now will be far ahead of competitors who did not make the necessary investments in technology and training.

The Internet

64K of memory should be enough for everybody.

—Bill Gates (1981)

The last few years have seen the Internet go from a backbone network for governments and universities to a technological and economic explosion without parallel in modern times. The Internet is rewriting the international economic landscape almost overnight and, in the process, is affecting our lives dramatically.

In 1993, when the Internet became officially commercial, early commercial sites were basically inoffensive pages of information and images on college and university sites. The early "business" sites were usually on inexpensive servers, often in someone's home office or basement. In less than five years, some of these "basement" companies have turned into billion-dollar Wall Street juggernauts! Yahoo!, the granddaddy of Internet companies is less than a decade old. The following information is taken from the Yahoo! Web site, *http://jobs.yahoo.co.uk/eurojobs/company.html*.

> Yahoo! started as an idea, grew into a hobby, and then turned into a full-time passion. Our chief Yahoos, David Filo and Jerry Yang, Ph.D. candidates in Electrical Engineering at Stanford University, started their guide

in April 1994 as a way to keep track of their personal interests on the Internet. Before long they found their home-brewed lists were becoming too long and unwieldy. Gradually they began to spend more and more time on Yahoo!.

Although there have been other technology phenomena in the 20th century, such as the automobile, radio, television, transistor, and jet engine, none have become as pervasive in our society as the Internet after being introduced as consumer products.

The relative inexpensiveness and universal availability of the Internet have ensured its phenomenal growth. The inexpensive transistor radios we today take for granted cost over $50 dollars in the mid-1950s when they were introduced. This is comparable to today's high-end PalmPilots. Although PalmPilots are quite popular, they are still far from being household items. It took 10 to 15 years before every teenager in America had a transistor radio of his or her own. The same is generally true for any emerging technology—except the Internet.

Previous consumer trends that form the usual S-curves (see Chapter 5, Figure 5–2) seem to be dramatically reduced in relation to the Internet. Since the Internet is not a consumer product, its direct impact on society cannot be measured according to units sold. In fact, people who have never used the Internet or even know what the Internet is (highly unlikely!) are still being affected by the Internet simply because it exists. Internet technology is revolutionary because it is one of the few technologies to go from *emerging* to *pervasive* almost overnight!

▶ What the Internet Is Not

The Internet is not a product; it is a service. Although it is used to sell products, the real economic value of the Internet is realized when corporations develop a business strategy for the Internet. To maximize its utility, the Internet must first be viewed in terms of its current role in the world economy as a whole.

The Internet is an information delivery system. Networks can be viewed as markets in themselves, but the true value of a network is its access to markets, and more importantly, the creation of markets. These markets, as they are created, define new generations of businesses. The concept of buying and selling dates back to the dawn of man. Who can say when the first Cro-Magnon bought a fresh new lionskin with a useful bone or piece of flint? Technology has allowed the idea to evolve steadily and measurably, becoming a part of our everyday culture and language. There was no such thing as "telemarketing" until the telephone came along. It took quite a while after the telephone was introduced to business before the term "telemarketing" caught on.

The Internet is comparable to what the telephone was 100 years ago. The phone was a useful commodity that, at first, only the well-to-do could afford and utilize. It was by no means the common household item it is today. A household with a telephone in the 1890s was similar to a modern-day household with a PC and Internet access. Today, the limit on the growth of household access to personal computers, and therefore to the Internet, is tied to price—approximately $2,000 for a well-equipped PC. This is still a lot of money to the average American household. Another price limitation is bandwidth: Internet service providers (ISPs) charge more for higher bandwidth because it enables faster Internet speeds. This was the case 100 years ago when the cost of a telephone and its monthly charges were prohibitive to the average American household with a $10 monthly income. And even if you owned a telephone, you could use it to communicate only as far as your local telephone company supplied service. Remember, at the end of the 19th century, Ma Bell was not yet born. Anybody who could afford to run a copper wire from one pole to the next could be, and often was, a "telephone company." Like today's ISPs, they were single-point providers to the much larger network.

The biggest problem, as the cost of owning a telephone decreased and the amount of households that owned one increased, was a lack of standardization. It took an act of Congress to merge these variant telephone companies into a monopolistic whole, finally creating the ubiquitous "Telephone Company" for the next 70 or so years. But once the standard was set, telephones turned from a rarity to a commonality. Prior to 1910, only the most wealthy and successful business tycoons had access to telephone lines. Twenty years later, practically every desk in the corporate world had a telephone. Today the concept of not having a telephone to do business borders on the ridiculous. One hundred years ago, using a telephone to do business was viewed as just as ridiculous. As the phone became more common in our private lives, it became more intertwined with business, whatever that business was.

Eventually, the telephone network allowed us to inform, receive, and distribute goods and services more easily.

Although the telephone network does not define the business, sometimes the business can be defined *by* the network. The Internet, like the telephone, represents a network to distribute products and services, spawning hosts of new businesses to promote these products, and more importantly, the network itself. To be more precise, the actual product or service the Internet lends itself to is information, and the Internet is slowly, but very surely, revolutionizing the information business. So, rather than watching the revolution, how do you actively and profitability participate in this revolution?

▶ Major Concepts

When formulating a plan to use the Internet for business, we must first fully understand how business has historically been transaction-oriented and how the Internet affects that orientation. We will look at six primary business concepts that have been uniquely combined by the existence of the Internet. Once these concepts and how they relate to each other is understood, we can define a successful business strategy for decades to come. These concepts are

- the economics of information
- Internet competition; the "lane" network concept
- the virtual economy
- the e-lance economy
- the information infomediary

▶ The Economics of Information

Before we can make money, what is it that we're selling? The hallmark of the 20th century in terms of business in general has been the leveraging of the industrial revolution and the economy's resulting rapid growth, relying on steadily improving "mechanized" technology. In just over a hundred years, most of the world went from agrarian, individualized economies based on close cooperation among farmers, land-owners, and markets to an economy based on rapid movement of both information and goods. The growth of an industrial-based infrastructure redefined the main units of the agrarian economy from a farmer/landowner relationship to the consumer/firm relationship.

In an agrarian economy, a single farmer would work either independently or with a group of other farmers to sow, nurture, and reap basic foodstuffs and cash crops. Farmers provided labor, landowners supplied land, and merchants provided both farmers and landowners with access to internal and external markets. How the food was grown and harvested, how the farmers provided for themselves and their landlords, and how the goods reached outside markets was left entirely to whatever arrangements these groups decided best met their mutual needs. Of course, this led to highly regional economies scattered no more than a few miles apart. Intertwining these autonomous economies was geographically difficult. There was mass trade, but localized economies were the heart and soul of every national, religious, or social state for centuries. Feudal Europe is a prime historical example. A common landlord allowed tenant farmers access to land to grow foodstuffs and other useful items to trade at a centralized marketplace. As marketplaces grew, so did the communities. Today, the shopping mall is a prime example of a concentrated localized economy in a specific geographical region. The technology of the car has made it possible to build a mall anywhere.

But during the last century, wind cutters, steamboats, railroads, the telegraph, and the telephone meant geographic barriers could be circumvented. Individual businessmen now found that they could maintain cause-and-effect relationships across mountains, rivers, and oceans that they themselves never crossed. The functions of trade and commerce were compartmentalized or absorbed. The hierarchical industrial corporation was born, subsuming a broad array of functions and often a broad array of businesses, quickly maturing to become the dominant organizational model of the 20th century.

Another hallmark of the 20th century has been the subtle change of value from material goods—food, clothing, shelter, and the like—to include a less tangible but no less basic item, information. As information has flown from region to region more freely and much more broadly, it has developed an economic value all its own, defining the Information Age. It is the economics of information that provides the vast frontier of economic opportunity that gives life to the hype surrounding the Internet.

What Gives Information Its Initial Economic?

If the Internet is based on a free global network that is available to anybody, how can real economic value be extracted from it directly?

The answer is simple; the economics of information are not the same as the traditional economics of goods and services, that is, so many units of one good (whether barter or money) for so many units of another good. Information, for the most part, has no units; the value of information is decided upon singularly, not collectively. One person may desperately need to know the latest bit of news or a stock quote and would gladly pay dearly for it; the next person wouldn't give a single penny for the same information. In a barter system, there is usually some universal sense of value between three pigs or two bushels of hay. With information, you are more likely to be dealing with a market of one, not the classical invisible hand of a free and more universally accepted market. With the business of information, the seller and buyer decide for themselves what is of value and what is not.

The new economics of information can change the rules of competition, allowing new players and products to render obsolete traditional sources of competitive advantage, such as a sales force, a supreme brand, or the world's best content. The new economy more closely resembles the agrarian economic model than the industrial. The scale of value has returned to small groups and individuals.

Corporations taking a traditional view of the Internet will discover that the old methods of doing business do not work. We cannot assume that a unit of information is going to provide $10 of value for each consumer. And we cannot predict value using traditional economic indicators such as unit costs, marginal cost, or marginal utility. As more and more companies launch Internet sites for distinct services rather than for a new form of access for the buying and selling of goods and services, thousands of new business models have been created worldwide, not just in the U.S., fueled by unprecedented amounts of venture capital.

So far this year, Ottawa-area technology startups have attracted enormous and unprecedented amounts of venture capital—grabbing $354 million in the second quarter alone.

—Christopher Guly, *"Venture Capitalists Invest $63 Million in Ubiquity Software: Kanata Firm Lands Record Funding"*

If we are selling information over the Internet, we have a whole new ballgame, but still a ballgame in which anyone can play. The catch is realizing that since there are no rules, the new game is to define the rules. In other words, if you want to move beyond simply allowing people to buy goods online (a noble and perhaps profitable goal in and of itself) to actually creating whole new businesses, you must first define and follow through on new rules based on old principles.

The traditional corporate structure depends on independent networks under one name and one system of management. These separate networks work together to gather, create, and distribute the materials that comprise a business. The automobile industry is a classic example of such a system. A single automobile corporation is divided into a number of divisions, each responsible for its own profitability. Each division, in turn, is broken down into various departments with their basic areas of responsibility and accountability. Each department, division, or business is ultimately judged as profitable depending on its economic performance over time. Collectively, they determine the economic value of the corporation as a whole.

Although separate and sometimes unique, each department is ultimately dependent on exchanging information with the departments, business units, vendors, and clients with which they interact. In doing so they create internal networks that expedite goods and services internally and externally. This defines the organizational value chain of the modern corporation.

Information, like any product, can be manufactured, packaged, and distributed. Once distributed, it can be marketed, and the traditional business concepts of marginal and unit cost and value are in effect once again. What changes with the Internet is the network defining the distribution of information. We no longer have to rely on transportation routes and shelf-space to get the product to market. We simply "post it" on a server and it is made available to anyone with access to cyberspace. Once everyone is connected electronically, information can travel by itself.

What is truly revolutionary about Internet connectivity is the possibility of "unbundling" information from its physical carrier. We can now define a direct value relationship between the information offered and whoever is interested in the information. In other words, there is no middleman to consider. Information can be split into two simple categories: information interesting to a few and information interesting to many. Most information falls somewhere in between but can be valued using the following definitions: *reach* and *richness*.

Reach describes who and how many receive the information. Information can be extremely valuable to one person and completely useless to another. Some information can have little value to any one individual but can be extremely valuable to large groups. For example, commodity traders specialize in the buying and selling of soybeans. One of the largest soybean farms in the world just lost half of its crop due to fire. This kind of information would have vast implications to all soybean traders, particularly the one who hears the news first. Anticipating an inevitable rise in soybean prices, any trader can buy up as much soybeans at its current price as possible before the news becomes widespread. When the news does reach the public, the trader could expect a considerable profit. But for me or you, except for possible empathy for the soybean farmer losing his crop, the news means very little in terms of personal gain, at least for now.

Richness describes what kind of information is being networked and in what form it can be delivered. Richness can be grouped into two general categories: *Customized information* is tailored to specific or general audiences. *Interactivity* describes how the information is targeted for those audiences. For example, a dialogue defines information interactivity by small groups; a monologue defines interactivity directed to large groups. In a dialogue, two people find the exchange of ideas, knowledge, or feelings valuable when shared only with each other. To these two, the information network is "rich" in value. In a monologue, certain information is extremely valuable only when disseminated to large groups and thus offers "reach" as its value.

Information economics is the trade-off of richness and reach. If graphed, its mathematical representation looks strikingly similar to the classical supply and demand curve, as shown in Figure 6–1.

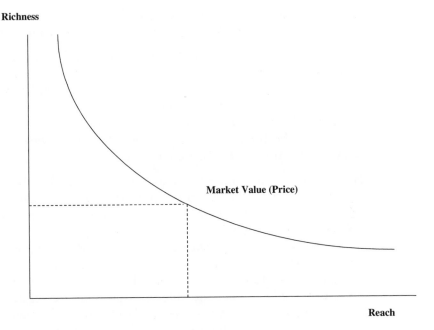

Figure 6–1 Need caption for this figure.

Mathematically, this diagram infers that the relationship is exponentially inversely proportional, i.e., the higher the reach, the lower the richness, and vice versa.

Traditionally, it was thought that the following axiom applied to all networks: *Communication cannot be rich and broad simultaneously.* Loosely translated, this is the reason why a cable network company provides value—everyone on a very broad scale wanting access can have access, as long they are willing to pay. A cable network has reach. Conversely, the Reuters news service is more or less limited by price and accessibility to financial professionals. Since Reuter's concentrates solely on financial information, it is valued for its richness.

But what happens when that rule no longer holds true? What if cable companies could broadcast specific shows to specific audiences at very specific times, or conversely, what if Reuters could provide financial information to anyone, regardless of whether they were in the world of finance or not? Part of the economic value of the corporate structure is that its internal structure provides the basic network required to do business less expensively than external networks. External networks, in turn, are comprised of corporate entities providing their own internal networks as an external service or good to parties willing to pay.

The boundaries of the corporation are set by the economics of exchanging information: Organizations enable the exchange of rich information among a narrow, internal group; markets enable the exchange of thinner information among a larger, external group. The point at which one mode becomes less cost-effective than the other determines the boundaries of the corporation. However, through the Internet, this trade-off is being blown up!

How does a corporation regain cost control of the information exchange between organizations and markets? By defining the rules of the exchange. Technical standards underlie the so-called Internet technologies *and* their growth. Most of these standards are "open," meaning anyone can access, support, and expand the Internet and its content according to those standards. This is how the Internet can send very specific information to a very broad audience. Over time, organizations and individuals will be able to extend their reach by many orders of magnitude, often with a negligible sacrifice of richness. Picture a multichannel world, where knowledge, entertainment, and services are at our reach from a single location, 24 hours a day. At our desk at work, we can pay our phone bill, renew our driver's license, watch the opening round of the Masters, follow stocks on Bloomberg, and talk to our spouse, business associates, and friends, all on one device.

More importantly, companies will no longer have to maintain an expensive and closed infrastructure to support their own information value chains. The replacement of expensive, proprietary, legacy systems with inexpensive, open extranets will make it easier and cheaper for companies to, for example, bid for supply contracts, comprise a virtual factory, or form competing supply chains nationally and internationally at a fraction of the cost.

▶ The End of Channels and Hierarchies

Unbundling the Corporate Infrastructure for the Internet Hyperarchy

The redistribution of the information value chain from the internal to the external leaves the average corporation with much less "protection" in the open market. Competitive advantage can disappear overnight. The Internet makes it possible to organize businesses in new ways, to offer new products and services, and to distribute those products and services to tens of millions of people almost instantaneously. And this holds for everyone with access to the Internet, whether they are Fortune 500 companies or lone individuals looking to sell their own talent or ideas.

No longer are internal proprietary networks creating natural barriers of entry for distributing information. Those proprietary networks were often patterned after the organization that created them. (For example, rich flow of information to the top and controlled specific flow to the bottom of the organization.) But information is now widely distributed to everyone and anyone with access to the Internet. Whether that access is provided at work or at home, it is as evenly distributed to the corporation's janitor as to the CEO. Of course, organizations can build artificial boundaries through intranets, virtual private networks, and filters, creating private segments of the World Wide Web for organizational use. But a corporate-wide web does not dilute, in any way, the overall power of the Internet as a whole.

The Corporate Structure Redefined

The corporation is based on hierarchy; the World Wide Web is a hyperarchy—*everyone communicates richly with everyone else on the basis of shared standards.* Thus, the Internet network goes beyond just being able to provide content to those that choose to access it; it can provide very *specific* content to as wide an audience as required! There are no organizational pyramids on the Internet. There is no flow up or down. The flow is continuously in and out—not on a two-dimensional plane, but through an ever-expanding three-dimensional cube. In fact, since the content of the Web is ever increasing over time, we can picture it geometrically as a four-dimensional hyperarchy. The concept of the hyperarchy challenges *all* hierarchies.

No single software program can achieve both richness and reach, *but for the first time in the history of networks, the Internet can!* As the Internet evolves from an informational model to a transactional model, it will have the same impact on the way the world does business in the 21st century as the assembly line did in the 20th. In other words, the knowledge model expanded exponentially through the Internet hyperarchy has the same effect on a commerce model. Someone can buy or sell just about anything without having to rely on traditional distribution channels. At one time, these channels more often than not played as great (or greater) a role in product pricing and distribution as the production of the product itself.

With the increase in software to create "state" transactions with standard databases, the Internet has matured from a large network of text-based knowledge and still image graphics to a transactional e-commerce model. In doing so, the Internet is revolutionizing how we do business and how we live our personal lives. Early e-commerce sites consisted of bulletin boards and auctioning software, allowing customers to announce their product requirements and accept bids. As security across the Internet improved, customers began to buy and sell traditional goods without venturing from their keyboards, drastically modifying the traditional economic basis for the consumer-producer model.

Historically, the producer-consumer model relied on the following economic definitions:

- **Cost of production:** finding, collating, and consuming various resources (including labor) to produce a singular or set of marketable goods.
- **Cost of distribution:** the means of offering these goods to the open market for consumption.

Although the Internet will have a profound effect on both of these, we will first concentrate on the latter. Intuitively, it is much easier to grasp why the cost of distribution should decrease dramatically with the advent of e-commerce. If a consumer can place a transaction directly with a producer without ever leaving home, this calls into question the need for one of the basic staples of any consumer economy—the store, or what we now call the brick–and-mortar business.

Traditionally, a typical distribution network consisted of a producer, or group of producers, manufacturing a durable good. Depending on the scope of their marketing and distribution, there would be a series of main distribution centers, or warehouses, at various geographical locations. Products would be shipped to these hubs in the most cost-effective manner. Simultaneously, as the goods arrived at these distribution centers, they would be sent to the applicable retail markets. Independent retailers were responsible for ensuring sufficient inventory to meet demand. Some manufacturers would use internal retailers, and most would supply as many external retailers as necessary to distribute their product. This is the conceptual model of the value-chain distribution network at work.

The *value* of the value chain comes from the fact that each unit in the chain has its own economic responsibility, which theoretically lends value to the overall producer-consumer network. Manufacturers must carefully measure the total and incremental costs of producing their product. Overproduction could result in spending more capital than can be recouped in sales. Low sales could result in underutilization of capital and a lower return on every dollar spent to produce.

Both the manufacturer and the distribution center must determine the most cost-effective way of transporting the manufactured goods to their designated locations. Since this "lane" exists between the two parties, both ends are responsible for maintaining the lane's economic viability. This is why, more often than not, most manufacturers also maintain their own distribution centers. These distribution centers, in turn, further distribute to the individual retail firms they supply. The distribution center's economics are based on its ability to successfully stock and supply these retailers at maximum economic efficiency. Optimally, the number of items going out should equal the number of items coming in. With no inventory, all costs generated by maintaining the network will provide incremental profit for each item distributed.

If the entire system is running at maximum efficiency, the retailer can net pure profit by selling exactly as many items that their regional market demands at any given moment in time. Of course, all this is an ideal. Each link in the value chain produces real value by maximizing, as much as possible, its ability to create and supply goods to a demanding market. There are considerable variations on this theme, as manufacturers, distributors, and retailers all develop business plans that best suit their individual needs. Barnes & Noble does not manufacture anything, but its distribution centers are the economic generator that power many widespread publishers. Conversely, Ford Motor Company manufactures and distributes product, but maintains no retailing outlets (though it would like to change this):

> Ford announced that it would invest an undisclosed amount in Microsoft's MSN CarPoint Web site. CarPoint will soon launch a "build to order" service that should let customers seek out exactly the color and features they want in a Ford. Although any orders will be filled by traditional dealers, CarPoint will sell aggregated customer data back to Ford.
>
> —Brad Trent, *"Remaking Ford"*

Occasionally, manufacturers rely entirely on outside distributors and retailers. Occasionally, individual distributors are purely middlemen. The entertainment industry has relied on this model for years. And, of course, there have been independents for as long as there has been commerce. But it is almost impossible to find a single organization or business that distributes, sells, and generates business successfully on a large scale.

The Internet is slowly altering all this. A manufacturer could theoretically use the Internet as a free, universally accessible distribution channel to sell whatever goods it or its partners could produce. In fact, add the concept of the real-time feedback loop, and said manufacturer now has to make only the amount of goods demanded at any moment. And although the potential of "on-time" manufacturing has yet to be reached by everyone, the impediments to reaching this pinnacle, personalized items on demand, are slowly but surely falling by the wayside.

As the basic economic models of manufacturing, distributing, and retailing are being redefined by the Internet, it is becoming clear that a provider's competitive advantage will be determined product by product. Therefore, providers with broad product lines will lose ground to focused specialists. The phrase "broad product lines" conjures up images of megalith corporations, keiretsus, and multinationals, but the category more commonly includes single-brand manufacturers or producers in a specialized field. For instance, a magazine publisher, a traditional brick-and-mortar company, has built a substantial business publishing magazines in a variety of fields and interests. Each title is strongly branded, advertising revenue is constant, and the distribution value chain (based upon a hard-fought and reliable network) is effective all over the world. But with the advent of the Internet, "frictionless" e-magazines are popping up everywhere. The issue for the brick-and-mortar company is how to leverage this new medium without cannibalizing its own healthy print product. (This is similar to the points of view of Manager A and Manager B in Chapter 2, "The Business of Technology.")

First, an aggressive strategy could be to cut the losses now, forget about print, and start "e-versions" of the current print product. This may seem a bit drastic, particularly since the major revenue source for print is advertising, and "e-advertising models" are still maturing. But any losses in revenue could be recouped by cutting costs in resource acquisition (paper, ink, etc.), printing, and distribution.

Writers and editors could simply publish directly online, cutting out the middleman. At the same time, new advertising models could be experimented with and refined.

A less aggressive approach would be to simply do both. Leave the print product as is and simply establish e-versions. This may sound simpler, but in actuality it is more complex. Although a magazine, whether print or electronic, is essentially the same product, a print version and an e-version will have two entirely different business models. The most obvious drawback is that if an e-version exists, why would anybody pay for the print version? In my opinion, the basic flaw in this argument is that for some reason, people assume that "e-products" are meant to replace brick-and-mortar products. In some cases it may happen, but certainly not across the board. There is a certain "stickiness" to some brick-and-mortar items that illusory e-products simply cannot match. In short, you can't read an "e-zine" in bed or in the bathroom. You can't leave one on your coffee table so guests can enjoy your unquestionably good taste. Interestingly, the difference between an e-company and a brick-and-mortar company is not that the products themselves are radically different, but the distribution of these products and their information, or more exactly, the distribution value–chains, are different!

The magazine publisher is selling not just magazines, but the *content,* or information contained within. That is what interests people. The print form is just a means of distributing that content. The more ways an organization can find to distribute its content, the more value it adds to the content. The key concept for our theoretical publisher to grasp is that the core value of its content, or product for a manufacturer, has not changed in regard to its market. Only the means of distribution has changed. But changing these means will inevitably change the business relationships of the traditional distribution channels. This is the real challenge our publisher and any mass-product manufacturer must face in the next millennium, the idea of value-chain unbundling.

All it will take to deconstruct a business is a competitor that focuses on any vulnerable sliver of information in the value chain. For example, businesses can now buy paper clips online to save a trip to Staples. If the principles of frictionless information can be applied anywhere along a producer-consumer value chain, a strategic advantage can be gained immediately. Since each link in the chain is responsible for its own economic efficiency (regardless of whether each link is part of the same organization or completely separate), each link will take advantage of this frictionless economy as it becomes available. Existing chains will fragment into multiple businesses, each of which will have its own sources of competitive advantage.

For instance, a shoe manufacturing concern finds it can order and track leather supplies via the Internet, therefore abandoning its costly, high-maintenance procurement system. This produces increased efficiency now that ordering can be "tuned" to fit projected capacities. These projections become increasingly accurate because, day-to-day, even minute-to-minute, the manufacturer can track inventories at some or even all of its geographic distributors in real time. In conjunction, each distribution center maintains its own inventory control by meeting the demands of retail customers via their internal intranet and shipping merchandise directly to customers using their e-commerce Web site. Amazon.com, for example, maintains massive warehouses that are constantly in touch with both suppliers and consumers. B2B and B2C commerce engines are only the tip of the Internet's growing role in how supply chain economics are evolving.

Although this producer-consumer economy still relies heavily on digital networks, the producer need only be concerned with producing its goods and content and maintaining whatever software is required to create and transport information up and down the value chain. The real advantage is that neither the supplier, the distributor, nor the consumer need to erect these units and support a costly digital network themselves. The network is frictionless. Via frictionless commerce, network economies of scale arise when individual business units are no longer dependent solely on internal networks that may or may not be well-defined and supported. Each business unit can act independently, knowing that the information it has available at any given time is up to date and accurate.

Businesses that broker information, make markets, or set standards are all taking advantage of a self-reinforcing dynamic. This dynamic is eventually measured in productivity gains, lower operating costs, and, most importantly, higher net profits. Unfortunately, although the idea is common sense, handing over this responsibility to the Internet is still a radical idea. Not only are the security issues daunting, but so is the relative maturity of the software and even the hardware that would have to support this type of infrastructure. Developers and vendors of the required software are relatively inexperienced as well.

Let's take a look at a theoretical but very possible example of using current business principles to redistribute a value-chain concept to the Internet. Every autumn across tens of thousands of college campuses in America and throughout the world, hundreds of thousands of college students begin new classes. Each class has required textbooks for particular courses. Publisher A will probably publish a good proportion of those textbooks. Traditionally, each student has to make a trip to the college bookstore, find the required text, and buy it. Even if used, these textbooks are generally expensive and have very limited use. In terms of information economy, *these texts are rich information items.* Yes, some of these books will become reference material for years to come, but most reach the end of their utility at the end of the semester. They will then be sold, traded, or eventually thrown away. The distribution chains between Publisher A and the bookstores determine Reach. This value chain comprises a static but very viable network. What would happen if Publisher A made every textbook that was published and distributed to the bookstores on its distribution lists available via the Internet? The distribution network would change overnight. The business economics of each college student, and of college education itself, would change overnight.

Instead of students having to purchase a $65 tome they may or may not need six months later, students could simply browse all pertinent passages on their PCs or computers in the campus library, for a nominal fee, of course. But would that fee be equal to the price of a bound and edited version? Even if it were, there would still be economic advantage to both student and publisher. The student would no longer have an overwhelming collection of books to store and maintain (unless, of course, he or she wanted to). The publisher could now extensively scale down, or do away with altogether, the costly expense of printing, binding, and shipping. And none of the economic value of the information would be lost. In fact, the economic value would be enhanced by actually removing the bookstore from the value chain and substituting a Web browser. Reach has been increased and richness" maintained, while expenses have been considerably decreased!

Bookstores may not like being excluded, but as they provide no added richness to the process, the advantages to producer and consumer are very clear. So why doesn't Publisher A, or any other major publishing company, leap at the chance to do this? Because like most hierarchically managed, traditional businesses, no one wants to cast the first stone.

Traditionally (and tradition goes back only five years or so), Internet business has been defined as fast, flexible entrants taking on dominant incumbents: Netscape vs. Microsoft, Amazon.com vs. Barnes & Noble, Schwab.com vs. Wall Street. Some businesses are merely looking for additional profit, not for a war, but although defining a Web-based approach to business does not have to be a war, it can often be a struggle some businesses aren't quite ready to take on.

Almost every business in the world is either affecting or being affected by the Internet. The popular vision of the ever-increasing e-companies is that they are rapidly multiplying and will eventually devour the great brick-and-mortar leviathans, but Internet companies still know their limitations. The only thing that is holding up the Internet revolution in terms of total convergence is the "traditional thinkers" being unwilling to make too many changes too soon. Fortunately for most Fortune 1000 companies (and them some), they can afford to take a more casual approach to radically changing their businesses. But not for long! A traditional, old-line Wall Street firm like Morgan Stanley can look pretty awkward chasing Schwab.com, but if Morgan Stanley has learned anything from being in business as long as it has, it's that slow and steady wins the race.

This may be sound policy for Morgan Stanley as a whole, but whoever is in charge of making its online businesses work had better look like a tortoise and act like a hare. Eventually, the sheer number of Internet startups will begin to affect traditional market share. The great attraction for venture capitalists, stock enthusiasts, and everyone else who is getting rich on the rapid ascent of Internet technologies is the mouth-watering concept of so many new ideas and business models coming to quick fruition. It used to take years for a sound business model to ferment into a solid business plan that would not only attract investors but the public at large.

The obvious attraction is all the economic advantages we've discussed. Any company that can maneuver in the currently turbulent Internet seas is automatically a good investment. From an industrial analyst's point of view, the average Internet company starts out lean and mean, with 10 to 30 hard-core developers led by some young and hungry entrepreneurs who are not yet hobbled by stockholder expectations, fickle markets, and closed corporate structures. Analysts apparently think that if these insolent Internet startups are competing head to head with brick-and-mortar Goliaths, so much the better! Smart Internet startups aim to turn their opponents' resources, strength, and size against them.

Authors David Yoffie from HBS and Michael Cusumano from MIT call this competitive approach judo strategy. They use the Netscape-Microsoft battles to illustrate the three main principles of judo strategy: rapid movement, flexibility, and leverage. According to Yoffie and Cusumano, in an article published in the *Harvard Business Review,*

> Judo strategy...is especially well suited to turbulent, technology-driven Internet competition.
>
> David B. Yoffie and Michael A. Cusumano,
> *Judo Strategy: The Competitive Dynamics of Internet Time*

The early lessons that have come to light have been based on the turbulence resulting from dealing with many unknowns. As Internet business moves into the mainstream of business, it will be expected to behave just as predictably and assuringly as legacy businesses. Investors may enjoy rollercoaster rides with a company a few months old, but will not tolerate it with a company a few years old, Internet-based or not. But the industry as a whole is still nascent enough to tolerate some unpredictability as long as e-companies are flexible and responsive enough to meet these changes head on. Their greatest advantage rests with establishing a new business that establishes a foothold, enabling them to be viewed as some kind of a success. Establishing a business model allows a company to be aggressive in defining its market, pricing, testing and distribution.

In fact, more often than not, that is the Internet business model! Just defining a product is an adventure, pricing even more so. Any business model extending beyond traditional buying and selling must rely on the enigmatic and Zen-like Netscape model of "an innovative pricing model...free, but not free," coined by Marc Andreeson, one of Netscape's founders. This, for obvious reasons, has been a pretty difficult model to understand in terms of real value, possible growth, and marketability. The original "blue-chips" of the Internet, Netscape, Yahoo!, Amazon.com, and others, were able to work this model into solid capital by sheer perseverance and by realizing the Internet's potential from a producer's side as well from a consumer's. Netscape demonstrated such business insight; according to Yoffe and Cosumano, Netscape had pushed its marginal cost down to zero by writing its browser from scratch.

Terms such as *Web portals* and *traffic-aggregating sites* weren't in anyone's vocabulary until Yahoo! came along and literally invented them. To capitalists, this is like opening the Louisiana Purchase to homesteaders. Early pioneers may face some hardships, but if they survive, they have new and fertile ground from which to reap rewards for generations to come.

7

Developing Technological Strategies

▶ The "Information-Based" Organization

"Being afraid of monolithic organizations, especially when they have computers, is like being afraid of really big gorillas especially when they are on fire."
—Bruce Sterling

[I]nformation-based organizations won't look like the pharaonic pyramid of the past but like, well, like what?
—Stewart T., *"The Search for the Organization of Tomorrow"*

Now that we have an idea of what is going to happen, how can we as individuals and as organizations, businesses, and groups, prepare for it? How do we structure today's organization to meet tomorrow's needs?

Let's step back and macroscopically view the present with some level of objectivity. (By understanding the entire forest, perhaps it's easier to contain the forest fire.) The nature of business as a whole has changed considerably in just the last 30 years. In digital technology, the speed of decision making creates more decisions for the decision makers. If we had more decision makers, then this would be a good thing—providing, of course, that most of the decisions are correct. Correct decisions would theoretically increase overall productivity since, in theory, more things would be undertaken and completed.

Business in general, and technology in particular, has increasingly allowed almost everyone to have some input in day-to-day business activity. This is a far cry from the assembly line days, when only a handful of people made the decisions for sometimes thousands of individuals. An assembly line worker could easily be replaced by anybody off the street. Labor was repetitious and uncreative. However, this was a plus for owners and senior management, since by and large it meant lower labor costs and thus higher profit margins. Labor unions aside, cheap labor was the primary force behind the industrial boom of the 20th century.

But as we eased into the economics of the 21st century, we found that when regional economies grew into national economies, and national economies grew into international economies, decision-making could not be left in the hands of a desperate group of middle managers who rarely spoke to each other and even less to those they managed. With the introduction of the personal computer, the fax machine, and wireless communication in the latter 20 years of the century, decision making had to be streamlined if organizations were to remain competitive. This combined with globalization means that technology's role in the modern corporation is on par with the people that comprise the organization. Different areas of any business, large or small, have to make quick, independent decisions on a day-to-day basis, based on information technology provides. As such, it has become impossible to separate the technology from the decision-makers.

In addition, Internet access to once privileged information has put all facets of corporation strata, or at least more people capable of making informed decisions, in the know. But this can give rise to a very different problem. For example, picture an assembly line economy of the 20th century where everyone is a foreman and nobody is a worker. As a result, nothing gets done. In today's corporation, although some form of hierarchical structure is required, strict stratification of roles is no longer efficient. The assembly line economy has to give rise to the hier-

Chapter **7** | Developing Technological Strategies

archical corporate structure that exists today, a complex, organic network of information interchange among internal and external sources and destinations.

However, no matter how large or complex this information network is, it still must rely on centralized decision making to achieve unified singular goals and deliverables. So the question for the 20th century is simple: How can a handful of people with a working knowledge of their business vision enforce that vision through a myriad of dispersed managerial levels, internal networks, and external supply chains?

Let's consider an example. The corporate board of an automotive firm decides it's a good time to reintroduce a retro look to its cars. By setting itself apart, the company hopes to establish a strong branding of its models among the car-buying public. By redefining each model's market niche with new designs, the company can, at least initially, dominate selected segments and reap the profits accordingly. If a retro market doesn't already exist, careful marketing will create one. In addition, using extensive extranets along the automotive firm's value chain, individual buyers can customize just how retro they would like their purchase to be.

Sounds like a pretty good plan when agreed upon by twelve or so individuals in a well-heeled boardroom. Two years or less later, 20,000 or so auto workers across the nation, sometimes across the world, including senior executives, managers, designers, engineers, distributors, and assembly workers, find themselves designing, making, and selling customized cars. Although they had no part in the original decision making, they have become vitally important in implementing this decision. Their job is simply to carry out their part of the grand scheme, regardless of its origin. Everyone involved, in their own right, in their own way, at their own level, acts accordingly. Some or even all of these individuals will think the return of retro is a great idea that should have been implemented long ago; others may think it's crazy. Whichever it proves to be, the real point is that huge organizations, using only "chain-of-command" policies, can mobilize vast armies of people to follow a very specific, well-planned policy for the benefit of the organization as a whole.

Up until the last 20 years or so, this model was more than adequate to forge and ensure the success of the corporate manufacturers and services that comprised the global economy. But changing technology has changed all these models. "Chain-of-command" works very well when there is strong, carefully defined leadership, or "head link." Part of the strength of hierarchical leadership, however, is its exclusivity. By definition, there always has to be some "head" at the top of the pyramid, either an individual or a group of board members. Even public companies must rely on the insight of the few to make strategic decisions for the many. In truth, this model is still in effect among most, if not all, the Fortune 500 companies. The face remains; the model is changing!

Although networks are becoming more and more complex and decision making is becoming more decentralized, it cannot be too decentralized. If it is, decisions will eventually conflict and the chiefs will spend more time straightening out their own quarrels than effectively delegating and engaging new problems. Fortunately, unlimited access to information (or even to technology) may allow individuals to feel like an Indian or a chief, but that doesn't mean they are. Even if every Indian does become a chief, some chiefs will still be bigger chiefs than others. This may not be utopia, but the point for all the newer chiefs is that they can now "live" like a chief, big or small. In short, we have now defined the basis for the New Economy.

No one will argue with the economic boom of the 1990s, an era when many economists of the 1980s were predicting gloom and economic depression brought on by the careless spending during the 1980s and the resulting "junk bond" economy. But it didn't happen. Why? Technology to the rescue! Now that a bicycle messenger has access (theoretically) to as much information as a corporate CEO, he can be more productive as a bicycle messenger. This in turn allows his dispatcher to schedule more efficient deliveries, allowing his district manager to cover more territory, allowing the district manager's vice-president to report increasing market share, allowing the CEO to make strategic decisions to exploit that growth. All the messenger needs to do is know which street has less traffic on a route at any given time via PDA, wireless phone, or other form of communication. Extend this scenario to hundreds of diverse industries, all affected in one way or another by the advances of computer chips, PDAs, cellular phones, and the like, and no wonder the United States, and to a lesser degree the entire world, is in the midst of the world's largest economic boom.

But although these changes have had an enormous impact on the way businesses do business, in no way have all of these changes been drastic. True, in the 1990s when companies such as Digital Equipment, Silicon Graphics, Apple Computer, once very profitable in the 1980s, did not make dramatic decisions, they found themselves in very precarious positions. However, other companies such as IBM, Hewlett-Packard, Sun Microsystems, when faced with the same problems, reacted to rapid changes in technology and their marketplace in a controlled, measured way, remaining consistent with their traditional business models and eventually profited from changes out of their control.

The speed of change strategies now undergo can create quite a bumpy ride. The companies that observed these trends and accepted the consequences made their transitions much easier. But other companies had a tougher time, floundering between the way things were done in the past and how things should be done in the future. This has always been a dilemma in business, but managers usually had a much greater cushion of time to make their decisions. With the introduction of Internet speed, corporations could make a decision one week and reverse it the next.

Even prior to the Internet, the speed of technological change was catching up to some of the older players. IBM's stock price dropped to a 50-year low in 1992 before IBM's upper management adjusted to a new business paradigm. That paradigm (no, not the Internet, but the client-server model) was changing the way corporations viewed technology and its applications. This model did not fit well with IBM's traditional view of application processing (ironically, IBM helped invent client-server technology, but only for IBM customers).

IBM had spent decades convincing a few key people at select corporations that IBM technology could handle all their needs. These key people were generally senior executives who comprised the so-called "old-boy" network. By the late 1980s and early 1990s, the first generation of technically savvy managers came into their own. No longer were techies or geeks or weenies prized for their technical skill alone; these up-and-comers could clearly see and state the reasons why their organizations could no longer afford the simple "one-stop" shopping provided by IBM, DEC, and Burroughs.

These fast-rising 20- and 30-somethings had no allegiance to IBM, and more importantly, had no interest in forging any. They wanted small, manageable, and powerful digital technology they could exploit for their own needs. If those needs were in line with their overall company objectives, then so much the better. Of course, initially, there was resistance by the established and steadfast who had built careers around legacy technology. But the dollars spoke for themselves. The maintenance and support costs for most mainframes for a year could pay the salaries of two programmer analysts.

This is when what we will call the second techno/socio-revolution occurred. The Steve Jobs and Bill Gates of the first revolution were the original "upstarts" who, through vision and sheer will, could determine the path of technology for years, directly defying older, more established paradigms. This reoccurred in the early 1990s, but with much less fanfare. The players were much less high profile than Mr. Jobs and Mr. Gates, but no less visionary and determined. These are the people who would become the Internet pioneers and who are still leading the endless charge of technology into the next millennia. The robber barons of the 21st century will be the John Chambers, David Wetherells, and Larry Ellisons. Why? Because the young seem to be the ones who best understand the apparent mish-mash of technologies, or perhaps, they're the first to try.

Traditional managers are faced with too much information to make strategic decisions within the models to which they are accustomed. By definition, even a senior manager in a specific field must be somewhat of a generalist. As such, strategic planning requires time to observe the factors that come into play in a particular industry. Through careful analysis and intuition, a sound-minded business strategist can typically propose a plan for advancing his or her company's role in that industry. The major benefit of the pyramid management structure was that, in general, more information flowed to the top than downward. Analysis could be made, decisions reached, and a period of implementation could take effect, followed by a keen observation of results. This information then filters back to the top, and the process restarts. Hence, the simplicity of the three to five-year business plans.

But today, once a strategy is assessed, decided upon, and implemented, it may already be obsolete. As a result, businesses have to speed strategic business planning to Internet speed by giving more people the ability to make more decisions. If some of the decisions don't pan out, they aren't as costly as a single, large, well-invested decision that doesn't pan out. In fact, instead of having one big decision that could easily backfire, more companies now find it palatable to make 10 small decisions. And even if six or seven of them go awry, the three that don't should make up any loss. The age of "empowerment" has arrived, and many large, centralized, hierarchical organizations have begun to flatten out.

Chapter **7** I Developing Technological Strategies

So, people are making many more decisions, and in most cases, the right decisions for what they are experiencing, where they are experiencing it. However, in a large organization with numerous branches, both national and international, these experiences can vary widely from location to location. Although individual regions, plants, or branches can prosper enormously from sound grassroot decision making, this isn't always beneficial for the entire organization. Ironically, the increased decentralized decision making also creates problems. All of this is not necessarily exacerbated by technology, but a large part of it is. Without the technology to make informed decisions at ever-increasing rates, empowerment would seem laughable, more a synonym for chaos than a sound business strategy. But as more well-informed, decisive managers and employees are making more and more decisions, good and bad, the traditional system of checks and balances may not be able to keep up.

There is inherent conflict in any organization that wishes to create an environment that fosters decentralized decision making but must still be accountable to some form of centralized control. By the end of the Roman Empire, the western Roman emperor had left so much of the day-to-day operation of the provinces to the various local governors that it was very easy for the provincial heads to lose sight of Rome's wishes. By the time the Vandals invaded, outer provinces willingly shepherded them to the capital as long as they spared the locals.

This, of course, is a bit of an extreme example, but similar situations arise all the time in business. Car manufacturers often find it very difficult to find new ways to market cars, since the actual selling is left entirely in the hands of individual car dealerships. Local dealers may follow some of the manufacturers' promotional ideas but still resort to what they think is the best way of selling cars locally. Organizations that are more hi-tech may be able to disseminate centralized information much faster, but that doesn't mean that information will result in the action planned by centralized management. In fact, the information flowing back to the center from so many different sources may seem like an endless stream of conflicting information that may or may not lend itself to quick decision making.

As we go further into the 21st century, organizations as a whole will continue to find ways to behave like small maneuverable Internet companies, whether they have anything to do with the Internet or not. This will be especially problematic for large, traditional organizations that have traditional networks firmly in place. Unless they can effectively find ways of freeing both creativity and productivity on a small scale, they will find constant erosion of their markets and value chains by smaller, perhaps Internet-based, companies that can work on a small scale. In the long run, even the largest, most self-contained corporations may have to depend on individuals in ways they never have before.

▶ Knowledge Is Power

So now we know the underlying management problems of the Information Age and the knowledge-based economy—more and more will be expected from the individual, as an individual and as part of a larger organization, in facing new and sometimes unique problems. How do these problems translate to you and me as individuals? What does all this revolutionary ability to inform, be informed, and stay informed mean to us? Let's look at a hypothetical, but very possible, scenario. Now that the bicycle messenger is "empowered" through technology, what does that mean to her? As we move up the value chain to dispatcher, district manager, and so on, does the messenger looking at these changes in relative terms feel as if empowerment is the same as progress? In realistic terms, no one can truly say but the messenger herself. However, in economic terms, there is a drastic change going on, generally measured in productivity.

> The shift to an information economy is generating a steady stream of enterprise. Innovation is throwing up new companies and new products faster than you can say "electronic commerce." Restructuring and downsizing are an obsession. Productivity is paying for much of the recent real gain in wages.
> *Business Week,* Does America Have a Bubble Economy? No

Productivity, at its simplest, is producing more with either the same amount of resources or less. In a knowledge or information economy, the more knowledge individuals obtain, the more valuable they are and the more value they produce in turn.

But in real life, most people do not go to work every day simply to gain and expound knowledge. The bicycle messenger's exposure to the Internet may tell her more about what's going on in the world, but it will not help her legs pedal any harder or faster. On the other hand, it could tell her the best route to where she's going. The mechanical harvester allowed the production of grain crops to increase exponentially, making farms more productive, but did it make farmer better at farming? In other words, who or what is actually in control here, the technology or its users?

The primary reason for such an incredible increase in economic productivity is the exponential increase in the use of network technology. Twenty years ago, even local networks were cumbersome and expensive. With the rise of the Internet, any dotcom can now be viewed as a global player. Why? Because knowledge, information, and productivity can be shared on a scale never previously known. Organizations were originally valued more by capital assets than by individual knowledge, even while that knowledge was amassed. Today, not only is collective knowledge essential to an organization's bottom line, but also equally significant is the ability to get that knowledge and information to those who need it, when they need it.

On a smaller scale, the bicycle messenger's empowerment revolves around her needing to be in constant contact with the dispatch office. If she has to change a given route due to an accident or some other detail in the course of a day, she immediately notifies her dispatcher. He in turn can immediately apply this new route to other customers that may need service earlier rather than later, and off they go, back up the economic food chain. The main advantage that centralized organizations (and corporations in particular) have always enjoyed are the vast internal networks that allow them to do business more efficiently than relying on external networks beyond their control. Now these global networks are available at a fraction of the cost via the Internet, and this principle comes into effect tenfold. However, although traditional client-server networks can still be directed solely for strategic purposes within a corporation, the broader, more diverse Internet cannot. This presents a series of both challenges and opportunities to everyone within and beyond an organization's value chain.

Managing all this knowledge and the empowerment it provides can be tricky. Look at how innovative modern corporations, both Internet and traditional, have become to attract and keep valued talent. Stock packages, equity, bonuses, and gifts are becoming the norm across the board for even entry-level talent. Not only are all our new chiefs going be able to think, act, and live like chiefs, to a certain degree they will want to be treated like chiefs, especially by other chiefs. Does this mean that our bicycle messenger can now make special demands of the dispatcher, such as informing him of what routes she prefers to take, what packages she prefers to deliver, and what time she chooses to deliver them? Well, yes and no.

Since it is the messenger that has the firsthand knowledge of the best way to deliver packages to her customers, her constant input is vital; however, if she doesn't understand the overall function of her organization in terms of delivering packages to customers as a business, then her personal judgments could be narrow, biased, or skewed by the smaller picture that encompasses her everyday duties. Although she may have no part in the design of her organization's business strategy, she now has become vital in its implementation, simply because she too has access to the network.

▶ A World of Chiefs

[F]irms must change the way they are organized, and employees at all levels must become "information and knowledge literate"—not just computer literate.

If someone wants to be chief, live like a chief, and be treated like a chief, he or she must also accept the responsibilities of being a chief. This has given rise to the next level of empowerment, termed *interentrepreneurship*. Managers, workers, and individuals can exercise a certain level of self-enterprise as long as this enterprise fits in with their organization's overall strategic goals.

> In its place he envisions a company in which executives run independent units—cut loose from a stifling bureaucracy, and held far more accountable for success and failure. And with a consumer focus at the heart..., he's banking on a future in which designers, engineers, and marketers someday will do a far better job of anticipating the wants and needs of car buyers."
>
> Brad Trent, "Remaking Ford"

However, all these chiefs must have a very clear idea concerning their boundaries and must understand that no matter how their individual

Chapter **7** I Developing Technological Strategies

strategic goals differ, their overall organizational objective must be the same. What is the biggest stumbling block to this utopian cooperation? Implementing networked and communication systems in a traditional hierarchical structure organization simply won't work. Although some level of hierarchy must be maintained if an organization is to survive as a single, cohesive unit, by doing so, traditionally, organizations run the risk of stifling their competitive advantage. "Matrix" management, on the other hand, allows greater flexibility but more friction. "Organic webs" are ideal in theory, but may need time to form in practice.

▶ The Executive Challenge: A Brave New World

In the real world, we are all familiar with the difference between a job and a career. A job infers a requirement to be at a certain place at a certain time to perform a required task. A career infers a serious commitment to achieve various goals, financial, personal, and professional, over the long term. These goals are usually quite abstract, but the idea is typically referred to as success. Like pornography, what success *means* is open to a broad spectrum of interpretation, but also like pornography, everyone seems to know it when they see it.

Success for individuals is of course highly personal. However, success for any organization, public, private, or nonprofit, is pretty clear-cut, basic survival. The blue-chip companies are not considered successful simply because they have huge operating incomes, profits, and capitalization. They are blue-chip because they have been around a while. In American terms, any strongly existing business more than 50 years old can be considered blue-chip, whether it employs a hundred thousand or a hundred. And although these organizations appear to have a life of their own, they would not exist without the concerted efforts of a great number of people working in a combined and usually anonymous way to give that organization life. In return, the organization, through financial means, compensates these individuals for those efforts and sacrifices.

However, in view of this utopian ideal of the working world, we are still, when you get right down to it, dealing with human nature and balancing each individual's self-interest with the overall benefit of the organization. If a key manager makes an incorrect decision to keep a bit of knowledge, information, or action to himself, as opposed to sharing it with the organization, the organization can suffer. With this in mind, how do organizations, particularly organizations whose general goal is profit, maintain a balance in the workplace? The answer is simple: rules and regulations. These are the only tools managers have to "tweak" everyone, from highly paid senior executives to college-age interns, into a semblance of united individuals working for a common goal. When we introduce capitalism, the general idea is to get people to work together by getting them to work for themselves.

This idea may seem contrite, but in reality this has been the most effective way in the history of mankind to drive economic growth. One of the reasons for its success is the constant reinforcement of technology meeting human needs and human need generating technology. But creativity, imagination, and even genius can be generated and nurtured by rules and regulations. With the need to maintain some rational infrastructure to keep people's self interests from breeding chaos, we need rules and regulations that do not, in turn, stifle the very things we are trying to encourage.

This seeming contradiction has been at the heart of business—business first in villages, then city-states, then empires, then corporations, and then conglomerates. The most successful businesses have been the ones to meet this challenge time and again throughout history, whether that history is hundreds of years old or, as in the era of Internet giants, just a few months old. All organizations, no matter what their goals or how they are organized, must have some kind of authority system to ensure whatever it is they are trying to do gets done. Slave economies were popular throughout the world, because they were simple. Authority was absolute—perform labor or be severely punished. Although capitalism has supposedly abolished this with a more democratic notion of *perform your labor, be severely rewarded* strategy, the need for an authority system still exists.

The result of the last 2,000 years or so of man's evolution, at least in terms of economic theory, is the result of his ability to use individual talents, skills, and insights for the overall benefit of an organization. If the organization happens to be large, then for the most part, most individuals will come into contact with only a very small percentage of other individuals within the organization. This contact is comprised either of proximity or the need for contact to perform whatever individual tasks require. The most successful organizations, therefore, generally consist of an authority system that generates sets of rules for general organizational behavior and mandates guidelines for how individuals perform their specific functions. Those who work well within these guidelines generally succeed; those who do not are usually weeded out of the organization. This is manifested by the traditional review, conducted in most corporations. Once a year, every employee's performance is critiqued. The idea is for these reviews to be objective, but people are people. Those who pass the muster year in and year out "get along." Those who don't get along, whether they perform well or not, rarely stay for long.

As a result, any individual who is a part of a "modern" organization has been mandated with some level of personal empowerment to meet whatever responsibility they have for the organization's benefit. In return, the organization financially compensates them. It is this empowerment (and the individual's ability to use it for the benefit of both himself and his organization) that anchors economic productivity. And digital technology has not changed this in any way, but it has gone a long way in redefining just what empowerment means.

Fifty years ago, well-trained executives at an average American institution would be well educated in engineering, scientific disciplines, or the arts. They would be expected to know how to conduct conversations, organize ideas, express these ideas efficiently and cogently, and take responsibility for both long-term and short-term decisions. Today, none of this has changed, but technology has. The executive of 50 years ago had a telephone, perhaps a voice recorder, and usually someone else to do labor-intensive tasks such as typing, copying, and arranging information. Today the average executive is expected to maintain contact via cellular, perhaps a PDA, a digital voice recorder, and of course the ever-present beeper. They are expected to have access to fax machines, copiers, and a vast variety of digital networks, both at work and at home. In short, technology has lifted the forms of empowerment to new levels. Add laptop computers and office programs, and the same executive from 50 years ago would be expected to do 10 times as much today, or at least to *know* 10 times as much. But although technology has changed how people do business today, it has not changed who does business. It is still people working with other people for the benefit of some kind of greater whole, be it the corporation or all of humankind.

▶ The New Corporate Culture

Like governments, businesses that use poor judgment in creating rules and regulations that comprise their authority system leave themselves open to problems. These problems can, and usually do, lead to serious inefficiencies that erode business growth and success. For instance, a small but growing technology company has cornered the market in widget-counting software. Its product, being a smashing success at its inception, has gained an almost 60 percent market share in just three years, with a 30 percent revenue growth rate to show for it. This success was achieved by a small group of skilled and highly dedicated programmers who were brought together by an insightful management team that foresaw the market for widget-counting software. This management team correctly surmised that if they could develop software that was open, flexible, and easy to manage, they could create a strong niche in terms of initial sales. Additionally, if they also delivered strong customer support to compensate for the lack of technical savvy in the widget-counting industry, this young firm could potentially position itself at the forefront, rapidly becoming the market leaders.

This was not difficult to do in traditional firms when technology was useful but not yet pervasive. Now that technology is becoming more and more pervasive in even the most nontechnology-oriented businesses, ideas on how to manage growth have to be more open and yet firm. The only way this duality can be accomplished is not by repurposing the need for control but by redefining what control means to a modern organization.

Of course, these types of controls are what most organizations, large and small, strive for. And over the last 10 years, one of the most successful organizations, IBM, had to readjust to its own limitations in dealing with just how rapidly the world was changing.

The era marking the "death" of the mainframe was supposedly the death knoll for Big Blue. This, combined with the collapse of IBM's PC business, made IBM look like a lumbering dinosaur laboring under its own weight. Out looking for sources of replenishment, as the global climate cooled under the effects of a client-server striking the earth, Big Blue apparently hit a dead end. This is a dramatic portrayal (but not inaccurate) of how the situation was portrayed in many business and technology magazines. However, IBM, although temporarily losing money in the mainframe industry, never accepted the popular credo of the time and continued to sell mainframes. It also began openly positioning its consulting and business branches as accommodating "open" solutions. IBM's senior management had the foresight to recognize that mainframe technology is a pervasive technology, and that client-server, despite all of its face-value advantages, was still emerging. Mainframes were expensive and difficult to maintain and program, but still necessary to large corporate structures that depended on hundreds of thousands of daily transactions. IBM began to develop more flexible relationships, both externally and internally, with their organization to create acceptance that two very different technologies can work together. Systems integration, despite what most people think, begins with people and skills integration.

Five years after the so-called death of the mainframe, IBM was selling more mainframes than at any time in its history.

> Consequently, IBM mainframe sales have thrived at the time many were predicting its demise. A 1996 study from Trish Information Services, of Hayward, CA, surveyed 100 mainframe shops with at least 200 MIPS of installed capacity and found that 87% plan to add more mainframe capacity; and 79% expect renewed demand to be a long term phenomenon.
>
> —Bill Carico, *"The Internet, System 390, and Serious e-Business Trimming Clients and Tiers Down to Size"*

But that was not the reason for IBM's successful turnaround. By adopting an open technology management policy, IBM used its ubiquitous position to leverage its technological knowledge even when using other companies' technologies. For instance, if an international bank was developing a universal foreign exchange PC-based client-server application, the bank found that it needed to retrieve and send information to the back-office mainframe. These customers found themselves more comfortable with IBM advising or supplying the software to do this than with the vender supplying the front-end client-server application. Soon, when the financial firm found itself dealing with a variety of venders, applications, and databases, IBM was there as well.

This new positioning was not without costs. To enable a shift to the open technology market, layers of middle management formed during the proprietary years were peeled away, often exposing an ill-prepared core of technologists.

The issue of reduced workforces is at the heart of reengineering's promise to do more with less. It deserves special mention, I think, because layoffs have affected so many of us and because the changes in exposures associated with downsizing or rightsizing can be very subtle. They show themselves in many ways:

> Morale problems often accompany lay-offs. Workers who are upset, under stress, perhaps concerned about their own job security, are more likely to have accidents.
> —James J. Conerty, *"Business Interruptions: Is This What Corporate Reengineering Left In Its Wake?"*

Through no fault of their own, many people, once secure in the all-embracing arms of Big Blue, now found themselves adrift in a rapidly changing technological environment. If IBM's senior management had been just a little better prepared to handle the client-server onslaught, a good deal of personal dissolution could have been avoided. However, no one foresaw just what explosive changes in doing business would result from IBM introducing the world of digital computing to the individual desktop. This is by no means uncommon. As we've already discussed, DEC, IBM's biggest rival throughout much of the 1960s, 1970s, and 1980s, was a prime example of what not to do when faced with the mounting pressures of technological change. As DEC's success meant almost phenomenal growth from the 1970s into the early 1980s, the organization itself began to feel some of the fallout of its own success. As a culture, DEC exemplified "engineering for engineers," unsurpassed quality, and ease of use.

However, its matrix, instead of producing a smooth exchange of ideas and solutions, complicated their implementation. Programmers and system managers alike fell in love with the vast and useful features available from both the hardware and software units within DEC. But this led to a reliance on systems that sold themselves; marketing and sales units primarily managed the demand for VAX systems, rather than acting as a focal point of gauging and monitoring that demand. With money flowing in so easily, product lines and the requisite workforce were expanded. DEC evolved from a minicomputer company to a network, peripheral, software application, database, PC, field service and maintenance, and consulting service organization. Business units grew and divided geographically, each with sub-units to deal with the now quite extensive DEC product line.

This system worked well as long as DEC was growing, but once it hit critical mass in the late 1980s, DEC began introducing products that made its older products outdated too soon. In the spring, they would sell a model that processed at 25 mps and, in the fall, introduce a model that processed at 30 mps, at two-thirds the price and half the size. Individual business units were developing competing products and a centralized sales force had to sell them to the same customers. Each business unit individually developed very successful control structures and internal hierarchies, but DEC's matrix management was never able to develop a central focus. Without realizing it, DEC had become a huge distributed network. Each business unit was a well-structured and efficient node. But with no central link, it became more and more difficult to provide the marketplace with a singular, well-defined entity with which to do business.

Ironically, DEC did succeed in creating a very powerful web of external DEC users, programmers, and enthusiasts. In fact, the demand for DEC's products was still growing as the 1990s began. But DEC's internal units began competing with each other. They began to develop and roll out new products faster than any other computer manufacturer, faster than the market could keep up with. What DEC lacked in marketing skills it made up for in manufacturing skills. But just manufacturing high-quality digital systems was not enough. Although DEC acted like a distributed network, it still saw itself as a centralized network. Although the company's president, Ken Olsen, was charismatic and highly intelligent, his view of the organization was as a traditional manufacturing concern as opposed to the technology company it was—and he expounded a central vision often in conflict with the matrix-confined management.

When the "open era" began in the 1980s, DEC maintained a proprietary approach to both its hardware and software. After all, its growth had been based largely on the one-stop shopping it had provided in the past. And, unlike Apple, which began to suffer from the same malaise, DEC had very little competition in its specific market, the minicomputer—at least, not until DEC itself forced the issue by becoming its own competition. At this point, DEC could have taken a quick lesson from IBM in terms of leveraging position in a technology marketplace beginning to take a direction out of its control. IBM, when faced with the same kind of crisis, adapted to change on the surface but never wavered from its core competency. By making the right statements to the press and cutting "deals" with would-be competitors to open up their own versions of Unix, IBM, instead of trying to dominate the market, extended it. By not trying to control the market, IBM let the business world assume that IBM was in control—at least of IBM. For a company the size of IBM, this proved remarkably effective. Although it was client-server computing that put the blade to IBM's neck, IBM was able to weather the storm until the danger had passed, and it still sell mainframes in ever-increasing numbers. IBM did not tangle with the client-server web, but simply became a part of it eventually.

IBM tried desperately to compete in the client-server market, but never quite caught on (see LotusNotes article in Appendix A for reference). But by at least maneuvering the behemoth to be a viable node in the ever-increasing client-server web, it found itself very well positioned for the next "craze"—the Internet—without even trying. In the past, IBM could afford to scoff at smaller market patterns since it believed it could dominate any market in technology anytime it chose. The PC fiasco of the mid-1980s taught it a valuable lesson: Mighty businesses from little acorns grow. DEC on the other hand did not learn this lesson until it was too late. DEC tried to compete with both low-end PCs and high-end workstations, and in the process, its core minicomputer business suffered.

DEC had always viewed itself as a world apart from its market competition and falsely assumed that as long as the market didn't change, DEC didn't have to change. And for the most part, this may have been true. There was no real player in the minicomputer market to compete against DEC up through the early 1990s. However, although there was little competition inside the market, there was plenty outside the market. IBM was fortunate that only mainframes can do what mainframes do. But as technology progressed, particularly at the chip level, PCs and workstations rapidly became able to do what minicomputers could do at a fraction of the cost. Instead of relying on strength in the minicomputer market, DEC tried to do too many things at once and lost hold of its prized minicomputer market, falling to third behind Hewlett-Packard by 1994. Hewlett-Packard, originally positioned to do business in peripheral and workstation markets, found itself thrust into the world of minicomputers, not so much by active choice but by DEC's choice to all but abandon it.

Could DEC have avoided any of this? Maybe, but its decentralized management philosophy combined with a very centralized business point of view kept DEC's senior management from clearly aligning the company's business functions with marketplace realities. Internally, DEC, in true 20th-century fashion, could design, produce, and ship a top-notch product efficiently and economically, but didn't always

Chapter **7** I Developing Technological Strategies

know what to do with it. In fact, it was so efficient, it had more internal units competing from within than external companies from without. DEC had grown into the unsinkable *Titanic*, but somehow lost its rudder along the way. In short, like the great ship *Titanic*, DEC simply couldn't avoid a glancing blow with an iceberg, the market for desktop computing.

> [H]ybrid organization...benefits of centralization and decentralization simultaneously...requires a fundamental shift in the nature of control from standardization and supervision based on compliance to a learning model that preserves flexibility and fosters commitment. Systems thinking, the ability to see a situation or problem in its totality, is at the heart of learning; it demands an understanding of the causal relationships between individual components of a system and the whole.

I doubt if IBM's senior management teams ever thought of their strategies to deal with crises as "organic webs," but in essence, they were. Those who survived had to broaden their goals and embrace open technologies that were not necessarily IBM's. At the same time, they had to find new ways of bringing IBM's technology to the open-systems table and make it work. Hierarchical structures can still be effective if it is agreed upon *in general* that every manager, regardless of position in the hierarchy, adopt an open point of view across the board. Individual managers are now free to incorporate some level of entrepreneurial decision making, depending on the level of their individual understanding of the technologies involved.

▶ Now That We Know What Not to Do, What Should We Do?

Original Internet "judo" companies like Netscape and Yahoo! have turned to absorbing smaller Internet companies as a way of meeting the challenge of a constantly shifting technology frontier. Since we are functioning in a knowledge-based economy, every area of business has become an area for specialization. The success of the industrial revolution was based on the concept of mass appeal. By singularly producing goods for a vast number of people, a business assured success by both reducing the overall costs of production and ensuring a large available market to purchase the final product. Competition among competing organizations was mainly a matter of elbowing for market share, whether that share was measured as shelf space in the local supermarket or car dealerships along Route 1.

But with the revolutionary concept of a mass market with very specific needs, almost every facet of knowledge has to be specialized to create market value. The challenge of any modern business is integrating the concept of rapid change into a cultural ethos that has always looked at radical change warily. The traditional business culture point of view is hard for large corporations to surrender because of the concept of centralization. As we've already observed, without some form of centralized policy and control, any company with more than a handful of employees will quickly risk drowning in chaos. Companies without some system of accountability will not be able to stay in business very long. But if there has to be some level of centralization, how does a business branch into a variety of specializations?

Interfunctional teams must have a centralized directive to be effective in seeking out and working with their specialized core technologies. For instance, Yahoo!'s business plan is to be an aggregate portal, with the aggregate branching into a number of areas that direct surfers towards pages based on their interests. An absorption of a specialized aggregate, say, a video broadcast site, will look and feel pretty much like just another page of Yahoo!'s total site. But behind the scenes is Broadcast.com—a completely separate business, run within its own business plan, under its own leadership, and with its own technologies. Yahoo! is an example of a modern "large" Internet business, a centralized aggregate of smaller, more mobile, specialized partners (this is similar to the concept of franchising).

But the Internet introduces the concept of "seamless" partnerships. An independent business can be accessed with a click of a mouse button on an icon on a single HTML page that may contain a dozen such links. To the consumer, a click is a click as long as the expected results come about; they have little interest in what goes on in the background. But with all this seamlessness, how do both business partners and consumers know that they are dealing with legitimate businesses? Even more importantly, how do businesses that are comprised of "virtual companies" know exactly what is real and what is virtual?

Virtual businesses can never replace the brick-and-mortar world where people organize to do business, whether the brick–and-mortar consists of a hi-rise office building or someone's apartment. Wherever business is being done, it will continue to require honest and reliable people to do it. But the relationship hierarchy will not be the same. It will no longer simply come down to "who's the boss." As mentioned previously, a true knowledge-based economy allows everybody to be his or her own boss, at least to a certain degree. Centralization must consider that course changes need not be cataclysmic but must be easier to control, and even more importantly, easier to understand. Technology projects frequently fail because when the decision for a particular technology is made by senior management, the decision comes down to middle management as a big surprise, possibly involving technologies that the middle managers are not comfortable with or simply do not know. This of course introduces unforeseen and little understood problems that filter their way back up the food chain as vague but inescapable delays and miscommunications.

But there are problems even with virtual businesses. The main problem with a group of virtual companies is a matter of who holds the upper hand. Currently, major aggregate sites like Yahoo! and AOL hold tremendous power by their ability to decide who can access their sites and how. This can actually exacerbate the problems of hierarchical control, because a few concentrated managers can make decisions concerning businesses other than their own. The potentials of abuse and mismanagement are obvious.

The Internet and its virtual relationships eliminate the middle-management tier but leave nothing behind to take its place. An economy of all bosses leaves very little ground for argument or room for error, and much less times to decide if a business is a success or failure. In other words, by cutting out the middleman, these companies eliminate buffer zones that absorb wrong decisions and re-gear to implement the right ones. Without these buffers, decisions have considerably more "sink or swim" implications. The Internet economies will force managers to "rethink the nature of authority...managers must successfully marry autonomy, control, and collaboration," according to ?????

The main question still remains one of accountability. Simply replacing Internet businesses on a whim may seem like a good idea, but this results in some chaos. Companies need a layer of either independents or organizations to implement the centralized decisions with the businesses they coordinate. These "cyber brokers," whether internal or external, will be essential for any Internet-based economy. Whether these brokers are authority figures or objective observers, they will be needed as much as middle managers are needed in the traditional, hierarchical organization, only their role will be more as arbitrators than as implementers.

The cyber broker can translate general business decisions into practical plans of action for a variety of businesses. For instance, if Yahoo! decides to promote more broadband access for their ISPs, each sub-portal (Broadcast.com, Shopping.com) will implement these policies according to its personal business model, with the cyber brokers keeping a close watch.

Developing Business Strategies

▶ **Understanding the Correlation Between Competitive Advantage and Organizational Alignment**

Those who master change are those who address themselves to the times. To those who address themselves to the times, even danger is safe; for those who master change, even disturbance is order.
—Bernard H. Boar, *Information Technology with Business Strategies*

What can an individual manager or other professional do in the face of all this technological change? The question any manager in any business is going to have to ask is simple: Is my business a part of technology, or is technology a part of my business? For instance, a book publishing company uses computers and networks between editors, writers, printers, and others involved in the publishing process. If an average publishing company lost access to this network for a day, business would certainly suffer, if not stop completely. However, although technology has been integrated into the world of publishing, it is not

143

the publishing business! From Chapter 2 we learned that digital technology has become ubiquitous in whatever business environment people find themselves. And, as technology continues to evolve, it will be difficult to separate the "office" from our personal lives. The question then becomes, as senior, middle, or junior managers, how can we handle this subtle but sweeping change in a controlled, reliable manner while still meeting whatever short-term and long-term goals our business demands of us?

Individuals are having a difficult time trying to decide what they should or should not do to keep up with ever-changing trends. When combining this individual confusion with an organization's confusion, the confusion escalates. Organizations must keep in mind what technological advances their competitors may use or bring to market, especially if they are technology companies. And, unless an organization has a firm understanding of its own commitment to technology, it cannot be effective in using or deploying technology for strategic advantage in whatever markets it competes. However, this understanding is elusive at best, mind-boggling at worst, for the technologists who must keep up with rapidly changing technologies.

Keeping up with these changes will be a full-time profession for many, perhaps as much as one half of the working population of America.

Can you imagine looking for a job five to ten years from now, not knowing how to find and interpret information from endlessly vast networks, communicate effectively and globally, or solve complex problems quickly? Our children of the very near future will not get good jobs without understanding how to navigate through and succeed in a world which is becoming very fast moving, fast changing, networked, global, and uses very sophisticated tools. We must all help prepare them for that life now. You don't have to be Bill Gates or Steven Spielberg, but our kids deserve from all of us the initiative of a Bill Gates and the creativity and innovation of a Steven Spielberg.

Even with all the existing craziness of life, when it seems impossible to add on more, we must. Don't wait for the training or staff development to come to you. Seek it out, make it happen. Read articles, experiment and play with the technology. It can be fun. Spend some time each week having your kids teach you some things you didn't know. Start small by using new technologies. Get comfortable, then push yourself forward. Take some risks, and, most of all, be bold. Our children deserve our boldness to give them the learning experiences they will need for their futures, even to the point where you are changing your ways so you are using those skills and strategies you think our students will need.

Don't wait to be told to learn new technology skills. Learn them now.
—Jeff Holte, *"Keeping Up with Technology. Yeah, Right..."*

If we can manage to put a human face on technology the way we do with most other facets of business we may not have to be so worried about reining in the bull. After all, a new data center or wide area network can be just as manageable as resupplying the office cabinet with staples and file folders, if we take the right approach. Not everybody has to understand every piece of technology they come across, but they do need to have access from time to time to those who do. It is now time to return to the old fashioned notion of "people" networks. These existed long before digital networks and, although not as speedy, proved quite effective for centuries from "runners" to the pony express.

If we work for a larger or medium-sized business, then chances are we are familiar with "tech" departments. These are usually the internal specialists whom you call when your PC is on the blink or the fax won't work or your telephone has lost its dial tone. If you work for a smaller company or for yourself, you are even more familiar with the external networks of vendors who can take care of these situations for you if you are unable to do it for yourself. The plumbers, the mailman, the electrician, comprise the "people-based," or organic, networks that comprise society itself. As technology becomes more intertwined with society, so do these networks, both in substance and in implementation. After all, each aspect of technology requires its own set of specialists. In addition, these "knowledge-based" networks may be technical, nontechnical, or a combination of both, but they are as much a part of professional life as the telephone and the sticky pad. This is the best place to start a new organic interface to business. Actually, there is nothing new about it, since people have always conducted business with each other. But the form these networks are taking in the 21st century will be radically different from the forms they have taken in the past.

▶ Aligning the Network

Networks have traditionally been viewed as chains or branches that extend from one point to another. As we examined in Chapter 7, it is the value of each node and the access to each node that gives value to the network as a whole. But if each separate business in a value-chain network is seen as a specific node of that network, then each business can be further broken down in the internal and external networks that comprise it. Soon we have networks within networks within networks, and a well-integrated, web-like, three-dimensional picture must replace our flat, two-dimensional notion of a network. According to Henry Mintzberg and Ludo Van der Heyden, in an article that appeared in *Harvard Business Review,* this new network diagram is called an *organigraph*:

> [The organigraph is] much more useful than traditional charts in show-ing *what* an organization is—why it exists, what it does. Organigraphs demonstrate *how* a place works, depicting critical interactions among people, products, and information....more web-like ones...need for nego-tiations of transfer of prices and the like...call for more decentralized approaches...different managerial mindsets throughout the organization. Chains are heavy, webs are light.
>
> —Henry Mintzberg and Ludo Van der Heyden,
> *"Organigraphics: Drawing How Companies Really Work"*

The organigraph tries to give value to the human element involved in the complex network structure that will be the earmark of business in the 21st century. Technology is allowing these networks to grow in both speed and complexity. These new networks not only intertwine among businesses but also integrate with how these businesses are managed. Business, in essence, is simply the flow of goods, services, and information between a provider and a consumer. The two parties agree on some form of value for the exchange and act accordingly. As businesses grow, these simple transactions will of course become both numerous and quite complex in nature. As suppliers produce more goods, they in turn become consumers, interchanging goods and ser-vices with other suppliers. Management, in simple terms, is the means of balancing both internal and external consumption and production to maximize profit. This, according to Bernard H. Boar, is *alignment*. How this is done can take many forms. One of the simplest, most effec-tive general business principles is the strategic and tactical direction. Strategic and tactical are defined by Boar as follows:

> [A]ctions of a strategic nature are dramatic, they require significant change and investment, and demand extended commitment. Strategic actions determine the character of a business in numerous dimensions

Chapter **8** | Developing Business Strategies

and are not something that can be done "now," especially if they would need to be conceived, designed, and executed immediately. Things that can be quickly conceived of and executed are tactical in nature.

—Bernard H. Boar, *Practical Steps for Aligning Information Technology with Business Strategies: How to Achieve a Competitive Advantage*

In other words, a strategic approach is focused on the long run; the tactical approach deals with the short term.

Because business generally takes place in a competitive arena, there is an economic Darwinism that eliminates companies that have difficulty formulating effective strategies and tactics. It is not unusual for business rivals to view this competition as war in the marketplace. This is a bit dramatic, but it is an effective metaphor. Any independent economic unit must establish some level of self-sufficiency either as an individual, a small group, or an international conglomerate. This allows a business organization to be *better positioned and able to revise strategy as times dictate,* according to Boar.

This is pretty straightforward in the traditional business sense, but when combined with technology's complexity, business management's problems begin to increase exponentially. In general, technology within business organizations, including organizations whose business *is* technology, has a tendency to isolate and manage those units or departments that focus on technology separately. These units have a tendency to implement their own strategies and tactics designed to interact with the business organization they are a part of rather than interacting with the open market itself. These strategies often take on lives of their own, leading to either success for the organization or debilitating results. The role of any business organization, large or small, is to ensure that all personalities, points of view, and different perspectives work together toward a common goal, resulting in an overall synergistic and profitable experience.

However, once a group is separated from a larger group and treated differently in any way, it is only a matter of time before the smaller group develops goals based upon its own outlook. Now, if these goals match the goals of the larger, more autonomous whole, then the business is internally aligned. If these goals are out of sync with the common mission, obviously the business is internally misaligned. This is a very easy principle to understand, but it has proven remarkably difficult to implement. Digital technology, in particular, has had a very difficult time breaking out of those glass walls that have defined its role in business since the 1950s. Even as computing became more personal, IT groups were viewed as outsiders much more so than other service groups. But either by definition or social bias, the world of technology usually creates a culture of its own, defined by insiders and technical "geeks" who interact with the real world only when absolutely necessary.

Fortunately, as the workforce as a whole becomes increasingly more technology literate, one of the major effects of a pan-technological society will be the eventual erosion of this technical counterculture. The worlds of technology and everyday life will become more and more intertwined. As this occurs, business strategies that do not include or originate ideas in accordance with this evolution will find themselves failing more and more often. And the businesses creating and implementing these strategies will be far more likely to survive the ever-escalating war of business competition.

▶ The Insider's View

Perhaps everything we believe is wrong. Perhaps.

—Descartes

Pan-technology is leading us and our businesses to a vast, highly volatile web of interactive specialists providing valuable resources to both businesses and individuals in a timely and efficient matter. This web will create value for each participant simply by its existence. Eventually, the organic web value chain of supply and demand will replace the static, heavy value chain relied upon by most organizations and corporations. The value created by each node will become the value of the network itself. With the entire world tied together electronically, people will create new value chains every day. These new chains are the driving force behind the productivity fueling the New Economy.

We are in the information age because of the explosion of worldwide communication. For the first five years after the Internet burst into the business world, most businesses saw only a trickle of what networks could do in terms of restructuring business. In the late 1990s, everyone was caught up in the flood, and quite a few investment dollars were producing quite a bit of capital and, ironically, quite a lot of revenue, even with little or no profit. Everyone saw the potential and wanted a piece of it. But like any gold rush, just knowing the gold is out there is not enough. You have to first know exactly where to find it, and then you must stake your claim and keep it. Finally, you have to actually dig the gold out of the ground. Unfortunately, there is only a finite amount of gold in any lode. But for now, most people are happy to be getting their fair share. However, as Boar puts it, *all good fortune is but temporary.* An Internet business, or any kind of value-chain business, whether Web-based or not, must be managed like any brick-and-mortar business. The dynamism required to manage this kind of enterprise can be exhausting, which is why the Web model works so well for small, "judo-like" companies, and will continue to do so into the millennium. But larger companies will find that they have a distinct advantage in experience and resources. A quick and changeable market can wound them, but they are awful hard to kill!

Now, let's return to our earlier lesson plan for PT-101. Strategic planning is one of the required courses of PT-101, and any manager looking to do business in the future must get a passing grade. Now that we have our internal and external networks, both digital and organic, aligned, how do we use them to maximize our business potential? By taking *strategic action,* defined by Boar as follows:

> A strategic action is an action, initiative, or move that, individually or in concert with other actions, has the ability to move the business from a current position to a desired future position. A strategic action is an action of sufficient force and consequence to make a compelling difference to the future well-being of the business.

Remember that strategy must be viewed over the long term, generally no less than three years down the road. But the Internet is a prime example of everyone rushing to El Dorado and having to build their own carts to carry them along the way. Generally, all a person needs is a few good Web servers and some capable programmers, and an Internet business is off and running. An Internet strategy is relatively easy to implement compared to traditional businesses. In the old brick-and-mortar world, implementation meant enormous investments in capital. For instance, if a shoe manufacturer wanted to open new markets, senior management would plan where the new markets should be and whether these new markets would require additional manufacturing capacity and new distribution links. Implementing the strategy would require building manufacturing or distribution facilities, forming partnerships and third-party distribution relationships, and putting management structures in place. But with the Internet, a person can put up one Web site and have global reach.

This may seem exciting, but with such a radical change in scope, all the rules for measuring performance and success are thrown out the window. What if nobody knows about or uses the Web site? If somebody orders a pair of shoes in Japan from a company based in Iowa, the Iowa supplier is now responsible for getting those shoes to the customer in a timely fashion. This may seem obvious, but the Iowa shoe manufacturer may not have necessarily built an infrastructure to support and pay for international exports. Our Iowa manufacturer only wanted to use the Internet to create new markets in the United States. It is very easy to forget that wanting to go global and building the infrastructure to support the idea are two entirely different things. Who will do the exporting? Who will do the importing? Who will handle the local markets overseas? And, what type of finance system must be in place before anybody can buy anything? This business operation paradigm shift forces managers to alter their planning a great deal. All the operational issues that have to be taken into consideration must also be able to work seamlessly together, be well integrated, and be aligned.

▶ Aligning the Organization

The nature of alignment must be twofold, addressing both internal and external alignment. Internal alignment requires internal business units and organic networks to work smoothly together. External alignment requires a business to seamlessly integrate with its outside suppliers, customers, and other members of its supplier chain. Additionally, alignment can only be obtained if every sub-node within the web is properly aligned.

This is made more complex with the fading of the line between consumer and producer. Producers are becoming consumers and consumers, producers. Both will comprise the ubiquitous, ever-present market in which they compete. Any business must be keenly aware of this if it is to be productive in this new, less-segmented marketplace. These principles are as true for brick-and-mortar businesses as they are for Internet businesses. However, compared to brick-and-mortar, Internet businesses work at the speed of thought instead of the months, even years, for which traditional business normally plan. With traditional planning, there was plenty of margin for error and even more time for execution. With paper-thin margins, rapid market volatility, and extremely thin barriers of entry, Internet companies do not have this luxury. Whatever the overall business plan, a Web company must find alignment right out of the blocks to be of any use. Reaching this alignment is problematic since there is very little precedence for knowing what an Internet "threshold" is. Today the largest and most successful e-businesses generally lose more money than they make.

The advantages may outstrip the volatility disadvantages of the e-marketplace. An organization needs static structures for accountability but also fluidity to remain competitive in the marketplace. This is the strength of any "judo-strategy" e-business as it maneuvers across the frictionless cyber-landscape. Maneuverability is greatly prized among Internet investors and venture capitalists. Because barriers to entry in any e-business are small, competition is ferocious. Many investors are looking closely at the management teams behind Internet enterprises and their strategies to cope with such an unforgiving environment. They are putting not only faith but money into individuals who must have a clear, concise knowledge of how the Internet marketplace works and how their company should be best positioned to exploit it.

Business is business, and the best strategies, sooner or later, attract competition. But even if these managers have no idea of where the Internet is going, they should have at least a good working knowledge of how to circle the wagons when an attack comes from all sides. In fact, the truly talented should be able to tactically counterattack at a moment's notice. This is the value of an e-company's maneuverability. E-business management teams can change business direction on a dime and generally at very little cost. If knowledgeable in both traditional business and the Internet business world, the leaders of the next Yahoo!s and Amazon.coms can quickly set up shop, capture the lion's share of a devoted market, raise millions in capital, and then hold on for dear life, whatever their market or business plan.

This explains why most of the field generals in this "global war of movement" are people in their 20s and 30s with longer technical dossiers than business resumes. Since they understand technology and the reasons for its success, it is much easier for them to recognize, follow, and even create trends in technology. The capitalists, or businesspeople, will keep a sharp eye on the business side of e-business—however, when it comes to maneuvering, the capitalists are more than willing to leave the battleground to the technologists.

Most of these technologists are already familiar with interpersonal business "chaining." Many have explored and rejected the regimen of formal corporations, often working as consultants or for startups or in a variety of positions where their individual abilities were far more important than their titles. You would be surprised at the number of "Silicon Valley" techno-giants who started out programming video games or thesis projects simply because it was fun; just look at Yahoo!'s Timothy Koogle. Their method of business relies on staying one step ahead of the next learning curve, individual ability, and a profound, hard-earned trust in those they collaborate with to accomplish both personal and organizational goals.

Most traditional businesses and corporations, on the other hand, still rely on hierarchical management structures to maintain direction when a few thousand people are working towards a goal that some are aware of but most are not. These companies are efficient in managing and utilizing intranets based on their own centralized computing systems, but feel somewhat awkward when facing the enormous uncertainty around the Internet. Traditionally, the glue that held most IT organizations was the mainframe. Mind you, there have been many a siege of mainframes in the history of IT, and the mainframe has survived, simply by luring the blitzkrieg armies into the trenches. This is much easier to do than to force an entrenched army into blitzkrieg. Once the war of attrition starts, the old-fashioned mainframe model may seem stoic, but it remains effective. This is one of the reasons why brick-and-mortar companies haven't been simply swallowed up by cyber companies. Many Internet e-companies are a fraction of the size of a traditional Fortune 500 brick-and mortar, but at one time demanded ten times their value on the stock market. In the end, blitzkrieg or not, everyone is still waiting to see what happens when all this limitless potential begins turning into real profit. The e-businesses that develop the strategies to get there first will be the Standard Oils and GTEs of the 21st century.

A major paradigm shift for both the e-company and the traditional corporation will be the new role of IT in terms of everyday operation and long-range planning. IT will be the first line of defense in the cyber marketplace wars and, therefore, the logical center for business planning. Its function will go from staff support to mainstream overnight, from cost center to profit center in a wink. Senior management of either an e-company or a brick-and-mortar will no longer be able to relegate IT to the lowly back office. It will be treated as the heart and soul of the business.

▶ Aligning for the Future

How do we incorporate traditional IT strategies with the new dynamics of the 21st-century marketplace? IT is currently the mainframe, PCs, and the networks that link them together. The optimum alignment of IT and the business occurs when business strategies are developed together, so that each can influence the other to maximum advantage. Misalignment, at any level, results in a dysfunctional relationship between IT and the business.

As internal networks begin to play a larger role in the extrastructure of the public Internet, as Boar points out, perfect strategic alignment between IT and the business occurs when IT can be used not only to transform business processes, but also to create dislocations in the marketplace and, concurrently, the means of exploitation of those dislocations. This can be visualized as the famous "You don't know me!" IBM e-commerce television commercials. Although marketing databases and demographics can be evasive, as the era of personalization begins to take hold, a good amount of information that was considered personal five years ago will become commonplace, almost mundane. For instance, our shoe manufacturer found success in e-commerce because its Japanese client began ordering shoes on a regular basis. After the first order, the client didn't need to enter its address, shoe order, or method of payment. The client merely makes the selection from a browser and the shoes are on their way.

All the traditional friction of shopping, parking, haggling, and standing in line to pay has been removed. But without the interpersonal connection, chances are the company or store will know more about the customer than the customer knows about the company or store. This knowledge becomes the source of a company's personalized customer database and the basis of its competitive advantage in the marketplace. Companies can now use this information to better service their markets, combining the richness with the Internet's reach. The customers' purchasing data, on the other hand, is stored in a database every time they buy a pair of shoes, or socks, or a Rolls Royce.

The dangers of this are obvious, but for the most part, most companies are only interested in using this information to develop some clear competitive advantage in the minds of customers. For instance, retailers used to compete according to pricing and atmosphere. Bloomingdale's has a distinctively different personality from Macy's. Each expects to attract a certain clientele and expects to address its clientele's expectations accordingly. Economies of scale used to depend heavily on the demographics of how, why, and where these targeted segments of the population did their shopping. A Macy's could try to set up a store in Beverly Hills, but rarely did Bloomingdale's consider opening a store in East Los Angeles. This may not be the best thing socially or politically, but it is the way retailers have done business for centuries. But what happens when the old adage "Location! Location! Location!" no longer has any meaning?

In cyberspace, Macy's and Bloomingdale's find themselves competing not for social or economic demographics but for each and every transaction, regardless of who commits it. Instead of focusing on the type of people buying goods from these retailers, the emphasis will be solely on what (and why) they bought. This knowledge will be vital in getting the same people to buy more similar goods. Macy's and Bloomingdale's will spend less time defining markets and more time trying to capture them, with technology leading the way. On the Internet, it doesn't matter if you buy Gucci or a bargain-brand; what matters is only how much the product cost and how soon it will be delivered. If a retailer can go beyond just selling goods to making the purchase of those goods a personal experience over the Internet, the retailer may gain some level of competitive advantage with each particular customer.

The Internet offers companies that compete with non-Internet companies an even greater sense of dislocation. If Neiman-Marcus never enters the "e-race," it may find itself selling only to those who like being seen in Neiman-Marcus. But when people really want to buy something, they simply go online. It is important to make the distinction between traditional business strategies and the strategies of the Internet era clear. Prior to the Internet, most business strategies to obtain alignment were internal, even so-called outsourcing. Downsizing and re-engineering were buzzwords in the late 1980s and early 1990s, but did little to solve intrinsic problems in most of the organizations that embraced them. Without clearly seeing the direction that technology was actually going, senior managers began addressing symptoms without understanding the disease. Some companies made short-term profits by downsizing to cut costs. Most could not stimulate the real remedy they were looking for: new business and growth. Some who did find the solution were no longer in a position to take advantage of it. Fortunately, in the early 1990s, America's period of market prosperity began due to newly created efficiencies in the stockmarket.

Many companies that downsized or re-engineered found that although nothing changed in the internal networks, the external marketplace was continuing to create networks around them. Companies also found that, at least to some degree, their preoccupation with internal strategies did enable easier adaptation to a changing marketplace it hadn't seen coming. Also, the individuals displaced by sometimes arbitrary downsizing began to redefine the American workforce, creating (or at least reinforcing) individual technologies by working either alone or in small groups. This helped pave the way for those Internet entrepreneurs that eventually got the ball rolling.

We now have the makings of a perfect business network. The advantage technologists enjoy right now is that they are well aware of one simple concept, which is well-stated by Boar: With the rise of the Internet, IT can reach a state of perfect strategic alignment when it achieves a reach/range/maneuverability architecture that has the following attributes:

- Maximum reach
- Maximum range
- Maximum maneuverability

In other words, the e-business understands that IT can be used to create marketplace disruptions on demand; the business doesn't wait for fortuitous situations, it generates them.

What does this mean? It's simple—businesses need to be more entrepreneurial, replacing the matrix with the web, and not just the web, but a marketplace web based on users and providers of services and knowledge. Both the business and the IT organization need to adopt marketplace styles, and these styles must be complementary. Now, as we've all seen from past expeditions by business organizations to improve their strategic alignment, this is much easier said than done. The most immediate problem is that if most senior managers missed the coming of the Internet as such an overwhelming business force, how will they realign their organizations without repeating the same blunders they made in the 1990s? Not every traditional corporation is willing to just hand over the reigns to 30-year-old technologists and say, "Lead us to salvation." And there is no reason why they should.

In truth, many of the problems these organizations face are directly due to their technologists. Not all technologists are fair-haired Stanford graduates from Mountain View. Hard-core veterans of the mainframe world and the politics that go with that environment have built brick-and-mortar companies. Turfdom and interdepartmental territories are not so easy to give up after years spent creating them. This is not entirely the fault of the technology managers; the blame must be shared with directors and senior managers who are responsible for the cost-center mentality that has allowed most internal IT organizations to develop their own little worlds.

Few senior managers understand, or even wish to understand, the intrinsic inner workings of the enigmatic IT department. This is sometimes due to simple economics. In 9 out of 10 organizations, according to Boar, various IT departments run under two separate economic systems: The business economic system determines the rules of exchange between the IT organization and its business customers, the internal economic system governs the exchange of services within the IT organization.

Once this is understood, managing these departments to achieve strategic alignment should be much simpler.

▶ Aligning the Unknown

Most business structures depend on a very political, eclectic system that combines, according to Boar, "the worst of centralized communism and medieval feudalism." Senior managers decide on the general direction and strategy of the company as a whole. By the time the goals are defined for IT, they have usually been shifted down several levels to the mysterious IT organization. Used to independence and a certain lack of accountability, these managers implement these directions pretty much in any way they see fit. If there is glory to be had, they will apportion it to those who are favored. If there is no glory to be had, then chances are this new direction will quickly become too expensive, too difficult, or take too long to implement. Frictions will grow and problems will be left unresolved. And this doesn't happen because IT managers are stubborn, or greedy, or evil. It happens because the system they are in has defined their roles usually incorrectly. As Boar states,

> Internal IT organizations tend to be governed by vertical smokestack organizations (defined by a technology), which rule over their domain and have complete control of their budgets. Employee's loyalties are to their vertical managers, and well-being of the community is directly proportional to the organizational leader's political ability to maintain the status of her technology.

Senior management and directors can create strategy but cannot implement it. They rely on middle managers (whose incentives are based on individual performance and direct loyalties to immediate superiors responsible for the assessment of that performance) to implement.

Directors act as if the organization is *a completely centralized economy* with a distinct set of planners (termed *planner sovereignty*) who will design the ongoing business strategy for the entire organization. However, these decisions are based upon interactions with *a decentralized economy represented by the organic internal networks that is driven by the marketplace dynamics between free and independent producers and self-interested consumers (consumer sovereignty)*. They are pressed to make the right decisions in the best interest of their stockholders, but these same stockholders have very little knowledge (nor do they want any) about how the organization accomplishes these goals.

This leads to imbalance because organizations, to maximize efficiency, have a tendency to create feudal-like monopolies that do the exact opposite of what is demanded by the marketplace in which they are competing. They do not cooperate easily or evenly with other internal groups seeking to maintain their own monopolistic approaches. This, of course, hinders efficiency and adds real and opportunity costs to the actual delivery of goods and services.

However, senior managers have a tendency to look at their organizations only in terms of *static efficiency*: the raw productivity of the economic system to convert resources to products and services. They only want to maximize their organization's ability to do this conversion in the most cost effective manner and, at the same time, introduce a degree of stability that will ensure some level of employee satisfaction and minimize disruption. If this can be accomplished, the organization now has *equity,* the degree to which prices provide a fair balance between producer costs and risk consumer assessment of value.

This works well in theory, but in practice, the best-planned systems are subject to intricacies imposed solely by the will of human beings. But some can be attributed to bad planning and lack of understanding of simple economics. IT departments are usually given a lot of leeway in how they do business, but are limited to finite budgets with which to do it. Given a fixed budget, fixed costs are assumed. We are also quite aware that change is expensive and the best way of eliminating extra cost is eliminating extra change. This can be attributed to many re-engineering projects of the past. So, let's take a closer look at the concept of a managed *resource (budgeting) system.* The driving question is, *do organizations have control over their own IT budgets, or does a central planning board allocate IT expense as overhead?*

However, there are institutions that deploy their IT departments as a *supplier system,* where a sole supplier takes orders (business services) or operates using the market processes of a competitive business. In other words, the IT unit, if responsible for managing itself, now has the added accountability for supplying their customers and producing results. This was originally the idea behind the DEC matrix, but although individual business units within DEC were supposedly independent, in reality, that was far from the case. Each department was given responsibility for results, but it could not make its own decisions and had to rely on the consent of other, often competing, groups. The matrix was effective when the units did agree because the technology that resulted was exceptional, but when they could not agree, the stifling effect far outweighed the creative.

Prior to the introduction of the matrix, some form of central planning committee made almost all real corporate decisions. Boar states that allocation is reduced to a political process where influence is the prime ingredient used to shape decision making. To minimize this political process to some form of controllable acceptance by everyone in the organization, standards for conformity are high. In general, people have to look alike, sound alike, and dress alike to avoid creating too much negative perception and to maintain some say in the overall political process. These organizations are not just business systems but strong social systems as well. In order to do well, the corporate culture has to exceed any other culture brought by individuals. For the most part, this is still the general gauge of corporate behavior everywhere else in the world.

Typical business economies seem to be heavily biased toward the centralized planning model. In a resource system, *the IT budget creates an artificial cap on demand* within the organization. It becomes far too easy to justify lack of ability to meet that demand with the inability to pay for it. Since IT does not have any direct input in strategic planning, it is excluded from responsibility for the results of that policy. Often, they may fail to even see the sense behind the policy, and often, as Boar states, *the IT organization is shielded from the unpleasantness of the marketplace. They share neither a sense of urgency nor the need for hustle.*

Often, departments without very strong leadership continually lag in some way as markets change—and the technology market will change, constantly. Most organizations prefer to continually allow these changes to occur and eventually decide which ones to adopt. This may seem reasonable at first, but it soon becomes hopelessly convoluted as either no technology is adopted or an entirely unsuitable technology is adopted.

Soon, even senior management finds itself starting to fracture, goals are reassessed, and earnings begin to decline. More policy is decided upon to catch up with the new set of parameters being presented by technology in the marketplace, and the cycle resumes. It is only natural that eventually certain inertia begins to set in and large, powerful companies become immobile monoliths. When *priorities are decided by an impersonal bureaucracy* the results will very rarely match the intended goals.

Already out of sync, senior management in IT begins to act as two entirely separate groups with their own policies, goals, and directives. They can take advantage of their position, since they alone understand what's going on. *New technologies are introduced on an IT schedule, not on a schedule of business needs.* This may have a devastating effect on the business of the organization as a whole. But with only implementation responsibility and no fiscal responsibility, IT groups are easily shielded by claiming lack of resource or technical expertise. Profits and losses are attributed to the financial planners and not to the IT units themselves.

The charging of IT services to overhead or to indecipherable IT units makes understanding costs impossible. Given the opportunity to develop their own internal economies as well as their own corporate culture, disequilibriums begin springing all over the entire organization. *Users engage in subterfuge to hide expenses and hire external providers, resulting in growing distrust between IT provider and customer.* Meetings are held to discuss interdepartmental partnerships and technology initiatives, but the only things committed to are the notes of the last meeting. This is not due simply to bad planning, a bad apple or two, or any grand conspiracy. People merely adapt to the set of circumstances they are given.

According to Boar, the best way to avert this is to "move to a completely free market system where the internal IT organization is just another equal supplier of IT services." But to do so, a manager must have a very clear set of formal rules to first define the marketplace and then define what the IT department's role is in regard to that marketplace. So we find ourselves back to the web-based chain of value. Before this kind of structure can actually thrive in a free market, it must first be tested in the controlled internal market of the business organizations that intend to use it. As Boar states, the internal relational governance mechanism permits the company to deal with the complexity of uncertainty of IT in an adaptive and sequential decision-making manner. It is no secret that most attempts, like DEC's matrix management, end disastrously. But a closer look will reveal a good amount of internal web-chaining has always taken place in spite of the restrictions of many functional hierarchies.

The Integration of Technology in Our Business and Personal Lives

▶ The Knowledge-Based Economy

In ancient times, skillful warriors first made themselves invincible.

—Lao Tsu

With limited competition in both the new industries and the old industries using new technologies, costs fell faster than prices and profits soared.

—Lester C. Thurow, *Building Wealth*

We are all witnessing a revolution, the direction of which we can determine, but the length of the road we still find mysterious. The Industrial Revolution brought great changes in the way people all over the world lived their lives, but even in the heart of that revolution, these changes took decades, sometimes centuries. With the digital revolution, these fundamental changes occur in just a few years, sometimes in just a few

161

months, overwhelming the most casual observer and the most hardened businessman. The best we can probably do is to try and achieve a sort of working equilibrium. If we somehow leverage these changes, we stand a reasonable chance of not just holding our own but perhaps even prospering.

The Industrial Revolution introduced the notion that creativity and inventiveness combined with the business principles of profit and loss could create, over time, enormous wealth. How this wealth was distributed or what resources were consumed to make these notions a reality was secondary to the advances they made. Hence, the Industrial Revolution could just as easily be called the Age of Invention. From the mid–18th century until now, the rapid growth of experience and knowledge in the sciences and engineering surpasses by far a millennia of preceding human invention. In the 20th century alone, we have gone from horse and buggy to space flight! While it took thousands of years for man to conquer the air, in less than a century we have gone from the Wright brothers to weekly shuttle missions into space. It took almost 400 years to move from the lateen sail to the all-metal steamship, but again, less than a century to move from the steamship to the nuclear submarine.

Not only is the very nature of technology changing, but also the pace of change is starting to approach staggering proportions. No longer is inventiveness and insight enough to make vast economic leaps—we have to predict when, how, and where these changes are going to come from before they happen. As a result, knowledge about technology has become almost as important as the technology itself. This Information Age has led to the creation of a knowledge-based economy. This is an economy where individuals must not only be educated but multi-talented in a number of fields. Our bicycle messenger, our publishing middle manager, and our hi-tech CEO must all be equally immersed in technology. One is either in the know or completely left out in the cold. The only problem is the overwhelming glut of things to know.

So, how do we determine what we *need* to know? Thankfully, although the nature of technology is rapidly changing, the principles of good business are still holding steadfast. "Buy low, sell high" is just as valid in an era of electronic trading as it was when Reuters was using carrier pigeons. This is the edge that we all have when trying to deal with change, whether we act as organizations or as individuals.

Let's start with the general assumption that everyone is in the same boat. Whether young or old, rich or poor, male or female, we are all consumed with the daily act of earning a living. As such, it's safe to assume that if you are deeply confused by everything going on, then so is the next guy. No matter how assured or secure the technical, the knowledgeable, the consultant, or the billionaire may seem, if he or she is human, then he or she has no more idea of what is going to happen tomorrow than you do. If this is so, then we can get rid of one of the more pervasive fears in a knowledge-based economy—the fear that we're going to be left behind. If no one has an exact fix on just where they are geographically, then there is no way to tell where behind, ahead, or even sideways actually is. The only thing you can be sure of is what might be ahead for *you*.

With that in mind, you should be able to put your own situation into perspective. Questions such as, do I want to get on the Internet? Do I want my own Web page? Do we need an ISP? and, should we be an ISP? are all valid to ask about our immersion into pan-technology. It is these levels of immersion that will dictate the future economic markets that businesses and individuals can exploit for economic benefit. While the industrial revolution made wealth by efficiently producing large quantities of similar goods, the digital revolution will produce wealth by efficiently producing very small, specialized quantities. In the future, technology will become a very personnel thing. This is why traditional brick-and-mortar companies continue to have such a hard time understanding what they should do in response to the rapidly growing e-conomy.

▶ Defining the E-conomy

But what is an e-conomy? There has to be something more to it than Web sites and banner ads! Let's start by looking at the nature of any economy, particularly simpler ones. Prior to the industrial revolution, our agrarian way of life did lead to a more individualized manner of living. One hundred years ago, since most of the clothes worn were made by the people wearing them, clothes accommodated economic necessity and individuality. Almost no one in today's society thinks of actually making his or her own clothes. Why? Since the invention of the automatic loom, the sewing machine, and the American system of manufacturing, clothes can be made inexpensively in large quantities, enabling even the poorest citizens to buy clothes rather than make them.

However, by consuming so many predesigned, manufactured goods, we no longer can personalize our clothes, unless we have them tailored. The best we can do off the rack is to look for clear product differentiation through designer labels: I'm a Bill Blass; you're a Pierre Cardin. But anybody with the same taste and budget can be just as "Pierre Cardin" as you. But what if the cost-saving methods of the American system of manufacture were combined with the individuality that results with the use of a personal tailor, or e-tailors? If you could go to a Web site and put in your measurements, type of clothing, color, and material, and two days later receive the goods, you would be the owner of a tailor-made jacket at an off-the-rack price. This is, in economic terms, true economic value.

The real problem is that since businesses are comprised of people, the work environment, technology-driven or not, is still a product of the ideas, perceptions, and eventually the culture of the people. Although just about any business school understands the concept of the corporate culture, it is usually reflected as a method for boosting morale, rewarding leadership, and inciting innovation. Rarely does a corporation think about what it is doing from any perspective other than business. The reality is that most businesses have a very short-term point of view. Good and bad is usually decided by Wall Street's reactions to particular quarterly earnings.

Because of this, most managers are almost forced to adopt a myopic market view, and although they may honestly believe that they are constantly reflecting what the market demands, only the smallest and most maneuverable companies can respond quickly—hence the lack of large- to medium-sized brick-and-mortar companies as drivers in the current Internet boon. The large players, such as IBM and Hewlett-Packard, have the market power to set standards but not the maneuverability to introduce them. Thus, IBM weds itself to Java, a Sun Microsystems product produced to compete with Microsoft, which instead of really innovating, must rely on its market clout to ensure its own market position until it is maneuverable enough to set the standard. If it has no clout in a particular market, it simply buys a smaller company that does, as reflected in Microsoft's purchase of WebTV and others.

The real concern for any individual living in the knowledge-based economy is the unknown. Traditionally, the idea behind entering a corporate environment was the notion of security. In the past, by following the rules established by both professional contract and the tacit acceptance of society, performance was not just rewarded financially, but ideally, by years of guaranteed employment as well. Two generations ago, workers joined corporations, manufacturers, and other small- and medium-sized businesses for life. Today, the notion of lifetime employment with a single organization no longer exists, and individuals are just as prone to imbalances in the labor market as businesses are in the commercial market.

Therefore, where employees only had to be concerned with what was expected of them within an organization to ensure some path of advancement, they now must be able to work within a variety of cultures that can only be assimilated by working for many different organizations. Interestingly, there are fewer glass ceilings, since individuals rarely stay long enough within an organization to hit them. Simultaneously, organizations have to deal with a much more liquid and demanding labor pool. The rules of compensation have begun to change drastically. After generations of demand-side control of the labor market, the market is beginning to tilt toward the supply side as individual knowledge and individual skills become paramount in terms of defining work in the 21st century. The challenge will be in learning how to actually go beyond thinking like an individual even while your work is being judged upon your being one.

In effect, each and every individual of working age and capacity should begin to view themselves as mini-corporations and act accordingly. Almost all corporations at one time were small businesses legally bound to follow certain rules that define a corporation as both a business and a legal entity. It is up to the corporation to produce a particular good or service, produce a profit, and ultimately pay taxes. They are simply a resource generator, using resources to either redefine or redistribute other resources to generate economic activity. Therefore, they must be organized, efficient, and, by all means, responsible.

Of course, for the most part, we assume the same for our professional lives. But let's face it, the vast majority of wage earners in the world are averaging 10 to 12 hours a day attempting to make enough money to keep ahead of their bills, regardless of the economy of scale. In my opinion, this is neither good nor bad. This is a natural state that allows humans to easily meet the necessities of life yet still overcome formidable obstacles. Theoretically, and perhaps philosophically, it is overcoming these obstacles that provides the additional economic value to any business or individual.

Obviously, one of the main areas where individual knowledge can be turned into actual capital with reasonably little friction is in the technology market, a market based solely on individual knowledge and skill. When this knowledge is collected, managed, and coordinated effectively, we have our modern technology company driving our new technology-based economy, even if that company is a company of one.

▶ A Company of One

You are now incorporated as Technology, Inc. You are the CEO, CIO, president, and treasurer. You are also in charge of public relations, development, and customer support. This is a pretty big undertaking for someone who writes code for a living, particularly if that someone is middle-aged and has been working at the same job for the same company for the last 15 years. Once, this was viewed as credible, but now it's, well, lame. But it is precisely the time to adopt this point of view. If you were the CEO of a Fortune 500 company, you would probably be about the same age but have more responsibility. Once individuals adopt the perspective that they are in charge of something larger than their job description, it becomes easier to at least see, if not always understand, where the road is going.

This may seem like we're a few steps beyond taking classes at the community college, trying to keep up with the latest hot language, or simply using the Internet more. We are. Misplaced overconfidence in the next few years could have a cataclysmic effect on individuals who become too complacent. It is relatively easy to stay on top of things, as long we are aware that the things we're staying on top of belong to us. The biggest drawback of hierarchical organizations is the presence of complacency. Complacency is usually equal to how enfranchised the individual feels in his or her organization. If workers, white collar or blue collar, feel like they are being exploited, then they will exploit. This results in a decline in their job interest, their performance, and their attitude—and if these feelings become widespread, the organization as a whole, large or small, will decline.

Since this is the extent of my behavioral and organizational psychology knowledge, I cannot delve into why all this is so. But I will suggest that the best way for individuals not to feel and act exploited is to assume they are working for themselves. If individuals cannot stay involved in the promotion of their careers, then they are probably not interested in anything I've said thus far. But if they are, they will find a certain freedom in decision making that is difficult to find when decisions are made for them. A change in mindset from employee to free agent will usually result in employees doing what is in their own best interest. If they do a good job, they become more valuable not only to their employer but to the job market as a whole—a large, hungry job market that is both demanding and rewarding. By doing a good job within an organization and keeping abreast of the business, an individual can invest in areas of opportunity as they arise.

Actually, knowing what's going on is difficult at best, and knowing what will go on is next to impossible. The New Economy provides much less friction in changing or applying a new professional outlook. Ten years ago, someone would be viewed as crazy for leaving a field they had been in for a decade and suddenly trying a new one. Now, although still not widespread, people almost view career changes as a sign of success. Not everybody has the imagination or drive to actually be an entrepreneur, but I believe everyone has the ability to think like an entrepreneur, because everybody looks after his or her own self-interests anyway!

Therefore, an individual who decides to think as an entrepreneur will find fewer barriers both within an organization and in the job market as a whole. As more and more businesses begin to adopt the core/contingent model of employment, a much broader, more demanding labor market will be created and employees will learn to manage their careers as if they were managing their own companies. This will be the basic knowledge requirement in the Knowledge Economy— knowing how to do business even if the business is simply showing up for work everyday.

Let's say you are a 27-year-old female. You are currently dissatisfied with being a legal secretary and decide, for whatever reason, that it is not the career for you. You decide that computers are the way to go. Twenty years ago, this would have required quitting your job and going back to school full time or taking laborious and expensive classes at a university or business school just to have access to a computer system. If your legal firm were large enough to have a computer, the idea of transferring to a department where it would have been accessible would have been deemed ludicrous. This would be true for a 35-year-old Caucasian male, a 21-year-old African-American, Hispanic, or Asian male or female, or just about anybody. And that is the point. Technology has changed the cultural values of our economy.

Today, if this same individual wanted to get into computers, it would be easy. She probably already has one where she works. If she can afford it, she will probably have a computer at home. She will spend considerable time reading and writing emails, shopping online, and perhaps pursuing programming as a hobby. She finds herself more attracted to how the computer can gather knowledge than to the knowledge itself. She first begins to study software pertinent to the legal profession and then software in general. In her spare time, she buys a Java package and begins to write some code. She gets rather good at coding and begins to write her own programs at work. Soon, every lawyer in her office begins to use her applications, and they begin to tell their colleagues at other firms about it. Our legal secretary is soon writing more code than legal briefs.

She mentions to her boss that she would like to spin off a company to sell her software. The firm backs her, and she finds she can't support the demand for her online, Web-based, object-oriented "Legal Secretary 2001." She has to hire additional people, and a venture capitalist invests enough to allow her to open her own office. Soon she is ready to go public and hires the venture capitalist to do the underwriting and her old law firm to handle the legalities for the "family and friends" pricing on the IPO.

Sound fanciful? It's not! As we've pointed out with the history of Yahoo!, personal interest in technology can lead to bigger and better things. Of course, in reality, nothing is this easy. Writing even the simplest program can be a vexing and time-consuming affair, but that is why it is considered so valuable. The major difference between technology today and 20 years ago is that it is so pervasive now that anybody can have access to it and, if they want to, exploit it! Nor does our legal secretary need a degree from Harvard Business School to find and evaluate a good opportunity. As a legal secretary, she couldn't find software able to do what she needed it to do; she realized she needed to create her own. This is the entrepreneur's first step. Now she simply has to determine whether this is a job she can do herself or she needs others to help. Since the software was relevant to her job, whatever time and effort she could invest, as long as she got her other work done, would likely be encouraged.

When given the leeway to pursue a technical solution to a perceived problem, she has become a business unit within the larger business. In fact, she is tacitly in charge of this unit and has to learn to manage both the time allocation and financing of this unwritten project to get something to work. If she persists, eventually she succeeds. She uses and tests her own product, inadvertently becoming a product manager. She promotes and supports the use of her software within her parent company. Her parent company uses it so extensively that it becomes a core product that the parent is willing to invest in. And, through all of this, the legal secretary is still a wage-based employee with a specific title and job description.

This is enough of an illustration to describe a real-life knowledge-based economy business situation that you or I can find ourselves in at any given time in any given company. What is important to know is not that we will find ourselves in this situation, but that we can and we must be prepared!

However, although almost every business has adopted some form of technology to do business, this doesn't mean that they all understand it or require activities as exploring better software options as part of their position requirements for secretaries. There are still many companies that eschew technology altogether. But these types of businesses are rapidly becoming the minority as they continue to create barriers where barriers are no longer needed. Organizations and individuals, unless this is a culture they choose, will simply go around them.

Another downside is that this form of economy, because of such low barriers of entry, is considerably more volatile when it comes to success or failure. Our legal secretary does fine after her whirlwind IPO, but now faces real market competition from larger, more experienced software companies just now realizing the potential of software in the legal secretary market. These companies are larger, have more money, and have a considerably larger installed customer base. In a matter of months, their software product surpasses hers in features and she begins to lose what little market share she had. Now the work *really* begins.

▶ My Technology, Myself

Regardless of the actual ups and downs of the technology business cycle, the ability to transform one's own career is greatly eased through technology. Specifically, it is the paradigm shift that technology is ubiquitous, somehow a good in and of itself. If it can be captured, harnessed, and put to good use, people seem to care less and less about who provides it. This is true not only for the new economy as a whole, but also within traditional corporate organizations, which would have viewed such behavior as counterproductive, even seditious, just a single generation ago.

And it is essential to every business, new or old, to continue to support and promote this type of initiative to maintain a competitive foothold in its own product markets and the ever-enigmatic labor markets. Most companies, although maintaining a somewhat hierarchical structure for the sake of definition and control, are becoming organic web-like structures that rely on interpersonal networks both within and outside of the organization. Ultimately, decisions must be made in terms of how much control is given to the modeled hierarchy and how much is given to the network. As the new economy evolves, the hierarchies will try to prevail but will eventually have less and less control of these networks. In time, we will have the 21st century equivalent of guilds—individuals, even if the individuals are full-time employees, will view themselves according to skill, experience, and choice. Organizations unwilling to accept this view will find it very difficult to attract and maintain quality labor. As these organizations change the way they view labor, they will simultaneously begin to change their view on how they produce goods for their markets. Like individuals, the real value of these organizations will be their ability to adapt.

For example, four of the five makers of vacuum tubes never successfully made transistors or semiconductor chips when transistors emerged to replace the vacuum tube—the fifth is today not a player.

These organizations did not stagnate because they were not aware of the impact that semiconductor chips would have on the world. Rather, they were so encrusted in the traditional hierarchies that they could not redefine themselves. Not being able to redefine themselves, they could not redefine their products. Without redefining their products, they could not redefine their markets. As their markets eventually vanished, so did they. But this is becoming the newest and perhaps the most difficult business requirement to face. It is natural to assume that if markets are changing, the formal social contracts that for so many years determined the true nature of management and labor relations in the industrial world will be maintained. Simply put, they will not. In the next century, there will be no one dominant scheme that will ensure what we can expect and what is to be expected for a day's labor. Gone are the days of the homogenous corporate culture that could determine and respond to homogenous markets. These markets were defined by the rules and economies of assembly-line manufacturing, and as the impact of this form of economy plays less and less of a role in the current economy, so will these rules play less and less of a role.

Technology allows individuals to remain individual even when working collectively. When all individuals have access to the technology that will define the economy of the next century, their influence and participation will play a much greater part than would have been possible on the assembly line. In the face of e-commerce, does this mean that the local store will disappear? Hardly. But the role the local store plays in our personal life and our economic well-being will change from one of necessity to almost one of recreation. If you can buy everything online, the only real need to get into a car and drive to a store is simply the pleasure of doing so. Although the role that technology will play in the future will reshape the way people do business, this change should by no means be disruptive. True, there will be transitional shock, but this is always the case as new technologies replace old ones faster than individuals want to or can keep up. Society will dictate new rules for business and personal success. Whether these dictates will be fair, humane, and effective remains to be seen. The only thing we know is that barring any large economic upheavals, these changes could be uncomfortable, but not catastrophic.

Since the baby boom generation still comprises the majority of working Americans, as they age and begin retiring, there will be a drastic shortage of labor, particularly in technology. The convergence of baby boom power and technological breakthroughs will guide who works where and who doesn't. The boomers, those born between 1946 and 1964, have dictated the products we make and the services we sell since they were in diapers. They'll continue to do so.

> Technology has revolutionized the labor force and the marketplace since the age of television in the 1950s. But in the coming years, the revolution will be in warp-speed mode. The better jobs will go to those best able to adapt to the technological landscape.
>
> —William Sokolic,
> *Shaping the Labor Market: Baby Boomers and Technology*

Although older professionals will not always be willing to adopt new technologies as soon as they appear, they will find the adoption process considerably easier, since pan-technology will make most of these changes seamless. A desktop will be a desktop, as well as a telephone, a television, an ATM, and whatever else one wants it to be.

The general structure of business, although radically different in process, will be pretty much the same in appearance. Offices and office buildings will not disappear overnight, if ever. Although individuals will have much greater flexibility in how they do their work, it must still be centralized to some degree to ensure that things get done in an orderly fashion. However, since the labor marketplace will become much more demanding without necessarily becoming more competitive, there will always be a fine line between corporate demands and individual responsibility. In short, individuals must show a much higher degree of initiative if organizations are going to allow a higher degree of flexibility. For most of the working world, just clocking in will be a thing of the past. Although "9 to 5" won't exactly disappear, it will become something of an anachronism.

Even in the manufacturing sector, renowned for punch clocks and time-tables, the demands of specialized production and just-in-time manufacturing will be far too great for simple piecemeal assembly-line work. It will demand a much higher integration of labor and technical skills. As the percentage of GDP that manufacturing contributes to the U.S. economy remains about the same, the percentage of the population in the manufacturing sector will actually decrease. This will obviously require considerable increase in individual productivity, demanding in turn an increase in individual initiative and skill sets. The burden of maintaining these skills will fall almost entirely on the individual. This will be true for both permanent core workers and various levels of freelance or contingent workers.

However, if this constant process of knowledge-building is to be successful, the organizations at the core of all industries must learn how to aggregate, manage, and understand the needs of individuals in a new way. Although long-range goals and financial planning must occur from a central body of senior managers and directors, the actual implementation of these plans has to be as fluid and dynamic as the individuals charged with carrying them out. Although the concept of business has always been competitive and dynamic, most corporations of the 20th century developed their own internal culture to provide a sense of direction to dozens, hundreds, sometimes thousands of employees. Without this type of conformity, organizations must reassess themselves almost as often as they assess the people that work for them. Undergoing such an assessment will be the only way these organizations will keep up with the rapid pace of new businesses and the organic web-like supply chains.

Again, the crucial point to remember is that both the organization and the individual will be pretty much in the same bowl of soup. They will be tied together in a much more intimate way than they ever have been. When businesses shift direction, individuals will decide whether or not to shift with them. When individuals shift gears, some businesses might find they have to shift, to some degree, whether they like it or not. Even large, more hierarchical structures will find that resisting too much change will create disequilibriums that their competitors will rapidly leverage. If the disequilibriums continue, individuals able to adapt quickly will exploit them, continuing the cycle.

It is relatively easy to throw around buzzwords like *era, age,* and *revolution*; such things do exist. They are defined by some event, discovery, or in our case technology, that alters the lives of everyone on earth to some degree. We today are just one generation removed from a world where a television in any household was extremely rare. This was a world where traveling by airline was reserved only for the exclusive and rich, a world where computers, at least the kind we have today, were found only in science fiction and Flash Gordon serials.

▶ The True Revolution

With the invention of the plow, the world of economics (and therefore politics, warfare, science, and religion) revolved around the earth. It was the earth that nurtured and supported mankind, culture, all that was held dear, and all that was feared. People would own land, build upon it, fight over it, and mold it to shape their needs for thousands of years, building societies, civilizations, and cultures that have all influenced mankind. There have been great technological revolutions in the history of mankind.

- The Agrarian Revolution

- The Industrial Revolution
- The Information Revolution

> After the first industrial revolution, energy replaced land as the basic building block underlying wealth. With the third industrial revolution, knowledge moves into the position previously held by land and energy.

With all this information flowing so seamlessly and freely, how can any person or organization possibly capture and control all of it in any way? As no one person or organization can be our information genie, we all must rely on small, special vesicles of self-contained, highly specialized knowledge. The Industrial Revolution freed the masses. The Information Revolution will eventually free the individual.

Every business, from international conglomerates to two- or three-person software power shops, will depend on individual skill and knowledge in the 21st century. Individuals will be judged by how well they disseminate and utilize their knowledge in reference to mass applications. Organizations will be judged by how well they manage and coordinate these individuals. Technology will simply be the link between the individual, the organization, and the application. If all three can be properly aligned at any given time, then the resultant harmony could lead to tremendous innovation, productivity, and realized economic growth. However, there has to be more than greed to sustain this kind of atmosphere. There has to be some fundamental understanding of how everything works before we can make everything work together. Knowledge is as varied as the individuals who gather it, analyze it, and apply it. Only now, in the beginning of the 21st century, do we finally have the means to truly share it with whoever wishes to learn it. The quest for knowledge must come from individuals and be encouraged by societies.

Some may argue that knowledge for the sake of knowledge is always a worthy cause. But some will also argue that many pursue knowledge for many different reasons, and not all of them good. Man has instinctively understood and even feared the power of knowledge—Pandora's box or the forbidden fruit that tempted Adam and Eve are good examples. In both cases, it was the combination of curiosity and knowledge that brought about ruin while simultaneously and profoundly identifying our humanity. Not that technology and religion must go hand in hand anymore than politics and philosophy, but there has to be some logical and moral pursuit behind the quest for knowledge. Collectively, it will lead to many things other than prosperity, and it cannot be abandoned for the sake of simplicity and order.

Some cultures, religions, and societies view nature as a neat and orderly place governed by rules of its own, perhaps with the guidance of a supreme deity. But in reality, all nature, including human nature, is hectic, chaotic, and unpredictable. Our earliest ancestors were awed and inspired by the simplest technologies (such as fire and the wheel) simply because these very simple tools could bring some level of control to the chaos around them. This is the instinct within us that has led to the invention and application of technology, whether any one of us understands it or not. However, far too often the tools of control become closely associated with the chaos. Sometimes technology, by trying to control chaos, becomes the source of chaos. With each problem solved by one successful technology, a thousand new problems may arise. The steam engine, the power plant of the Industrial Revolution, was large and dangerous, and finally gave way to the gas-combustion engine. The combustion engine relies on fossil fuels that release pollutants into the atmosphere. Nuclear energy has been seen as a way of creating clean, nonfossil-fuel-based energy. But radioactive wastes pose a more serious pollutant problem than fossil fuel ever could!

In ancient times, discovering and harnessing fire was a boon at first, but as jealous and aggressive outsiders fought for this gift instead of sharing it, the heavy burden of war, fear, and death vastly overshadowed the good. But should we extinguish all fires in the hope of peace? Of course not, for someone, somewhere, will come up with a good idea and once again mankind will be off to the races.

However, in doing so, we must also discard the need for generalities and black and white dualities. When individuals are interviewed for a COBOL position in the 21st century, they will be judged not only on how many lines of COBOL code they have already written but also on how many lines of code they've written in C or Java, or, even more importantly, in English. After all, the ultimate programming language, at least in English-speaking countries, would be a program written in plain, simple English—a program anybody who knows English can actually read. You would not need a computer science degree; you would not need Boolean calculus and algebra. You would simply need to know how light or dark you want your toast.

Tomorrow's technologists will still need to be imaginative and creative engineers, scientists, or artists. Politics and society will determine the structure, but the desire for knowledge will still determine the function. Putting creativity to good use has always been a challenge for economists. In the world of finance, profit and loss determine how successfully an organization or an individual meets this challenge. How do we actually produce profit in a knowledge-based society?

> Selling knowledge so that others could make products that came from it has never been a profitable strategy.

The main difference between skill and knowledge is that skill is learned and applied over time to a particular and usually static objective. The more the skill is applied, the more timely and effective the individual that applies it becomes. Of course, in the process of acquiring and perfecting one skill, other skills can be learned and applied in their own right, perhaps to other objectives. But knowledge is much more synergetic. A little can go a long way in a very short time. Being able to add numbers quickly is a skill; being able to understand and apply the Pythagorean theorem is knowledge. Both skills and knowledge can be gained purely from experience, but only knowledge requires insight.

In the knowledge-based world geared towards personalization, self-creativity, and the ability to adapt, the dynamic of both our social and economic life will take on a vitality all its own, essentially becoming a never-ending moving target. This can be an awesome challenge, but it is also the reason why the rewards for succeeding are so great! As our skills in applying knowledge increase, we are able to control chaos that currently exists as well as the chaos created by the control! Let's look at it simply. We all must balance our checkbooks every month. Now, some of us don't like arithmetic or having to balance our checkbooks, so we don't. Therefore we are often overdrawn at the bank, we receive constant notices, our credit becomes shaky, and we are summarily outcast from society, and our lives are ruined. On the other hand, by acquiring the skill of balancing a checkbook, by education, by training, by just hard practice, our bills are paid on time and we acquire the *knowledge* of just how much money we have or do not have at any given time. We now have the means to forecast future investments and activities, to actually plan what we will or will not do tomorrow, today, or next week. This knowledge can actually allow us to increase our revenue through saving and investment.

Now that these very personal principles have found their way up the economic evolutionary ladder, they are here to stay. Every individual, every organization, though still measured long-term by growth, will be measured in the short term, by "What can you do for me today?" Eventually, these ideas filter into the labor market, as timeliness becomes synonymous with flexibility. If we are confronted with an entirely new set of problems day by day, then we must acquire whatever skill set is required to solve these problems day to day. The old world of learning by rote will have no value if the skills acquired are no longer applicable by the time you apply them. Workers who have the ability to learn new things quickly will be prized over those who do not.

The major organizational change will be the "organic web" domination of the business landscape; small, flexible groupings will become the norm. Whether these groups exist in relatively large, even traditional, corporations, or in many separate independent companies, it is clear that the era of size for the sake of size is over. Even the ancient Japanese keiretsus are evolving their own form of organic webs in order to become more competitive with the European and North American economies. In fact, the Europeans may have a decided advantage, since their Economic Union is organized as a number of separate entities in terms of culture and language, working towards common ends. We'll see if there are any tangible fruits from such a revolutionary and compelling program, but if there are successes, than chances are they will be enormous ones. Conjointly, where there are failures, they are likely to be catastrophic. But once again, the Rubicon has been crossed, and there can be no going back.

So, not only in America is the era of subsidization and patronage ending—it's also ending all over the world. As a result, *downsizing is a way of life even in good times among profitable companies.* And once this is accepted, the psychological fear of unemployment, changing jobs frequently, or what was once viewed as uncertainty and instability will lose its stigma. Both organizations and individuals will come to view change as not just inevitable but desired. This adaptation will enable everyone to have his or her own ideas about what's changing and where the change is headed. These ideas will differ greatly between individuals and corporations.

▶ Most Frequently Asked Questions

1. What's in it for me?

   What's does any professional have to gain by taking the time to fully explore and understand technology? The answer is simple: everything to gain and nothing to lose. For any individual with at least 10 years of experience in the working world, technical skill is *essential* to taking part in even the most minimal level of business activities, almost regardless of the type of business. For managers, both IT and non-IT, this is doubly so.

   Although technology seems a bit ubiquitous and overwhelming, it is merely the ability to understand how tools, hi-tech or low-tech, can be exploited for economic gain. It has long been tacitly assumed that "techies" were a breed apart, competent at designing, implementing, and maintaining complex software and hardware systems, but incapable of decisive business management skills. That stereotype is rapidly falling by the wayside, as more CIOs become CEOs. And even those who do not obtain the top spot in businesses, companies and organizations still find their role in top-level management decisions becoming increasingly more important.

   It is easy to get caught up in the myth that technology is the playground of the "super hip" who are under 30 and who spend every waking hour behind a computer screen. True, they are the future of technology in business, but it is those who are already in decision-making positions, whether 30, 40, 50, or older, who have to make the decisions today.

2. Should I have access to the *Internet?*

   Should you have a telephone? Should you have a washing machine, or a hairdryer, or any other common household item? What do you think?

3. Should I get my own Web site?

   Not every individual needs a Web site. As with any technology, the determination of how far you should go depends on how far you want to go. If you are actively thinking of incorporating Internet technology into your business, or even just pursuing it as a hobby, having your own site is the best way of finding out how the Internet functions.

From a business perspective, depending on the size of your company and how much money you have to spend, it is without a doubt the best way of learning to manage an Internet site, whether that site is internal or off-site. Of course, not everyone is interested in managing their own technology, but becoming involved with the early stages of a Web site helps considerably later on when discussing and planning Web technologies as they become more integrated as a business.

If you are not interested in understanding what's going on behind the scenes of a Web site, there will be nothing to hold your interest.

4. Should I have access to the Internet at work?

If you don't have access to the Internet by now, you are already behind the eight-ball. In a few years, working without Internet access will be like working without a telephone. Amazingly, there are still a lot of companies that feel access to the Internet is more of a distraction than an aid. They worry that employees will spend more time surfing recreational sites than sites required for work. Indeed, there is always that possibility, since employers have only limited control of the Internet. However, as the knowledge-based economy grows and is acknowledged as such, being able to attract and maintain good workers will be directly dependent on these workers being able to access the Internet. In fact, as organic value chains become more complex, it will become next to impossible to even do business without the Internet!

5. Should I provide Internet at work?

See the answer to question 4.

6. If I'm a programmer, what languages should I know?

This question is not a new one, but still holds the same validity in the New Economy as it did in the old. Obviously, Java is the "hot" language of the Internet right now, but the need for faster, in-process languages like Perl and C++ will continue to exist. The best approach from a programmer's perspective is not to concentrate solely on learning everything about a particular programming language. If programmers learn and fully understand the concepts and techniques of object-oriented programming, they will be prepared to deal with any language designed to operate within the Internet space.

Although a good understanding of programming techniques was necessary for traditional third-generation modular languages, such as C, FORTRAN, and Basic, these languages were considerably more insular and each had to be studied in its own right. But object-oriented languages all have a common thread when it comes to reusing code, class libraries, state transitions, and other programming features necessary to make the Internet work.

The tools and the platforms will dictate the areas of expertise any individual programmer will pursue. That is, will the application be UNIX-based or NT-based? Will programmers be using open languages like Java, JavaScript, and JSP on the more universal UNIX platforms, or will they require the proprietary languages, such as Microsoft's Visual Basic, VBScript, and ASP? As their names imply, these languages basically work with the same principles but on different platforms. As the technology market matures and both operating systems and languages become more interchangeable (led by different flavors of UNIX), even these differences will eventually become moot.

7. If I'm an investor, what should I invest in?

When it comes to the world of business and finance, unlike technology, the old rules still apply. Invest only in companies, products, and services that supply a real and measurable value to the economy as a whole. Of course, this is much more easily said than done, but if you have read this book carefully, some points about what is going on today should lend some valuable insight into what will happen tomorrow.

For example, the explosion in the use of cellular phones means that investing in the companies that provide these services—Qualcomm, Sprint PCS, Nokia, and a host of others—is a sure-fire hit. But what about the wireless markets yet to be tapped? Internet access from your car or portable Web browsers and email from your Sony Walkman are capable of popping up tomorrow. The true value of the New Economy is the fact that there are many innovations and products yet to be created. Now, unlike any other time since the turn of the century, investors not only can follow trends but also have the power to create them!

8. If I'm not in a hi-tech job, should I be?

That can only be answered on an individual basis. These days it seems the lion's share of glamour and prestige goes to the hi-tech sector of the economy. The images of nerdy engineers with horn-rimmed glasses and white lab coats has been replaced with well-moussed executives driving limos and sports cars and making millions with one swoop of the IPO. It all seems pretty glitzy, but the old rule of "you don't get something for nothing" still applies.

Being a successful technologist takes just as much hard work, dedication, discipline, and training as being a successful doctor or lawyer. If you want to go into hi-tech just to make money, chances are you won't. The secret of success hasn't changed. You have to be good at what you do, and the best way of ensuring that is making sure you love what you do. Most of us never get the chance to do what we love, which is one of the reasons most of us aren't rich. But even if great wealth is not our goal, every individual, now more than ever, can pursue their own goals in ways that didn't exist 20 years ago. Technology only gives those with imagination, fortitude, and desire that chance to pursue what they want to pursue.

9. I don't want a hi-tech job. Am I doomed?

   See the answer to question 8.

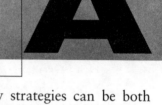

Following is an example of how technology strategies can be both unpredictable and frustrating. Lotus Notes is a very powerful application given birth to by client-server technology and then taking on a life of its own. At its inception, it was seen as a universal business tool that could and would solve a plethora of business problems. However, although successful and still widely used today, it never became as universal as Microsoft Office, though it is arguably a technologically superior application.

The late 80s also issued in the "open" era of digital software and hardware. Open software has been one of the driving forces behind the rapid development of the Internet and the entrenchment of digital technology into both the average workplace and our personal lives. The digital environment we live in today is due in no small part to the technology and business innovations founded in the late 1980s and early 1990s.

Lotus Notes, the Emerging Technology that Stayed that Way

The Year to Go Nuts about Notes

Back at the dawn of the personal computer era, excited friends insisted that I had to see something called VisiCalc on an Apple II. Their inability to explain just what it was didn't dim their enthusiasm, and seeing was, indeed, believing. The spreadsheet turned out to be the program that marked the evolution of the PC from a hobbyist's toy into a vital business tool.

In the months to come, you will likely run into similar evangelism boosting Lotus Development Corp.'s Notes. Fans of the "groupware" product will not be able to tell you quite what it does, but they'll swear that it has completely changed the way they do business.

Believe them. Notes may not have the revolutionary impact of VisiCalc (or Lotus' own 1-2-3 spreadsheet), but this may be the year that the program, with about 1 million users at 4,500 companies, really breaks into the big time.

Holy Grail

Notes runs on Windows and OS/2 PCs, on Macintoshes, and on many Unix machines. It incorporates elements of email, bulletin boards, and databases to give far-flung workers access to a broad variety of information. While Notes looks superficially like a snazzy communications program, it can change business practices in a way that led International Data Corp. to say in a 1994 study: "Notes may be the elusive Holy Grail of white-collar productivity."

What makes Notes unique, and particularly well-suited to today's *business,* is a *technology* called "replication." Computer networks have revolutionized intraoffice communications. But many people spend much of their time away from the office, disconnected from the information stored on the computers at the hubs of the networks. Notes allows identical copies of information to be stored on multiple computers, including laptops. Instead of transferring all the information, Notes sends only the bits that have changed since the last time the user tapped in. Thus sales reps in the field only need access to phone lines to keep their inventory lists up to date.

Given such obvious appeal, why has the program, which debuted in 1989, taken so long to build up momentum? One reason is that you have to see Notes in action to appreciate its power. Another was Lotus' original decision to make the minimum purchase a 250-user package whose $62,000 price tag made it accessible to only the biggest corporations.

Notes' revised pricing policy will help. You can buy a starter kit—software for two users and a server—for $995. Pricing for bigger networks is even more appealing: Lotus estimates that the typical cost is about

$300 per user. But the biggest impetus could come from a partnership between Lotus and AT&T. Network Notes, now being field-tested, will make it simple to extend a Notes network beyond corporate walls, linking Notes-based companies with their customers and vendors without them having to solve the tough problems of getting their networks talking directly to each other.

PEEK-PROOF

In one test, software retailer Egghead, Inc. is using Network Notes to handle orders from its corporate customers. Compaq Computer Corp. is using the system to give product and price information to customers. Notes' security features ensure that prying eyes cannot find out how much the customers are paying.

Notes is attracting some heavyweight competition. Microsoft's oft-delayed Exchange Server will offer many of the same features. Novell is trying to integrate Netware with the Word Perfect GroupWise message-handling product it acquired last year. Banyan Systems Inc. is building a rival it calls BeyondWare. But Notes, with an enhanced version 4.0 now in final testing, enjoys a huge head start. So business computer users who need to work more closely with their colleagues, vendors, or customers should check Notes out today.

Edited by Stephen H. Wildstrom The Year to Go Nuts About Notes, January 23, 1995.

The introduction of the "open" era also introduced new and unique problems on the business side of organizations heavily dependant on digital IT. Freed from the sometimes oppressive world of the mainframe, business managers realized they could do the same jobs in some cases at a fraction of the cost with smaller, powerful microprocessers and PCs. However, senior managers soon realized that there was a lot more involved in this mini-revolution than changing computer platforms. Whole business cultures and the individuals that comprised them had to be redefined.

This was no small task since most IT departments were used to acting autonomously, almost independently. Most senior managers were quite surprised at the level of resistance some "re-engineering" movements generated. Following is an example of a successful re-engineering project, but by the mid-1990s, the term "re-engineering" was slowly phased out of most corporations' vocabulary, although the process continues to one extent or another in almost all IT departments today.

CIGNA Corporation: Laying New Organizational Roots with Reengineering

by Vicki J. Powers

We have found that only about 50 percent of the reengineering efforts succeed in the first go around even if you have senior management's full backing. We've had our share of victories and defeats. We have lost battles, but we have not given up on the war. Reengineering is about trying and trying once again.
—Chief financial officer, CIGNA

For six years, CIGNA Corporation has used re-engineering as a tool to achieve breakthrough innovation focused on customer needs. It is not about tweaking at the edges. To CIGNA, re-engineering means laying new organizational roots.

CIGNA, a Philadelphia-based provider of insurance and related financial services, has maintained momentum with business reengineering in its nine business divisions in nearly 70 countries. Each division has completed reengineering projects, some with mixed results. Overall, however, reengineering has saved CIGNA more than $100 million, which illustrates the organization's dedication to this effort.

During CIGNA's experiences with reengineering, it has discovered two important realities:

1. No two reengineering projects are alike, and
2. There is no secret methodology for reengineering success.

The key is persistence over time. CIGNA has latched on to these beliefs and created its own success story. The following details its experiences and lessons learned from reengineering the organization.

Creating a New CIGNA

In 1988, CIGNA's income had declined nearly 11 percent from the previous year. A new chairman stepped into a troubled environment. As chief information officer, Raymond Caron initiated a review of the systems organization and its support in the strategic direction of the business. He found that sophisticated applications did not meet CIGNA's high standards.

"It wasn't that the applications weren't built well," Caron said. "But in implementing them, we hadn't spent enough time in developmental work to focus on the process. We had to reengineer the process to effectively implement technology. It was as if we had been looking through the wrong end of the telescope for all these years."

At the time, there was not much information about reengineering. Caron, who introduced reengineering to CIGNA, suggested a pilot project in one division to learn more about it. Management selected CIGNA Re, the organization's smallest division, which ensures other insurance carriers against loss on large life, accident, and health insurance policies.

In the pilot project with CIGNA Re, the team created initial objectives to dramatically reduce costs and enhance the technology infrastructure. Employees asked themselves this question at the beginning of the project: "How do we effectively implement technology?"

"They quickly found reengineering has to do with the entire organization," Caron said. "Reengineering is the ability to implement radical change and organizational transformation. It is major changes with an organization's capability and direction. And I can't emphasize the word major too much. There can be lots of incremental changes without major improvements."

CIGNA decided to invent a methodology for reengineering to help with the CIGNA Re project and others that would follow. The organization worked with Michael Hammer, famous for cowriting the 1992 publication *Reengineering the Corporation*, who was just getting started in reengineering at the time, too.

In a nutshell, the CIGNA reengineering methodology includes three phases: the fly-by, diagnosis, and implementation. During fly-by, the organization determines where the problem set might lie, not to solve it, but to determine key issues and financial benefits. The next phase, diagnosis, can last two to six months with a focused study of the specifics targeted in the fly-by. The last phase, implementation, is the execution of the strategy to achieve the new vision.

Although the CIGNA Re reengineering project had a couple of false starts, it demonstrated tremendous success. After 18 months, CIGNA

Re had implemented new work processes and cross-functional customer service teams. It cut operating costs by 40 percent and compressed a two-week underwriting procedure into 15 minutes. In addition, the number of application systems decreased from 17 to 5. But according to Caron, perhaps the most significant change was the new culture that emphasized accountability and customer orientation.

"Nothing is really unique about our success with reengineering. We've had our setbacks, too," Caron said. "We've had really good projects with tremendous impact and others that didn't work at all. But the timing was right to think about change. CIGNA was at the right place in thinking and mindset."

But Caron strongly emphasized results beyond the financial value. "There are many benefits much more important than our $100 million savings; we've created more revenue, more retention in business growth, and a new mindset. The major impact is we've changed the method of operation at CIGNA. We think more of our customers, focus on teams, and integrate process and technology."

Once the CIGNA Re project moved into action, reengineering projects sprouted up throughout the company. Some of the other reengineering projects focused on CIGNA International, Global Risk Management, Property and Casualty Claims Systems, CIGNA Technology Services, and CIGNA P&C. These areas experienced hearty results, as well. For example, highlights include 75 percent improvement in quality, 100 percent improvement in cycle time, 50 percent improvement in customer satisfaction, and focus as a team-based organization.

Key Reengineering Lessons

During CIGNA's experiences with benchmarking the last six years, the organization has recognized some key learnings. These include

- Learning from failure
- Fostering commitment and ownership
- Exploiting green field opportunities
- Focusing most of all on a mindset change
- Assessing the cultural fit of reengineering
- Ascending to higher forms of reengineering
- Moving with lightening speed
- Communicating broadly and using multiple forms
- Selecting the right people

"A prerequisite for success in reengineering is a corporate environment that promotes learning, including learning from failure," Caron said. "And if you can get engaged with sponsorship, then you will have a better chance of success. Corporate management at CIGNA played a key role. They also ensured that when a project was derailed, the focus was on the discussion of what needed to be done to get back on track, rather than who was at fault."

Reengineering at CIGNA has grown right along with the projects. Reengineering projects that emphasized the internal operations represented the first form of reengineering: operationally driven efforts. As other areas became involved, they emphasized revenue enhancing activities in addition to streamlined operations. Later, one area, CIGNA P&C, needed to go beyond basic operations and revenue improvements to improve its overall financial posture. This third level, transformational reengineering, is an attempt to focus on shareholder value with new markets and new customers. The costs and requirements of transformational reengineering are much higher than the first two forms, but equally higher are the benefits.

"Reengineering was something we had to try to do. Doing nothing was not an option," Caron said. "If we continued on our path, we wouldn't have been around for long. It forced us to think of our problems on a scale we hadn't traditionally done before."

The integration between business and technology can be a very tricky business. Sometimes it is not enough for a technology to simply improve the way things are done. In many cases, this improvement can be seen as a threat to entire industries as well as individuals. This is obviously a crucial factor in the adoption of any new technology on a personal, business, or cultural level. When the television was introduced, both the film and radio broadcast industries were "threatened," but both eventually adapted to the world this new medium created and all three media thrive to this day.

In 1996, Congress passed the Federal Communications Act of 1996 opening up the installed telecom infrastructure to the new world of broadband, Internet access, and all forms of digital communication. Going into the 21st century it appears this law has created more problems than it has solved.

Competition: Walking the Walk and Talking the Talk

One of the great missions of the United States government is to pursue the goal of open and competitive communications markets in all countries, especially, of course, our own. To this end, we at the FCC are doing all we can to assist the United States Trade Representative Charlene Barshefsky to negotiate a successful multilateral agreement in the World Trade Organization. I recently returned from London where we were comparing notes and strategies on this goal with our counterparts in the United Kingdom.

Thanks to the United States Congress and the Administration, I was able to say that here in the U.S. we are not only talking the talk, we are walking the walk. Indeed, our policies now have a great deal in common with the procompetition policies of the United Kingdom and leading states like Illinois, Wisconsin, Ohio, and others. The rest of the world, I might add, for the most part has a long way to go in order to catch up to the U.K. and the U.S.

The goal in all states in our country, in the United Kingdom, and in the WTO negotiations, is simple: As to the pro-monopoly policy in telecom, to paraphrase a Rolling Stones song from my distant youth, we used to love you, but that's all over now. For industries such as shoes or soap or software or salsa, government should not champion monopolies, restrict investment, or set retail prices. The same can be true for communications services, if we reject the old monopoly regime and embrace competition.

In short, our ultimate goal for communications should be *no rules*. The only exception should be, ironically, the rules that get us to this goal.

All countries should agree on this goal. Certainly all states of the United States must agree on it, because Congress has made this the law of the land.

But today, 94 percent of all world communications revenue is earned by monopolies. And every state plus D.C. still relies principally on a local service monopoly.

Telecommunications policy historically embraced monopolies because economists taught that telephone networks are natural monopolies. Innovation and insight has revealed that networks do have vast economies of scale and scope, but the only thing natural about communications monopolies is that naturally the companies with market power will try to keep that power unless governments, through rules, constrain their potential anticompetitive impulses.

That's why, in the great new telecom law passed in February of this year, Congress asked the FCC to write new rules of competition to check such "natural" impulses.

But our ultimate goal is to reach the sunny uplands of deregulated markets in which the prices and output of telecom services, like software and soap, are set by markets and not governments.

Already the FCC has almost completely deregulated the long distance business: 500 long distance companies make for enough competition that we don't any longer regard AT&T as the dominant carrier.

In mobile communications we have preempted state regulation of retail prices and used auctions to distribute quickly and fairly hundreds of new licenses to firms that will provide at least a handful of choices for mobile carriers in all markets. And we haven't restricted the use of these licenses. Whether you want to use the airwaves for fixed wireless or mobile services, for voice or data, we are committed to keeping the government out of the business of telling you how to run your business.

Our competition policy will accelerate the wireless conversion to digital, break the back of duopoly pricing in cellular, and stimulate innovation as new entrants seek product differentiation and first mover advantage in niche markets.

Ultimately, wireless will not just complement wire phone service—it will substitute for it. This is a reason why at least one Bell company is withdrawing from a wireless trade association.

The way to the sunny green fields of vigorous deregulated competition in local telephony is to focus on facilitating entry by new firms and in liberating existing firms from unnecessary restraints. Congress made brilliantly clear in the new law that new entrants need to be able to lease portions of the telephone company networks. And they need the right to buy the telco services at wholesale in order to resell at retail in competition with the incumbent. And they need to connect their own new networks and new customers to the existing telephone networks.

The job of the FCC and its state counterparts is to write fair rules that make these rights real and practically exercisable. Our interconnection order of August 8 is one part of a three-part trilogy that will set forth the code of procompetition rules. This code, when put in place in every state, will lead eventually to the elimination of thousands of pages of state and federal rules that are designed to control monopolies instead of promote competition.

Anyone familiar with contests like investing or football, sales or baseball, will recognize that basic rules of competition make the games fairer, faster, and even more fun. And you will be gratified also to know that our interconnection rules, 48 pages in length, are in word count only 61 percent as long as the rules of Little League Baseball. Whether they are as important is a value judgment each person must make on his or her own. I will acknowledge that more money is riding on the interconnection order and that the Eighth Circuit is not sitting in judgment on the Little League. At least not yet, as far as I know.

Our four dozen pages of interconnection rules could be followed in all countries as the right way to get from monopoly to competition. After all, economics is like physics: Its laws don't vary from state to state or country to country. It is also true that you prove the truth of the laws of physics and economics by experiment, but all experiments in competition in communications indicate that the monopoly policies of the past hamper growth, harm productivity, and hamstring all sectors of the economy—because all depend on efficient communications in our Information Age.

If we saw competition in all communications markets, we would see also a vast increase in worldwide revenues for telecommunications: Right now it's about $550 billion worldwide; it could quickly be a trillion. And the $50 billion market for international communications alone could double in only a few years if competition policy were put in place worldwide. Most important, the growth of these markets would greatly stimulate all other aspects of world economic growth.

Of course we will never persuade the rest of the world to accept our competition policy if we don't implement it right here at home.

As I mentioned, our code of competition will have three parts—interconnection, universal service, and access reform. Only the first part is written so far—our interconnection order published on August 8.

Merrill Lynch said that by this order, "the FCC has smoothed the way for...local market competition." Morgan Stanley called it "even-handed." CS First Boston said that "the FCC order hits the mark," and that "the FCC is set on the right course." The stock market has reacted with equanimity. And I bet that those of you with investment hopes overseas would love to have these rules in, say, France or Germany or Japan.

Notwithstanding the widespread acceptance of our order by the Street, 23 states and all the Bell companies have taken us to the 8th Circuit Court of Appeals in protest.

So we live in a country of lawyers. What else is new? What is most important about these legal challenges is that they have no merit and they must not be permitted to delay our country's progress towards deregulation and competition.

In any event, I do expect that by the time we finish the trilogy almost every communications company will have sued us about something, and we will have won all cases.

Meanwhile, I am counting on all 50 states this fall to write every aspect of the interconnection order into the specific terms and conditions of the interconnection arrangements between each would-be new entrant and the incumbent telephone company. These contracts between new entrants and incumbent are the documents that will give the new entrants the rights to lease parts of the existing networks, buy services at wholesale, and connect the new entrants' customers to the telco's customers.

Under the new law, the states arbitrate these contracts where the parties cannot negotiate an agreement. And in those arbitrations, the states must adhere to the terms of our order, even if they disagree with the congressionally ordered competition policy. Barring the disruption of the whole congressional plan by a court (something that would be an economic tragedy for our country and a serious blow to our trade policy), by the new year these arbitrations will enable the long distance companies and any other new entrant to compete fairly in local exchange markets.

There are two things our interconnection order does not do. First, it does not take away incentives to maintain and invest in modern networks. Our order should, must, and certainly can be read to state that anyone who wants to operate a network will be able to obtain a fair return on their investment, whether by selling services to retail customers or having their networks leased by new entrants.

As a result, we very well may see companies splitting into wholesale and retail providers. For example, in the wireless world, Nextwave plans to be primarily a wholesaler. Some or all of the Bell companies may very well adopt this same approach and split into separate wholesale and retail affiliates.

We should also see telcos moving even more quickly into delivering big bandwidth—by ISDN or ADSL or wireless solutions. Indeed, any state that firmly follows our interconnection order should also consider deregulating enhanced telecom services. Is it necessary for Maryland to fix the price of ISDN so that Bell Atlantic cannot raise or even lower its prices without a lengthy approval process? Under our interconnection order, isn't there enough potential for entry to trust that the market will keep ISDN at a reasonable price? After all, you can hardly argue either that regulation has effectively promoted this long-overdue service or that ISDN is a basic commodity that should be priced by rule at affordable levels. Why not give deregulation of ISDN a chance?

The second thing our interconnection order does not do is set any specific prices new entrants will pay for leasing elements of the existing network, like unbundled loops and switching capacity. These will be set in state arbitrations or through negotiations between the parties.

We did tell states that they must determine the prices on a forward-looking basis, instead of historic cost. But no business in a competitive marketplace is guaranteed a recovery on past investment, and Congress did not include such a guarantee in the telecom reform law.

Only forward-looking cost concepts are consistent with a competitive market, because any other approach either makes the new entrant pay a tribute to the incumbent for the privilege of entry, or creates disincentives for the incumbent to invest in the network.

The second and third volumes of our deregulatory, procompetitive trilogy are called access reform and universal service.

We will issue a Notice of Proposed Rulemaking on access reform in the fourth quarter of 1996. We will bring home a completed Order in the first quarter of 1997. A joint board of state representatives and FCC Commissioners will make recommendations on universal service in November. The FCC will issue an Order in the first quarter of 1997. These orders might take our new paradigm of competitive rules to about the length of the Little League Rules, but they will usher in a Major League explosion in billions of dollars of investment, millions of new jobs, and a reduction by thousands of the pages in state rules managing the local phone companies. At the very minimum, this will be for equipment suppliers a benign version of what war is for arms dealers: a good time to be in the business.

And competition will deliver increased bandwidth to many more Americans than monopoly regulation could ever do. Starbucks is successful because coffee is a lawful, socially acceptable, but addictive, product. Thanks to the Internet, bandwidth is the same sort of product: You can never get enough of it. Our trilogy will let hundreds of firms enter the business of specialty bandwidth provision—and if state regulators relax their grip, the telcos will also gain substantial revenues from such value-added services.

Meanwhile, basic dial tone will get cheaper and cheaper to provide because costs will continue to decline. For now, government policy must keep the telco's delivery of basic phone service at today's low, eminently affordable rates. How do we know basic phone service is affordable? Because 95 percent of homes subscribe.

Congress and the FCC and the states want to keep subscription rates at least as high as they are today. Indeed they should be much higher for demographic groups that are far below that average, such as Hispanics, African Americans, and kids and teachers in classrooms. (The last group has a penetration rate of about 10 percent, for example)

Already today, a subsidy in the range of billions of dollars is necessary to sustain affordable basic phone service. But today a large part of that subsidy comes from access charges. Access is the charge paid by long distance companies to connect to the local exchanges. The FCC has set access charges for interstate traffic; the states, for traffic within state lines. Everyone agrees that these charges are far higher than forward-looking cost would dictate. The difference between actual charges and forward-looking cost-based prices is measured in the billions of dollars.

How should the access subsidy be raised if access is priced competitively?

Similarly, states set the price of what are called vertical services, like call waiting, far above their actual cost. Again the purpose is to generate revenue to subsidize other services. Call waiting and caller id and call forwarding will sell like hotcakes when the prices go down about 90 percent—and that's what competition will cause.

But then another source of subsidy for basic phone service will disappear. New revenue sources will be rapidly exploited by telcos, but it won't be wise to create a discontinuity in the revenue streams of our leading telephone companies as we transition from the old monopoly regime to the new competitive paradigm.

Fortunately, under Section 254 of the communications law, Congress gave the FCC the authority to create a durable, effective universal service system that will meet the three goals (everything comes in three) of keeping basic phone service low priced, compensating fairly any company for providing basic phone service, and making sure that new entrants and existing telcos each carry a fair share of the financial burden of keeping basic phone service affordable.

Here are some of the key principles of what ought be our new universal service plan, in my view.

The goal should be to pay for a modern communications network built out to every American. Every American should be able to be connected and to get some basic usage at an affordable price—and those Americans who need extra assistance to subscribe should get it. We must break down the barriers that keep everyone from being connected.

Chairman Reed Hundt
Federal Communications Commission
Alex. Brown & Co.
"Media & Communications '96 Conference"
Waldorf-Astoria Hotel, New York
September 17, 1996

Following is an example of the impending integration of digital media into a common interface. As the coming infrastructure to support broadband slowly falls into place across America and then the world, there will be a veritable explosion of services and products that will become just "one touch" away.

Couch Potatoes, Remain Seated

Headquartered in Mountain View, California, and incorporated in the British Virgin Islands, OpenTV develops software for interactive digital television systems, the little black boxes that sit on top of televisions and are currently used primarily to access cable programming. With OpenTV software embedded in the set-top box, couch potatoes can use their remote control devices to surf TV channels and access interactive services, such as shopping, banking, and email. According to the OpenTV pitch, viewers can even control camera angles and instant replays during sports broadcasts.

There is a lot of demand for such services from the advertising industry. They salivate to imagine viewers using the remote control to purchase a favorite player's jersey. "Program guides, enhanced broadcasts, and TV-based browsing is likely to generate $20 billion by 2004," says Josh Bernoff, principal television analyst at Forrester Research (Nasdaq: FORR), a technology research firm. "If you break it down, that's $11 billion in advertising, $7 billion in online sales or transactions, and $2 billion in subscriptions," he explains.

Advertising hasn't yet played a big part in the fortunes of OpenTV. Its prime revenue-generators are royalties and fees related to its software platform. In its latest financial report, the company stated that for nine months ended September 30, 1999, losses declined to $8.5 million, down 20 percent from $10.6 million in the year-ago period. The company also reported that during the same nine months it had revenues of $17.6 million, up 187 percent over the year-earlier period, when it reported revenue of $6.1 million.

Many Channels of Funding

The potential of the burgeoning market has made OpenTV attractive to some big-name investors. Sun Microsystems (Nasdaq: SUNW), which was a founding shareholder in OpenTV in 1994, now holds an equity stake worth approximately 19.5 percent of the company. The largest shareholder, however, is OpenTV's parent, MIH (Nasdaq: MIHL), which holds a post-IPO stake of nearly 70 percent. MIH is a multinational provider of pay TV services and technology, operating in Africa, Asia, and the Mediterranean region. However, there are a couple of twisty turns for investors who want to know who really owns OpenTV. The company's lineage breaks down as follows: MIH Investments owns 53 percent of the voting stock of MIH Holdings, and Naspers owns 100 percent of the voting stock of MIH Investments, along with direct ownership of 13.2 percent of MIH Holdings. Naspers is a South African media house.

Recognizing what some analysts call a ground-floor opportunity in late October, investors gave OpenTV a quick $31.25 million cash infusion through the private placement of an undetermined amount of convertible preferred stock. Those investors included America Online (NYSE: AOL), General Instrument (NYSE: GIC), Liberty Digital (Nasdaq: LDIG), News Corporation (NYSE: NWS), and Time Warner (NYSE: TWX). Sun Microsystems also participated in the convertible preferred equity investment.

Indeed, the investments from AOL, Liberty, News Corporation, and Time Warner will help OpenTV in its efforts to enhance its position in the U.S. and to expand the range of interactive applications available to its global client base. OpenTV already boasts that its software is used in more than 4.3 million digital set-top boxes. To date, the company says, 13 television networks use its software, including UK-based Sky Broadcasting and France's TPS.

"There are two standards, if you can call them that," says Mr. Bernoff. "In the United States, interactive TV is based on Internet-compliant protocols. Europe doesn't care what's inside the box as long as it works. But among other things, in order for OpenTV to establish a viable presence here, it will have to tweak its software."

The investment by General Instrument may help the company do just that. General Instrument, along with Scientific-Atlanta (NYSE: SFA), is one of only two companies in the U.S. making the set-top boxes. Also, Time Warner's experience with its failed Time Warner Full Service Network Five provides a helpful guide around potential pitfalls.

Interactive Intricacy

OpenTV faces stiff competition from AT&T (NYSE: T) and other cable companies that expect to begin offering their own set-top television, Internet, and telephone packages sometime next year.

Also in the fray are two other publicly traded companies with similar heavyweight backing. At a share price of $42, Wink Communications (Nasdaq: WINK) has a market cap of $1.2 billion and equity participation from the likes of Electric Capital, Capital Partners, Toshiba, Microsoft (Nasdaq: MSFT) cofounder Paul Allen's Vulcan Ventures, and General Instrument. Liberate (Nasdaq: LBRT) is another big player in the field. With its stock price at $162.50, Liberate has a market cap of $6.8 billion and institutional support from Oracle (Nasdaq: ORCL), which owns approximately 48 percent of the company. Both are recent IPOs, with Liberate launching in July and Wink in August. In addition, the satellite market is seeing a lot of activity. Echostar's (Nasdaq: DISH) Dish Network is scheduled to launch interactive services using OpenTV software in the U.S. next year. DirecTV has teamed with OpenTV to develop a satellite-based set-top box that would compete directly with Microsoft's WebTV.

AOL is straddling the fence, making numerous investments in competing companies. In August, AOL invested in Tivo (Nasdaq: TIVO) and partnered with that company to expand its interactive TV business. AOL also recently made a $1.5 billion investment in Hughes Electronics, parent company of DirecTV and satellite Internet service provider DirecPC.

"Even though you really can't call this a market yet, the cable operators appear to be leaning toward Liberate, while among the satellites it's a free-for-all," says Mr. Bernoff.

By *Redherring.com*, November 24, 1999

Technology Paradox

When Computer Associates International, Inc. introduced an accounting program, Simply Money, in 1993, it picked a daring price point for its first million copies: zero.

Toshiba Corp. happily admits that its forthcoming digital-movie player will never earn back the investment poured into it.

Order service from Teleport Communications Group, Inc., and a Teleport crew will install a dozen optical fibers with a million times the capacity you wanted—at no extra charge.

Are these companies crazy? No, they're obeying a new set of rules— seeming paradoxes that only make sense in light of the ongoing revolution in the price and capability of digital technology. To wit: Computer Associates gave away Simply Money software on the theory that favorable word-of-mouth would outweigh the trivial expense of making the diskettes—and persuade customers to buy upgrades and related programs. Toshiba plans to recoup its development cost for digital video-disks with spin-offs in other products, from high-capacity audio players to storage devices for laptop computers. As for Teleport: Optical fibers are so cheap that it makes sense to install enough capacity to last a lifetime.

That's the technology paradox: Businesses can thrive at the very moment when their prices are falling the fastest. "The only thing that matters is if the exponential growth of your market is faster than the exponential decline of your prices," says George M.C. Fisher, chairman and CEO of Eastman Kodak Co. The challenge is enormous, he says.

"Companies have to project out: 'How will I be competitive in a world (in which) technology will be virtually free?'"

Vanishing Point

High tech has had its own inverted economic logic ever since the invention of the transistor at AT&T Bell Laboratories in 1948: Power goes up and price comes down in lockstep. In the past few years, though, cheap technology has crossed an invisible threshold to assume a central role in economies around the world. In 1994, Americans spent more on home PCs than on TV sets. Cyberspace became a middle-class suburb. *People* magazine named Internet guru Vinton G. Cerf one of the 25 most fascinating people of the year. Five thousand Vietnamese owned digital cellular phones. Wounded by the microprocessor revolution, supercomputer giant Cray Research, Inc. saw its stock fall to barely 10 percent of its 1987 value.

The business world, in short, is being stood on its head. This creative destruction has fractured rock-solid principles of commerce of decades past. Among the casualties: 10-year plans and deliberate pacing of product cycles. Clear distinctions between custom and mass markets. Giant soup-to-nuts systems from single companies—such as IBM's long-dominant mainframe computer networks.

The new rules require more than ingenuity, agility, and speed. They call for redefining value in an economy where the cost of raw technology is plummeting toward zero. Sooner or later, this plunge will obliterate the worth of almost any specific piece of hardware or software. Then, value will be in establishing a long-term relationship with a customer— even if it means giving the first generation of a product away. This won't happen with cars and other products built from bulk materials such as steel, but it's already happening with the electronics systems that are increasingly becoming an integral part of these products.

No single set of rules works for every player. A strategy of domination and control befits the likes of Intel Corp. and Microsoft Corp., which own vital standards and charge handsomely for them. There's also money to be made at the other extreme, in pure commodities, from basic disk drives to plain-vanilla consumer electronics. Dynamic random-access memory (DRAM) chips, for example, perhaps the purest example of a commodity, have once again become the biggest source of profit for Japan's hard-pressed electronics giants as huge demand has propped up their prices.

For most companies, however, the technology revolution dictates a middle course—latching on to a standard rather than creating one, and then putting in a little something extra to elevate one's product above commodityhood. Compaq Computer, Dell, and Packard Bell Electronics survive the PC wars by tweaking the Intel-Microsoft standard to boost the speed or enhance ease of use. Sharp Corp. made a best-seller out of an ordinary video camera by building a flat-panel TV screen into it.

To companies struggling to adapt, this brave new world isn't so wonderful. Their high-tech crown jewels are suddenly all but worthless. AT&T has taken billions of dollars in charges since 1984 to get rid of obsolete jobs and equipment. IBM, DEC, and Wang Laboratories are still trying to recover from the blow dealt by the microprocessor.

Japanese companies have been hit especially hard. The country's consumer electronics industry has been mired in single-digit growth since the mid-1980s. Who needs a $500 camera when disposable models come with panoramic, telephoto, and underwater lenses? Dime-store digital watches keep time as well as costly chronometers. And the sound on cheap portable CD players is so good that savvy Tokyoites plug them into speakers in lieu of buying fancy audio systems. "How do you assign prices or value in a world where quality is perfect and nothing breaks?" asks Yotaro Suzuki, senior vice-president of the Japan Institute of Office Automation in Tokyo.

From Nibble to Chomp

The wave of downsizing that swept the computer industry is about to come crashing down on telecommunications gear. Companies such as Cisco Systems, Synoptics Communications, and Cabletron Systems stole a march on the likes of AT&T, Northern Telecom, and Siemens with equipment that links PCs in networks. Says Daniel Lynch, chairman of Interop, Inc., which runs trade shows: "The new guys start out nibbling. The big guys never notice. And then, boom!"

Successful strategists soak out costs, cut prices, and then wait for business to roll in. Step 1 is a price decline—say, in DRAM chips. At first it causes chaos, as in the early 1980s, when American producers fled the DRAM market amid cries of Japanese dumping. In Step 2, the market finds a new use for the cheap resource. Case in point: Windows software, which is ubiquitous and gobbles megabytes of DRAMs. Unit prices of the chips may fall, but gross revenue soars—a point that is lost on those who once again predict doom for commodity chipmakers. The next wave of chip demand will come from the likes of computers that obey spoken commands and communicate in 3-D images. After that? Believable virtual reality and intelligent artificial intelligence.

The new rules of "techonomics" practically guarantee that high-tech product gluts will be temporary. That's because the economy and society will reshape themselves to take advantage of the cheap resource, whether it's computers that talk or satellites that track stolen cars. Demand for digital resources—unlike demand for, say, food and clothing—is almost infinitely elastic. Witness the hockey-stick shape of graphs plotting usage of online services. Marvels Steve Case, president and CEO of America Online, Inc.: "Things take a while to coalesce, then they explode."

Even the ubiquitous microprocessor was once seen, by its own inventors, as a niche product. Intel cofounder Gordon E. Moore rejected a 1970s proposal for a home computer built around an early microprocessor. "I personally didn't see anything useful in it, so we never gave it another thought," he later recalled. In a list of possible uses for its 286 chip, written before the success of the IBM PC, Intel omitted the personal computer, thinking instead of industrial automation, transaction processing, and telecommunications. But then, history is replete with overlooked opportunities, from microwave ovens to fiber optics.

The signs that the old way of doing business was failing first became apparent in the mid-1980s. Electronics seemed like a dead-end street. Intense global competition had ripped profits out of the consumer electronics industry, and the chip and computer industries seemed destined to follow. Says Mark Rosenker, vice-president of the Electronic Industries Assn.: "We were walking around with our heads in our hands saying, 'My God, what's happening to us?'" Many theorists argued that the only way to win was to emulate huge, vertically integrated Japanese conglomerates, which could afford to make all their own components, lose money launching new products, and weather debilitating price wars.

The pessimists were proven wrong. By the early 1990s, a new strategy took shape in the chip, PC, and communications wars. To survive, smart middle-tier companies, which were neither owners of a standard nor pure commodity players, stopped focusing on the product alone.

They started concentrating on whole "architectures," or grand schemes for integrating many products into smoothly functioning systems. The approach required an intimate knowledge of customer needs, the ability to read technology road maps three to five years off, and a willingness to look beyond easy opportunities in the current mass market.

Small chipmakers such as LSI Logic, Cirrus Logic, and VLSI Technology couldn't sell a new PC microprocessor: Intel had that business sewn up. So they took aim at so-called chip sets that added sound and visual effects for PCs and on emerging-device areas, such as digital set-top boxes that link up to the Information Superhighway.

Fitting In

Europe and Japan offered fertile ground for these American hotshots. Open up a Canon single-lens reflex camera, a Ricoh fax machine, or a Philips Magnavox television, and you'll see specialized U.S. chips. Sony Corp.'s much admired game machine, the Play Station, runs on a chip designed by LSI Logic.

Companies don't have to create a new architecture—only fit into one. That's how C-Cube Microsystems gained leadership in the fast-growing field of digital signal compression. Managers didn't even think of protecting their two and a half years of work on a powerful video-compression chip behind a wall of patents and copyrights. Says C-Cube founder Alexandre Balkanski: "The whole trick is to get in quickly and run as fast as you can. There are no birthrights."

Digital satellite TV provides a glimpse of the strategies that will work in the future. A band of companies led by General Motors Corp.'s Hughes Electronics began planning it four years ago, after calculating that the necessary components—then far too costly—were about to become affordable. They were right: Partner RCA, a unit of France's Thomson, was able to offer a home dish and decoder starting at $699. Since last June, more than 400,000 American homes have signed up.

The confidence to take the gamble on satellite TV came from the designers' familiarity with the unique economics of silicon. Every 18 months or so, improvements in chipmaking technology make it possible to double the performance of silicon at no increase in price. More compact circuitry makes chips faster because electrons have less distance to travel. And as chips get smaller, more of them can be stamped out of the same slice of silicon. Consequently, single chips have taken over functions that used to be performed by refrigerators full of diodes, triodes, and capacitors. And chipmakers have assumed roles once performed by a wide range of companies, from makers of discrete electronic components to suppliers of software. "The food chain is collapsing," says Gilbert F. Amelio, CEO of National Semiconductor Corp.

The ascent of chips means that rules of play that originated in Silicon Valley are governing an ever-growing segment of the economy. Around 2000, high-volume microprocessors will crack the "bips barrier"—execute more than a billion instructions per second. That will provide a playground for designers to come up with an almost limitless range of products, from holographic videoconferencing to Oracle Corp. CEO Lawrence J. Ellison's pet craving—a personal digital assistant that alerts your cardiologist if your company's stock falls. But manufacturers beware: These miraculous devices will be subject to the same punishing cost curves as PCs and cellular phones.

Advances in optic fiber will mirror the miracles in silicon. Engineers continually upgrade the capacity of hair-thin glass fibers by jacking up the pulse rate and splitting the light beams that carry information into multiple wavelengths. Already, the cost of carrying one more phone call is practically zero, making the call a tricky product to price. Some long-distance carriers have even adopted "postal pricing, in which the cost of a three-minute call is the same anywhere in the continental U.S.

The same is true of software. The incremental cost of manufacturing one more diskette or CD-ROM containing software is close to zero. Consumers know that, which is why many feel justified in making illegal copies. Some idealistic programmers, like those affiliated with the Free Software Foundation in Cambridge, Mass., even argue that copying should be free. To help counter that movement, software publishers know they must give customers something more than a platter of bits. Makers of mainframe software are stressing customization or 24-hour maintenance agreements. Entertainment-software companies are acting like magazine publishers, building brand names by churning out titles frequently at easy-to-swallow prices.

'Splendid' Pirates

There's an old joke about a dim manager who brags to his boss that their company is losing money on every sale—but making it up on volume. In the era of "free" technology, that manager doesn't seem so stupid anymore. With the production cost of hardware and software so low in comparison to the development cost, it actually can make sense to give stuff away in order to establish a market toehold and start a profitable long-term relationship.

Michael Goldhaber, president of the San Francisco-based Center for Technology & Democracy, sees these grabs for mind share as the early manifestations of a coming high-tech "attention economy" in which attention from others is the scarcest and hence the most valuable commodity. Makes sense: Bits and bytes are virtually unlimited, but there are still only 24 hours in a day.

Media baron Rupert Murdoch understands that. In India, pirates steal the signal from News Corp.'s Star TV satellite and profit by reselling the programs to people over cable. "Some cynics have said this will be fatal for Star. We disagree," Murdoch said in a speech last year in Melbourne. His logic? The pirates—or "splendid entrepreneurs," in his words—are simply broadening the potential market for Star TV and allowing Murdoch to raise advertising rates.

If attention is the most precious resource in a free-tech economy, then it makes sense to throw battalions of cheap bits into capturing a share of it by making products exciting, easy to use, or preferably both. Work on the interface between human and machine already consumes three-quarters of the development work on electronic products, says Gary A. Curtis, a Boston Consulting Group, Inc. vice-president and leader of its worldwide information-technology practice. Nonetheless, technology keeps getting more costly in terms of the time required to master it. Consultant Gartner Group, Inc. calculates that the lifetime cost of owning an ordinary corporate PC—troubleshooting, training, and all—comes to more than $42,000.

In Goldhaber's attention economy, attention is reciprocal: Producers get it from consumers by showering it on them. Success will hinge on "letting customers define what they want to buy," then building it to order, says Roger N. Nagel, deputy director of Lehigh University' s Iacocca Institute. The cost of the parts will be almost incidental to the price of the final package, which includes service and follow- up modifications. Those who offer attractive packages can virtually give away their hardware, says Nagel: "Tomorrow's factories will sell customer gratification, not things."

Ultimately, companies will "mass-customize" their products, which means serving the mass market with products that are nonetheless tailored to individuals. Dell Computer Corp. already bundles each PC with software and peripherals that the customer demands—a level of customization previously reserved for cars and houses. The goal is to live in a commodity marketplace without serving up a commodity. Says Kodak's Fisher: "Every unit coming down the line should be capable of being different from the one that preceded it."

This, after all, is where the Japanese went astray. Much of their electronics universe is analog and electromechanical, with high-priced paraphernalia of spinning platters, motors, shutters, and lenses that take teams of experts to modify or enhance. So while American companies rushed forward with customized, multifunction chips that formed the heart of high-value, new product categories, Matsushita, Sony, and Sanyo—the original commoditizers—were endlessly mired in low-margin "box businesses." Their VCRs and microwave ovens could not exploit the economies of the silicon curve.

Nintendo Co. was one of the first to find a path out. "There's no way to charge a premium on hardware," says Nintendo president Hiroshi Yamauchi. So the world's leading video game company charted a business model in which the game consoles would be "given away" to consumers at cost, or even below, to boost sales of software. Virtually all of Nintendo's considerable profits flow from sales, license fees, and manufacturing charges on the game software.

Free technology demands that engineers learn a whole new discipline: wastefulness. Makers of custom logic chips regularly stitch together quick and loose designs on silicon, squandering what used to be precious "real estate" on the chip, to get products to market faster. It's hard on designers who take pride in writing tight code and building efficient systems. But why waste time and effort making efficient use of something that isn't scarce? The logic also applies to software. Microsoft's Windows 95 will be huge and slow on today's PCs. But Microsoft knows that customers will simply buy new computers or add memory to their old ones.

To be sure, there will always be some sectors, such as video transmission today, where shortages of capacity make efficiency a winning strategy. Efficient software for data and video compression, for instance, is a boom industry. But compression only creates more room—on a disk or over a phone line—for some other programmer to be creatively wasteful.

212

While free technology makes room for creativity, it also intensifies global competition. Cheap communications mean chipmakers in Silicon Valley can farm out work to Taiwan or Tel Aviv. "We have no monopoly in this country in 1994 on technology smarts and capabilities," says Warren McFarlan, senior associate dean of Harvard B-school. A visit last summer to four software companies in New Delhi opened his eyes: "They are dominated by Harvard and MIT PhDs and are every bit as good as any firm I've looked at in the U.S."

Yet it's misguided to worry that in a free-tech economy, all manufacturing, service, and even engineering jobs might migrate to low-wage nations. Where product cycles are shortest, such as in PCs, factories have remained inside the biggest markets—such as the U.S. and Japan—to save shipping time. Engineers also prefer to be close to the largest, most sophisticated markets. Taiwan's Acer Inc., one of the most aggressive PC price-cutters, is moving most of its assembly for the U.S. market to San Jose.

Information technologies will never be literally free—just when they start to seem so, someone finds a way to consume so much that they start to seem scarce all over again. Then the cry goes out for still more capacity and speed. That virtuous cycle promises to keep rolling as long as there are people with the imagination to envision something better.

The New Rules of the Game

The advent of "free" technology is forcing companies to master some slippery concepts. Warning: Not every rule is appropriate for every business.

Products are most valuable when they're cheapest. The niche for high-priced products gets ever smaller. Low prices and high volumes are the way to go. Just ask Compaq Computer.

Make money by giving things away. High tech loves shaving economics—giving away the razor to sell more blades. Mosaic software for the Internet started out free. Now, its creators sell it as Netscape.

Teamwork conquers all. The complexity of the latest electronics gadgets—such as digital satellite TV—requires the kind of collaborative systems design that used to be the province of general contractors on aircraft, ships, and moon shots.

- Mass-customize. To avoid the me-too commodity trap, use agile manufacturing techniques to make each product off the line unique. That's how Dell sells PCs and Matsushita sells mountain bikes.
- Hurry up and waste. Engineering efficiency in product design may be nice, but with computing and communication resources so cheap and speed to market so essential, quick-and-dirty is often the best route.
- Don't fear gluts. Demand for individual products rises and falls, but hunger for such things as computing power is, in the long term, insatiable. Memory chips are fantastically profitable despite being lowly "commodities."

Bibliography

Boar, Bernard H., *Practical Steps for Aligning Information Technology with Business Strategies/How to Achieve a Competitive Advantage*, John Wiley & Sons: New York, 1994.

Burke, James, *Connections*, MacMillan London Limited, 1978.

Chesbrough, Henry W., and Teece, David J., *When is Virtual Virtous? Organizing for Innovation*, Harvard Business Review, Jan.-Feb., 1996, pp. 65-73

Coates, Joseph F., Mahaffie, John B., and Hines, Andy, *2025. Scenarios of US and Global Economy Reshaped by Science and Technology*, Coates & Jarret, Inc, 1997.

Kim, W. Chan, and Mauborgne, Renee, *Fair Process: Managing the Knowledge Economy*, Harvard Business Review, July-Aug., 1997, pp. 65-75.

Malone, Thomas W., and Laubacher, Robert J., *The Dawn of the E-Lance Economy*, Harvard Business Review, Sep.-Oct., 1998, pp. 144-152.

Rifkin, Glenn, and Harrar, George, *The Ultimate Entrepenuer. The Story of Ken Olsen and Digital Equipment Corporation*, Contemporary Books, 1988.

Spar, Debora, and Bussgang, Jeffrey J., *Ruling the Net*, Harvard Business Review, May-June, 1996, pp. 125–133.

Thurow, Lester C., *Building Wealth*, Harper Collins: New York, 1999.

Yoffie, David B., and Cusumano, Michael A., *Judo Strategy. The Competitive Dynamics of Internet Time*, Harvard Business Review, Jan.-Feb., 1999, pp. 71-81.

Index

D

da Vinci, Leonardo, xv-xvi
Dark Ages, 2, 3
Data processing center, 53
Datatrieve, 76
de Vaucanson, Jacques, 18-19
"Death" of the mainframe, and IBM, 134-36
DECNET technology, 36, 71
DECNET V, 75
Dell Computer Corp., 207, 212
Descartes, Rene, 148
Desktop applications, in a knowledge base economy, 95
Desktop computing, 72
Dhebar, Anirudh, 15
Digital Equipment Corporation (DEC), 28-30, 67-72, 124, 207
    Alpha chip, 76
    case study, 63-66
    competitors, 74, 137, 138
    as a culture, 136
    database division, 76
    decentralized management philosophy, 138-39
    DECNET V, 75
    and desktop computing, 138-39
    fall to legacy category, 75-76
    marketing strategies, 35-38
    matrix management, 136-37, 160
    matrixed networks, 67-68
    service and support organization, 76
    software, 71
    storage product division, 76
    success of, 136
    ultimate failure of, 78
    VMS (virtual memory system) operating system, 70-71
Digital networks, 145
Digital satellite TV, 209-10, 213
Digital technology, 17, 147-48, xvi
    and changing society, 18
    defined, 17
    deployment of, 20

    pervasive nature of, 81
    as set of tools, 18
DirectPC (Internet service provider), 203
Distribution networks, 111-13
Doriot, Georges, 65, 67, 76
DOS, 70, 74
Dot coms, 32, 55
Downsizing, 154-55, 177
Duran, Jennie, 60
Dynamic random-access memory (DRAM) chips, 206-7

E

E-business management teams, 151
E-businesses, 32
E-Commerce: The Third Wave (Fingar), 94
E-conomy, defined, 163-66
E-magazines (e-zines), 114-15
Echostar, 203
Eckert, John P., 25
Economic Darwinism, 147
Economics:
    as "dismal science," 96
    of information, 104-10
    and rules of competition, 106
Edison, Thomas, 16, 64, 85
Egghead, Inc., 185
Egyptians, 10
Electric Capital, 203
Ellison, Lawrence J., 126, 210
Empires, 3
    and technology, 4
Empowerment, 128-30
Engels, Max, 21-22, 62
Engineer, digitized, xvii
ENIAC, 25-26, 85
Era of Personalization, 91
Euclid's Elements, 9
European Empire, 4, 8
Executives, yesterday vs. today, 133